LUKAS & STERNBERG, NEW YORK 015

NIKOLAUS HIRSCH IS AN ARCHITECT BASED IN FRANKFURT AM MAIN, WHO TEACHES AT THE ARCHITECTURAL ASSOCIATION IN LONDON; IN THE PAST, HE HAS ALSO HELD POSITIONS AT THE INSTITUTE OF APPLIED THEATER STUDIES AT GIESSEN UNIVERSITY AND AT UPENN IN PHILADELPHIA. HIS WORK INCLUDES THE INTERNATIONALLY ACCLAIMED DRESDEN SYNAGOGUE, THE HINZERT DOCUMENT CENTER, THE EUROPEAN KUNSTHALLE IN COLOGNE, AND UNITEDNATIONSPLAZA (WITH ANTON VIDOKLE) IN BERLIN. HE CURATED "ERSATZSTADT: REPRÄSENTATIONEN DES URBANEN" AT THE BERLIN VOLKSBÜHNE. HIS WORK HAS BEEN AWARDED A NUMBER OF PRIZES, INCLUDING THE WORLD ARCHITECTURE AWARD 2002, AND HAS BEEN SHOWN IN EXHIBITIONS SUCH AS "NEUE WELT" AT THE FRANKFURTER KUNSTVEREIN, "NEW GERMAN ARCHITECTURE" IN BERLIN, "UTOPIA STATION" AT THE VENICE BIENNALE, AND "CAN BUILDINGS CURATE" AT THE AA IN LONDON AND THE STOREFRONT GALLERY IN NEW YORK.

NIKOLAUS HIRSCH
ON BOUNDARIES

LUKAS & STERNBERG, NEW YORK

Nikolaus Hirsch

On Boundaries

Publisher/Verlag: Lukas & Sternberg, New York

© 2007 Nikolaus Hirsch, Lukas & Sternberg

All rights reserved, including the right of reproduction in whole or in part in any form.

Text Editor/Lektorat: April Elizabeth Lamm

Translation/Übersetzung: Steven Lindberg, Allison Plath-Moseley

Design/Gestaltung: Markus Weisbeck, Indra Häußler, surface, Frankfurt am Main/Berlin

Printing and binding/Druck und Bindung: Druckerei Otto Lembeck, Frankfurt am Main

ISBN 978-1-933128-10-8

Lukas & Sternberg is an imprint of Sternberg Press.

Sternberg Press

Caroline Schneider

Karl-Marx-Allee 78, D-10243 Berlin

1182 Broadway # 1602, New York, NY 10001

mail@sternberg-press.com, www.sternberg-press.com

CONTENTS/INHALT

ON BOUNDARIES
OR THE DIFFICULTY OF LOSING CONTROL

9

PLANNING THE UNPREDICTABLE
A DIALOGUE BETWEEN NIKOLAUS HIRSCH
AND WILLIAM FORSYTHE

21

OBJECTS VS PEOPLE

31

EUROPEAN KUNSTHALLE
NICOLAUS SCHAFHAUSEN INTERVIEWS
NIKOLAUS HIRSCH ON THE RELATIONSHIP
BETWEEN ART AND ARCHITECTURE

35

THE ARCHITECTURAL THING
THE MAKING OF "MAKING THINGS PUBLIC"

47

UNITEDNATIONSPLAZA: BUILDING KNOWLEDGE
MARKUS MIESSEN IN CONVERSATION
WITH NIKOLAUS HIRSCH

51

ERSATZSTADT: REPRESENTATIONS OF THE URBAN

63

THE ARCHITECT AND HIS BOUNDARIES
DAVID ADJAYE IN CONVERSATION WITH NIKOLAUS HIRSCH

73

GEOPOLITICAL TECTONICS
TBILISI OR HOW TO FIND A CONTEXT
FOR YOUR ARCHITECTURE

81

GROUNDED TOWERS

87

WALDSTADT 95
A DIALOGUE BETWEEN MICHAEL HIRSCH
AND NIKOLAUS HIRSCH

PERMANENCE AND SUCCESSION 109
MONUMENTAL QUESTIONS REGARDING TRACK 17,
BERLIN-GRUNEWALD TRAIN STATION

ARCHITECTURAL WORKS BUILT 119
FOR NATIONAL UNIFICATION

MATERIAL TIME 125
NOTES ON THE DRESDEN SYNAGOGUE

* * *

GRENZEN 161
ODER ÜBER DIE SCHWIERIGKEIT,
DIE KONTROLLE ZU VERLIEREN

DIE PLANUNG DES UNVORHERSEHBAREN 173
EIN DIALOG ZWISCHEN NIKOLAUS HIRSCH
UND WILLIAM FORSYTHE

OBJEKTE GEGEN MENSCHEN 185

EUROPEAN KUNSTHALLE 189
NICOLAUS SCHAFHAUSEN BEFRAGT
NIKOLAUS HIRSCH ZUM VERHÄLTNIS
ZWISCHEN KUNST UND ARCHITEKTUR

DAS ARCHITEKTUR-DING 201
THE MAKING OF „MAKING THINGS PUBLIC"

UNITEDNATIONSPLAZA: WISSEN BAUEN 205
MARKUS MIESSEN IM GESPRÄCH MIT NIKOLAUS HIRSCH

ERSATZSTADT: REPRÄSENTATIONEN DES URBANEN 217

DER ARCHITEKT UND SEINE GRENZEN 227
DAVID ADJAYE IM GESPRÄCH MIT NIKOLAUS HIRSCH

GEOPOLITISCHE TEKTONIK 237
TIFLIS ODER WIE MAN EINEN KONTEXT
FÜR SEINE ARCHITEKTUR FINDET

WIE DIE TÜRME STEHEN 241

WALDSTADT 249
EIN DIALOG ZWISCHEN MICHAEL HIRSCH
UND NIKOLAUS HIRSCH

PERMANENZ UND SUKZESSION 263
MONUMENTALE FRAGEN ZUM GLEIS 17 /
BAHNHOF BERLIN-GRUNEWALD

ARCHITEKTURWERKE, ZUR VEREINIGUNG 273
DER VÖLKER ERBAUT

MATERIALZEIT 279
NOTIZEN ZUR SYNAGOGE DRESDEN

ON BOUNDARIES
OR THE DIFFICULTY OF LOSING CONTROL

Architecture was once the mother of the arts. Today, architecture might still be part of the art family, but the old hierarchies have definitely changed. It would seem that the other arts have grown up, and architecture has become the family's control freak, mainly preoccupied with its obsessively protective character: order, stability, control, safety, security, authority, hermeticism, institutionalization. These reassuring yet implausible fantasies of protection delegate a crucial role to the boundaries negotiating between phenomena of inside and outside. In fact, these architectural boundaries have a double nature: the professional limits of the discipline and the physical boundaries of a "shelter." Indeed, the shelter for art embodies the obsessive and perverse character of architecture and, likewise, enhances the possibilities of creative resistance. Both conditions collapse into extreme architectural models such as the white cube and the black box.

It is no accident that architectural models of extreme protection are referred to within the realm of art. The increasing autonomy of art has led to the construction of paradigms of environmental control that define the condition of the contemporary institution and their physical expression. In this respect, the protective shelter acts both as a systemic self-reflection and a material condition. Yet the secure limits of these self-referential systems are today being questioned – from the outside by social and economic forces that change the basic conditions for art; and from the inside by artistic strategies that increasingly lock into external realities. The inside-outside conflicts inherent within the hermetic model of a museum or a theater, thus, create a situation in which architecture and the architect inevitably assume a critical role.

HAVING A PLAN
What is the notion of "protection" in architecture? Maybe it is more and more about a double logic: on the one hand, the physical condition of architectural tectonics, on the other, a discourse in which the role of the architect himself becomes a primary source. We are

witnessing a critical moment in architecture: in a world of late capitalism in which the material condition of a building becomes increasingly arbitrary, exchangeable, and contingent, how can someone who organizes matter – one is tempted to say "just inert material" – have cultural relevance?

The discipline of architecture has an ambiguous reputation. According to Aristotle, the essence of the discipline lies in foreseeing and predetermining a future end state, a *telos*. The primacy of *telos* is based on a procedure that predetermines and subordinates the various elements of a building. The architect is more than a technician, a *tektonikos*. Following etymology, he is an archi-tect, dealing with both *archè* and *technè*. He establishes *archè*, his strongest weapon: a principle, an authority that is closely related to the political field.

The architect's basic instrument is the plan. Essential is the double sense of it, as an accurate description of the layout of a building and as a means of controlling the future. This is what is inherent to all architectural operations. A plan designs an object, unifies diverse, often contradicting, factors into one language and establishes control "towards" the future. A project becomes a projection thrown into the future.

Though, as a pretension of stable conditions, architecture seems more and more like a built anachronism, like an inert object with serious problems of adapting to an increasingly unpredictable future. The question is how to build in an epoch without a *telos*? To pose such queries is already to displace Architecture with architectures. It is to transform a tradition into a site of translation. It is to render the potential universality of a project particular and specific: where to build is not merely to impose a vision but to narrate and construct a habitat. This would involve withdrawing from the confident grammar of the former and speaking the conditional languages of the latter. Rendering such a situation critical could be seen as one of the more relevant architectural questions today: not a product of a hermetic system, signature or authorship, but rather a re-territorialization into specific situations and cultural phenomena.

LOSING CONTROL

The problem of making – willingly or unwillingly – something readable is a difficulty that once puzzled Henri Lefebvre, the father of recent urbanism debates. He insisted on the complex relationships between the spheres of physical and mental space on the basis of everyday social praxis, while being unsettled by the "dominance of the readable and visible" in the interpretation of space. Interpretation, according to Lefebvre, has to come later – as an afterthought of the production of social space, so to speak. "Reading" follows production in every case except those cases in which space is especially produced in order to be read.[01] Yet, this exception describes accurately the problematic position of the architect. He is reading all the time. He constructs spatial products to be read: a speculation on the world with buildings. How could the architect overcome reading and speculating? How to get rid of the architect's most powerful weapon: an authority that guarantees his authorship as such? How to build doubt? How to lose control?

Throughout the past decades one of the most common, yet problematic answers to these questions used to be the "non-plan." Acting as a correction against the protective mechanisms of architectural systems, it seems to deliver a privileged access to a reality that is understood as heterogenic, open, unplanned. Within this approach, the city and its streets become the arsenal for metaphors of the concrete and the real. Temporary strategies in the tradition of Situationism leave the narrow cages of cultural institutions and appropriate existing territories and empty spaces in the city, and yet,

[01] HENRI LEFEBVRE, *THE PRODUCTION OF SPACE* (OXFORD: BLACKWELL, 1991), PP. 141-147.

in doing so, run the risk of being ensnared by a "festivalization" in line with the premises of neoliberal deregulation. The euphemistic "non-plan" becomes another version of capitalistic laissez-faire.[02] In this respect, it is doubtful whether the attempts to reject the very idea of institutions – in a reflex of Foucault's genealogical work on institutional bodies such as the asylum, the hospital, and the prison – have been successful. The anti-institutional off- and sub-cultural movements tend to become as stable and protective as their ideological enemies.

The opposite strategy attacks the problem from the other side, i.e., from the inside of the hermetic shelter. Since the 1990s, art institutions such as museums, galleries, and theaters opened themselves towards the phenomena of the street and other organizational configurations. Spatial models such as the flea market,[03] the camp, the school, and the workshop have entered the Palais de Tokyo in Paris, the ErsatzStadt at the Volksbühne in Berlin, the conversion of the Bockenheimer Depot in Frankfurt, and the failed Manifesta 6 School in Nicosia. Yet work in the expanded field has two sides. What could be seen optimistically as a strategy of opening and risk is – seen rather pessimistically – just another turn in the ongoing differentiation of systemic boundaries. What seems to be a subversive infiltration or a process of "smuggling"[04] might turn out to be a sophisticated integration. A more or less unconscious expansion of what used to be out of reach and out of control.

---

[02] JONATHAN HUGHES, "AFTER NON-PLAN: RETRENCHMENT & REASSERTION," IN *NON-PLAN. ESSAYS ON FREEDOM, PARTICIPATION AND CHANGE IN MODERN ARCHITECTURE AND URBANISM*, EDS. JONATHAN HUGHES, SIMON SADLER (OXFORD: ARCHITECTURAL PRESS, 2000), PP. 175-178.

[03] SEE NICOLAS BOURRIAUD, *POSTPRODUCTION. CULTURE AS SCREENPLAY: HOW ART REPROGRAMS THE WORLD* (NEW YORK: LUKAS & STERNBERG, 2002), P. 22.

[04] IRIT ROGOFF, "SMUGGLING. A CURATORIAL MODEL," IN *UNDER CONSTRUCTION. PERSPECTIVES ON INSTITUTIONAL PRACTICE*, EDS. VANESSA JOAN MÜLLER, NICOLAUS SCHAFHAUSEN (COLOGNE: WALTHER KÖNIG, 2006), PP. 124-127.

The difficulty today is that the strategies of opening the hermetic cage of the cultural institution and developing concrete social projects is not the exclusive project of curators, but has become an explicit element within state politics. When Tony Blair stated in his foreword to New Labor's manifesto ("Because Britain Deserves Better ") that "The arts are central to the task of recreating the community," it became apparent that the original avant-garde struggle to radicalize culture by linking art and life has been appropriated over time, and today runs the risk of serving a utilitarian demand on culture. In a certain way, it seems as if the art institution is fulfilling a historic evolution from hard to soft boundaries – from the notion of a museum that appeared in the late 16th century which introduced a severe separation between everyday life and the cultural artifacts; to the establishment of the public institution (when the Assemblée Nationale decided to convert the Louvre into a publicly accessible gallery three years after the 1789 revolution); to the museum that makes pretensions towards the dissolution of the boundaries between art and life. Eventually, the construction and critique of hermetic models run the risk of leading to the construction of an architectural rhetoric of soft boundaries. And worse, the politics of accessibility generates a new form of social engineering.

PLANNING AS CONFLICT

Professional boundaries are at stake when the main actors collaborate on the construction of the art space. Artist, curator, and architect are caught in a love-hate-relationship fighting for control over the same space and, ultimately for the protection of their authorship. The boundaries of the disciplines are questioned and renegotiated. What starts as a collaboration forms an explosive mix – and possibly ends with friendly fire. But what defines these relationships on a systemic level? How much distance and how much proximity are possible?

Historically, the boundaries of the disciplines have rather blurred contours. Art and architecture were not distinct professions, per se, but intensively intertwined for centuries. Art is still an open discipline, whereas architecture is now a protected profession – in the assumption that architects provide a shelter and protect people from harm, just as doctors and lawyers do. In the Renaissance, architecture was a product of the manifold work of genius: Michelangelo, Brunelleschi or Alberti were architects, painters, sculptors, and writers all folded into one. Beginning in the mid-nineteenth century, when architects began organizing themselves into a professional category – with the "invention" of their profession – their social and cultural position was legitimized by seemingly opposing aspects of their work. On the one hand, architects prided themselves on their knowledge of spatial organization and engineering; they were directly involved in supervising the building process. On the other hand, they took pleasure, nevertheless, in the artistic aspect of their work. However, with the modernization of the building industry and competition created by engineers, the architects of the modernist avant-garde subordinated their "art" to the engineering, an entirely new twist: with the aid of building technology and increasingly efficient production methods, architects were able to redesign the boundaries of their profession – the architect, as it were, with this re-newed engineering muscle behind him, was indispensable until the 1970s. But the success came at a high cost: the complicity with industry interests and state politics in the modernization of space (and modernist "mega-projects," in particular) has seriously damaged the legitimacy of the architect. Today alongside the increasing status of the arts in contemporary culture, the "art" in architecture seems to have been rediscovered, and the weak aspect, in turn, has become its strong.

As a result the field of architecture is becoming narrow: engineers like Cecil Balmond are pushing the evolution of architecture much further than any "star-architect," while artists like Olafur Eliasson construct an actual phenomenology of space – a difficult feat, even for the most sensitive of all architects. In this critical situation, the architect – the traditional specialist for the construction of shelter – is searching for his own protected space. But old protectionism does not seem to be a reliable solution; nor does architecture's interdisciplinary character, the first aspect that Vitruvius described when he was launching architectural theory. Most probably, the architect has two options. Either he waits for a further differentiation and eventual collapse of the professional boundaries into *Baukunst*, i.e., a fusion of architecture and art, or he shifts the category of boundary conflict to the scale of a building and the micro-politics of planning processes.

NEGOTIATED MATERIAL: PROTECTION AND EXPOSURE
The architectural implications of border conflicts provoke different models of spatial separation and porosity, i.e., strategies that define environmental conditions of opening and closure. In this context, the notion of the environment operates directly with the concreteness of architectural material and in its inherent capacities to mediate the instability of physical environments. Elements like the ceiling, floor or wall are interpreted as material transitions between system and environment, as boundaries that define opening and closure. By using and abusing the contraction between the instability of external fluctuation and the stability of internal concentration, the material strategy generates an architecture based on different rhythms and gradual phenomena. As a tectonic detail, the material concretizes different modes of perception – degrees of visual protection and exposure, rhythms of speed and slowness, noise and silence.

In order to properly conserve art objects, the museum usually has the task of prohibiting the everyday conditions of the exterior environment. The museum has the unusual task of "freezing" an ideal object condition. For eternity. In contrast, continuing the "life" of an object by extending the original environmental conditions would, in the long run, inevitably lead to its decay. Stability used to be the main parameter of an art space, but now – as a result of "participation" art and interaction – the notion of instability has become increasingly relevant.

Yet, if the negotiation between protection and exposure – or to put it in a drastic way, the conflict of "Objects vs People" – should ultimately construct the new typology of an art institution at risk, one has to ask: how do we negotiate the physical material in architectural practice? What is the status of material? To say that building techniques and materials like glass, steel, and concrete set the rhythm of architectural evolution is trivial. Less banal is the suspicion that recent developments are less focused on material technology than on the organization of a building as such. Construction industries have relinquished the ambition of revolutionizing the shell, the raw construction, and, for the last thirty years, the shell structure has fulfilled its archaic destiny. The main changes happen instead in the material applications, particularly in surface and security technologies. These new systems have nothing in common with traditional tectonics. Most often they are multilayered, hybrid conglomerates of material with precisely defined areas of use. The interface of the raw structure is controlled via sophisticated technologies that join one material to the other. Eventually, building becomes a problem of interface. This situation then confronts the architect, the traditional specialist of material organization. Distanced from the production process of a new conglomerate material that is beyond his tectonic control, he becomes a moderator of systems.

MODEL WORLD

How soft or hard are the boundaries of architecture? Since the 1990s, some of the most advanced architectural practices shifted their focus away from the subject of representation, meaning, and language towards those of organization, production, and technique as potential generators of form. The flow of informational tools into design practices shifted an important part of architectural debates into "parametric design" by proclaiming an architecture of emergence. However, as the potentials of production increase exponentially, a gap seems to be growing between a seemingly infinite range of formal, material, and organizational possibilities and their actual performance within political, social, and economic contexts. They are pure planning processes, not knowing when to stop, ultimately excluding the critical moment of "decision." Today the old question of whether buildings are pure material emergences of the autonomous discipline "Architecture" or whether they should relate to external systems beyond their mere organizational nature, appears with renewed force.

We are witnessing a soft language. A politics of accessibility. An architecture of the soft boundary. A new form of social engineering. In this respect, I would argue that the role of architecture is neither to secure the division between art and life, nor to overcome it. It is neither pure exclusion nor pure inclusion. It would be naïve to neglect the impact of protection and dismiss the tradition of the architect's *archè* and promote a borderless approach to spatial production. Maybe it is time to acknowledge the perversity of the architect. Certainly, the architect can critically investigate his involvement in all the modern constructions that served as models for Foucault – the hospital, the prison, the psychiatric ward – and add them to the pathology of the museum. But overcome it? Get rid of it?

Maybe all the clichés about architecture are right: order, stability, control, safety, security, authority, hermeticism, institutionalization. Yet, paradoxically, these very clichés seem to be the very reason why architecture is relevant and, in an uncanny way, attractive for the arts. It creates resistance and critical discourse. To overcome the problematic traditions of architecture would dissolve the discipline as such.

Or at least make it uncritical. In order to maintain its cultural relevance, it seems to be unavoidable to keep the critical, often uncomfortable, position of a specialist for spatial control and protection. A builder of shelter – always on the thin line between literal physical protection and the model world of metaphors. The categorical problem could be its greatest potential: architecture as a medium in which political metaphors and physical manifestations collapse into one phenomenon. Ultimately, it is this double character that makes the architect a political figure – whether willingly or unwillingly. The architect is a figure who has been given the tools to both simulate order and develop models. Those models must be both utopian and inhabitable.

FIRST PUBLISHED IN *PROTECTIONS*, EDS. ADAM BUDAK, CHRISTINE PETERS, AND KUNSTHAUS GRAZ, COLOGNE 2006, PP. 186-203.

PLANNING THE UNPREDICTABLE
A DIALOGUE BETWEEN NIKOLAUS HIRSCH AND WILLIAM FORSYTHE

NIKOLAUS HIRSCH In the Bockenheimer Depot, we collaborated on something that oscillates or shifts between determination and indetermination. I am still not quite sure how to describe our role: Did we design the space, in a literal sense of predetermining or designating?

WILLIAM FORSYTHE Is it design? Not yet. It is probably something like protodesign. The first decision concerned the floor. In a way, people should get back to the floor. That's why the space is very floor-oriented.

NIKOLAUS HIRSCH Actually, the floor – with its felt carpeting and other felt modules – made the space softer; besides its impact on the human position, this had an enormous impact on acoustic conditions.

WILLIAM FORSYTHE Another aspect is a size that has no orientation towards specific age groups. In other words, it works for tall people, tiny people, for babies, young people, old people. They can design their own comfort themselves. So what did we make? If anything, we designed opportunities for people.

NIKOLAUS HIRSCH The making of these opportunities was, from an architectural point of view, a process of planning, of making drawings. But, compared to other projects, the collaboration with you worked in a completely different way.

WILLIAM FORSYTHE I wouldn't say completely, that is probably too absolute. Architects are always creating spaces for bodies. In this case, we were focusing very much on bodies in public spaces. Even in industrial architecture it is still machines and bodies together. How are people usually constructed by public space? They are standardized. Their movements are determined. The challenge for us was to say, "This should be a non-standardized room," because visitors do not come in one standard bodily state.

NIKOLAUS HIRSCH I think this approach is even apparent in the detail. For instance, when we discussed benches, dimensions…

WILLIAM FORSYTHE …corners of things…

NIKOLAUS HIRSCH …and proportions. I remember a meeting in the ballet rehearsal space when we tested relations between the body and the modular elements. Space. It was very much about finding spatial proportions and sizes that do not determine specific positions, but which allow for unpredictable positions of the body.

WILLIAM FORSYTHE How you arrange your body physically is social, psychological, but in this case we never wanted to be far from the floor, because it is very much a dancerly room in this respect. So the question was: how can we get people to react differently to this room? And one of the ways was to say that they do not arrange their bodies according to a situation, but that they arrange the situation according to their bodies. All of our benches and tables are a little bit wide – they are wide enough to do other things than just sit on. They don't define just one specific position or function. You see how people spread themselves out; they are more curvilinear in their postures. They are using more than just their backbones to support themselves. They are spreading their bodies out, their weight is differently distributed – different muscles are required.

NIKOLAUS HIRSCH As an effect, the edges of the modular elements tend to disappear through use: they become soft. They are rearranged in unpredictable configurations, being folded and unfolded. What one may call "architecture" is permanently in process. The spatial concept was intended as a research between stability and instability. How do you see the relationship between architecture and dance? In a rather reductive way one could say that architecture is rather about stasis, whereas dance is more about movement. These disciplines seem to be quite opposed.

WILLIAM FORSYTHE For me it is rather hard to think of architecture as not made for bodies. And dance is just a way of being body. We are always body, day and night. We have beds, pillows. You can have a comforted body, punished body, body in fitness studios, hospital body, kung-fu body, rehabilitating body. What we are suggesting in the space at the Bockenheimer Depot is that there is more than one way of being body. And what, then, is a body in public space? And how could a body be in a less defining space? Architecture is always making us body in a certain way. The choice of using stairs, elevators or ramps alone is an authoritarian way to say, "Be body this way, be body that way."

NIKOLAUS HIRSCH We said that the space that we created is less about a fixed form, less about determining specific positions, and more about allowing an undetermined process. How does that refer to your own practice as a choreographer?

WILLIAM FORSYTHE Every choreography establishes a certain number of parameters. Usually, one does not try to accomplish every possible movement that the human body can do. You have to choose a series of categories that are discursive. Those movement categories are your resources for that particular work. What we are looking for in the Bockenheimer Depot is to present the space as a resource.

NIKOLAUS HIRSCH In fact, the concept of space as a resource is a very political question.

WILLIAM FORSYTHE I thought that if we can afford to make theater here, perhaps we can afford to live publicly here. Everyday life in public space is usually orientated towards consumption, but here we have a space where one does not have to consume.

NIKOLAUS HIRSCH People bring their own food, their own drinks, their kids, their bikes.

WILLIAM FORSYTHE We don't usually think about living in public. The project is an attempt to turn this around. Away from the private body and towards the public body. Usually physical behaviors of bodies are very regulated. In that sense, we wanted to have space that allows one simply to be body, rather than a space that requires specific behaviors of the body. The aim was to create a space of unregulated time. The body is not only physical, it is also temporal. What we choose to do with our body – what we do with it in time – is a very important subject. And that is perhaps very choreographic.

NIKOLAUS HIRSCH The use of time reflects the architectural approach of our concept: on one side of the hall, there is a rather formal theater space (including auditorium and stage) and its scheduled time, on the other, we have a rather informal space and an unregulated use of time. The two spheres are negotiated through a huge vertical element made out of felt – something between a wall and a curtain; between creating autonomy and providing exchange. The element is flexible in longitudinal axis, so that informal and formal spaces can be changed in size, i.e., reciprocally shrinking and expanding. In terms of temporal use, there are important repercussions between these areas. Like the ballet performances of some members of the Ballet Frankfurt that extend from one space into the other, or Louise Neri's arts program, "Public Life," that uses both spaces, or Ekkehard Ehlers and Olaf Karnik's music program, "Under Construction," that uses and abuses the felt elements of the undetermined space. These are phenomena which occur even on a smaller scale when visitors manipulate architectural elements according to their own individual rhythm of time.

WILLIAM FORSYTHE People can have a nap, be lazy, do nothing.

NIKOLAUS HIRSCH It is interesting how modular elements are reconfigured into beds, blankets, pillows, in an almost unpredictable way. Which, in fact, is something that interests me a lot: how something that we planned is able to disappear as a design. An oscillation between something planned and something that evolves. Something seemingly contradictory: Planning the unpredictable.

WILLIAM FORSYTHE You are describing a paradox.

NIKOLAUS HIRSCH The paradox between planning and evolution is something important for our project. Traditionally, at the very center of architecture as a discipline is "planning." In that respect, the work at the Depot was extremely interesting: we had to deal with quite different rhythms of production, of making. The work in the context of a theater – and especially your approach – is very much about process, which is actually quite different from what architectural discussion understands by process or processual planning. Yours is a kind of directness, a true search with all its consequences: going back and forward, starting again in a 1:1 scale in the workshop. I remember moments when we as architects had a real problem with control, when we had to create coherence in order to keep to schedules and costs. In these rare moments, we were thrown back into the classical role of architecture: no improvisation, but a determining strategy towards the future.

WILLIAM FORSYTHE Yes, completely teleological.

NIKOLAUS HIRSCH In contrast to this was the collaboration with you. It seems to me as if your approach is very much about maintaining openness, a process of the making. Does the notion of openness play a role in your work as a choreographer?

WILLIAM FORSYTHE The staging of public space is not different from what I do on a theatrical stage in terms of its strategies and organization. You certainly have different resources. The players are your public, the stage is the public space. When I am doing a piece for a stage, I usually want to know how big the stage is, how high it is, how deep it is. You have to know the rules of the space, what it can do. That comes through practice. When I worked with Daniel Libeskind in Groningen, it became clear to me that there is a difference between something that is going to last for a long time and something that lasts a short time – i.e., something that has life in the moment of its appearance but which disappears in the next moment.

NIKOLAUS HIRSCH The performativity of a building is quite different from the performativity of an act or a movement.

WILLIAM FORSYTHE How does the present perform? We first assess our resources and then ask: what are the properties of *this* present? And by *present* I mean the political present, the economic present, the social and psychological present. The question is: how can I best serve this situation? How can something appear that has a different kind of value, not a monetary value, but a purely ontological value; a way of being?

NIKOLAUS HIRSCH I am interested in the process of making a piece from the beginning to the end. Is there something like a "plan"? How do you create coherence? It seems that the notion of memory is quite important in that respect. In architecture, to a certain extent, you have to make drawings. This is a medium that guarantees and stabilizes memory, which is important in the translation from drawing to building. In dance, however, it seems to be much more about a memory that does not depend on other mediums like drawings. It is a different way to communicate spatial phenomena.

WILLIAM FORSYTHE The common thing is *threshold*. Architects have to make plans, they have to have a direction. Our threshold in choreography is much softer. You, as an architect, have this two-dimensional version. It is interesting how many things are determined by surfaces. Much of the industrial world is oriented to the idea of surface. The only surface that we have is the floor. We don't have to have the same kind of linguistic logic, but we have a coordinational and physical logic. But it is not a "plan." We don't go through the actual materialization of an idea in the same way. We go straight from the idea to the structure. It happens in process. Therefore, I say it is a soft threshold – it is hard to say when you have passed over from one state to the next.

NIKOLAUS HIRSCH Is translation from drawing to choreography, or vice versa, a tool that you use?

WILLIAM FORSYTHE No. Choreography is in itself "graphy" – a drawing. We are not drawing. We are drawn.

NIKOLAUS HIRSCH There is no intermediary. This direct, procedural approach, which seems to be one of the main characteristics of dance, became part of our architectural approach.

WILLIAM FORSYTHE The idea of procedure can be shifted around. If the Depot lobby is now a choreography, the procedure is taken over by the public. The public's awareness of this is not crucial to the enterprise. In other words, the awareness does not always have to be focused on that in order for its meaning as choreography to be present. It can lie in the organization of the architecture itself.

NIKOLAUS HIRSCH In the Depot, people reconfigure what one can call architecture.

WILLIAM FORSYTHE What they leave behind is a very interesting organization. At the end of the day, when you leave the room, it is a spectacular situation.

NIKOLAUS HIRSCH And it is interesting to look at it the next morning. There is a gap, as if things have lost their lives.

WILLIAM FORSYTHE That is probably the difference between a space and a place. What happens is that people come into a space and turn it into a place. A place has a meaning, it is personalized, whereas a space is relatively abstract.

NIKOLAUS HIRSCH The distinction between space and place is probably quite useful when we refer to the question of utopian spaces, as some comments did in the context of our work in the Depot. Is it a utopian space or not? The idea of utopia is very much about space and its ideal organization. In fact, I believe that the abstraction in classical utopias created authoritarian tendencies.

WILLIAM FORSYTHE I think so too. Classical utopias were highly determined. The lack of determination here creates a place. Although, the Depot is not really a place until people have an effect on it.

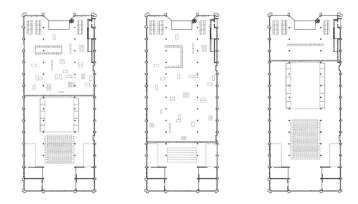

THE DIALOGUE HERE WAS PUBLISHED ON THE OCCASION OF "UTOPIA STATION" (VENICE BIENNALE, 2003) IN THE BELGIAN MAGAZINE *JANUS* 14 (2003), PP. 64–68. THE CONVERSION OF THE BOCKENHEIMER DEPOT THEATER IN FRANKFURT AM MAIN WAS DESIGNED BY ARCHITECTS NIKOLAUS HIRSCH AND MICHEL MÜLLER IN COLLABORATION WITH WILLIAM FORSYTHE.

OBJECTS VS PEOPLE

Once an object enters a museum, the nature of its existence changes. Accosted with a new and possibly hostile physical environment, the object's original conditions are modified or even lost in the new context. But there is an imperative for objects of every age, composition, and condition: conservation. The museum assumes the responsibility for maintaining the object's physical stability, for slowing down the processes of decay.

If the ambient environment in the museum was simply geared to the needs of the collection, the rate of decay of the objects would be slow. But museum spaces are not solely occupied by objects; there are also human beings to be housed – staff and, in significantly larger numbers, visitors. Both people and objects are sensitive to the environment; they even respond to the same physical variables of environmental change, but there is a crucial difference: people are primarily temperature sensitive, whereas most museum objects are humidity sensitive. A 4% relative humidity (RH) change has the same effect on objects as a 10% change in temperature. The same change in RH has the same effect on people as a 0.1° change in temperature. This means that objects are a hundred times more sensitive to RH than people.

Museum visitors can take action to influence their environment; they can adapt to, and recover from, a thermally hostile environment by changing the pattern of their activities or by moving from a place where they feel uncomfortable, or by reducing the amount of clothing they wear. Visitors wear heavy outdoor clothing, which may cause them to overheat and perspire as they walk through a space that is kept warm enough to provide thermal comfort for lightly clothed guards. On rainy days, people wearing wet raincoats cause even additional moisture gains. The solution to the problem is simple: they could leave their clothes at a cloakroom. Objects, though, have no such control over their environment. They are rather passive recipients of the ambient environmental conditions that people help to create and are unlikely to recover from completely after being subjected to a hostile environment.

The conflict is fundamental: with their very presence, human beings produce changes in their immediate environment. Human metabolic functions such as breathing and physical activity such as walking alter the conditions of temperature and humidity in the air and effect the objects. A visitor releases approximately 60 grams of water vapor per hour, and at least 60 watts per square meter of body surface as heat. Can this be prevented?

Note: There is no reliable relationship between human comfort and the suitable environment for an artwork.

THIS TEXT IS A CONTRIBUTION TO HANS ULRICH OBRIST'S PROJECT "OUT OF EQUATION."

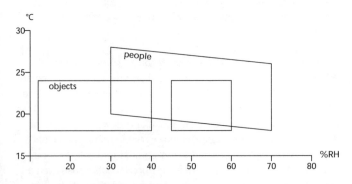

RH in the museum: objects vs people

EUROPEAN KUNSTHALLE
NICOLAUS SCHAFHAUSEN INTERVIEWS NIKOLAUS HIRSCH
ON THE RELATIONSHIP BETWEEN ART AND ARCHITECTURE

NICOLAUS SCHAFHAUSEN Architecture plays an increasingly hypertrophied role in contemporary art institutions. You have been researching this issue for many years at the Architectural Association and other academic contexts. In your practice, you have developed spatial models for institutions such as the Bockenheimer Depot Theater in Frankfurt, an experimental theater at Gießen University, the Manifesta 6 school in Nicosia, unitednationsplaza, and currently a cultural lab in Dehli and – not to forget – our collaborative project, the European Kunsthalle. How would you define the role of architecture in art institutions?

NIKOLAUS HIRSCH The impact of spatial strategies on institutional debates is crucial. On the one hand, this is because art institutions have become strategic instruments of urban planning and marketing expected to reactivate entire regions and cities. This phenomenon, known also as the "Bilbao effect" assigns a dominant role to architecture. An alternative position is taken by strategies that – in a more or less explicit tradition of Situationism – temporarily appropriate existing territories in the city, somehow avoiding architecture at all. In institutional debates, you confront a schizophrenic situation in which architecture is expected to be either the solution or the problem. This rather simplistic dichotomy reflects a fetishization of architecture on both sides: architecture is the absolute good or the absolute evil of institutional critique.

NICOLAUS SCHAFHAUSEN When we started the European Kunsthalle, I did not give you a specific brief, neither to design a new building, an intervention into existing spaces nor a temporary infrastructure for an exhibition. The commission was to develop a spatial strategy for the European Kunsthalle in Cologne, i.e., for a new institution without a building. How have you approached and structured your work?

NIKOLAUS HIRSCH On the basis of our research at the Architectural Association in London and a workshop at the RWTH Aachen, we – Philipp Misselwitz, Markus Miessen, Matthias Görlich, and myself – have launched the study *Spaces of Production*. Its focus was not only the obvious question of display of artworks in a gallery, but a *Kunsthalle* as a space of production on different levels. Case studies on institutions as diverse as Witte de With, Iaspis or Artangel were analyzed in terms of spatial configuration and materials, organizational and financial models, cooperation networks, temporal sequencing, and programmatic thrust. The most striking result of this research was the critical proportion between the heavy luggage of architecture and the light luggage of exhibitions.

NICOLAUS SCHAFHAUSEN This proportional problem seems to be reflected in the key notions of your work for the European Kunsthalle: "stability" and "instability." Can you elaborate on this?

NIKOLAUS HIRSCH Indeed, the dilemma between architectural stability and instability is crucial for our study *Spaces of Production*. Stability versus instability, i.e., the question of architectural duration, opens up different fields for action and yet also sets limitations. The question is: how much coherence must an institution possess? What does "stability" mean with reference to the physical conditions of exhibiting art, i.e., the perfect control of light, air, and the surrounding elements? There are institutions that determine a highly controlled environment, a neutral and unchangeable interior of a stable building. On the other hand, there are art spaces that blur into the everyday life of the city: institutions with changing, dynamic boundaries, sometimes altogether invisible in terms of gallery space. Both concepts have their own history and traditions, but now they can be re-thought and re-combined as a model that provides both protection and exposure. In fact, in our research it became clear that today the rhythms and durations of both models tend to approach one another. The opposition seems to be rather ideological. Unstable typologies require more and more structure in terms of technical equipment and manpower, whereas the seemingly "stable" Kunsthalle is destabilized by the ever-shorter life span of buildings, by ever more frequent refurbishments due to the fast change of artistic direction and spatial ambitions, by an ever more accelerating rhythm of artistic formats (such as exhibitions, lectures, and performances) and their diverse spatial requirements. Thus, our concept aims at a Kunsthalle whose architecture is interpreted as a material cycle.

NICOLAUS SCHAFHAUSEN Shifting from the research to the program of the European Kunsthalle: can you describe your role in our discursive program *Under Construction* and the exhibition "Models for Tomorrow"? What was your approach to these temporary formats of an institution without a fixed space?

NIKOLAUS HIRSCH We understood these formats as a sort of applied research. They are neither pure practice, nor pure research. Both formats were temporary and dispersed throughout the city, yet they had a precise structure in time and space. For "Models for Tomorrow," we created a spatial inventory of such diverse sites as call-shops, banks or gyms, on the basis of what you have named *post-public space*. All the 22 spaces were different in terms of their organizational structures, opening hours, and logics of inclusion and exclusion. Accessibility becomes a crucial criterion of any future institution of contemporary art.

NICOLAUS SCHAFHAUSEN The urban configuration of these spaces did not produce a situationist or improvised pattern, but a specific form. You insisted on the formal character of the institution.

NIKOLAUS HIRSCH You are right: the spatial strategy was to create coherence within the idea of temporariness and fragmentation. We wanted to be clear about the fact that the exhibition is not an improvised event, but a structure that is a piece of planned architecture on a different scale and that works as a model for an institution without building. Consequently we referred to the *parcours* as one of the characteristic logics of the museum. We literally created a loop with a diameter of exactly one kilometer.

NICOLAUS SCHAFHAUSEN As a final step you have developed a new model for a Kunsthalle that integrates stable and unstable parameters. In what sense does this approach present a new typology of a Kunsthalle? How does it react to a cultural situation that is characterized by an increasing withdrawal of the state and by volatile private interests?

NIKOLAUS HIRSCH Unstable and stable parameters are combined as if something provisionary solidifies over time. The Kunsthalle is created by accumulation. The project is not about inventing or designing the ideal Kunsthalle. It is not the belief in an absolute master plan, but rather it is about a strategy of conceptual pragmatism, if not a radical opportunism. Every building project is – before the start of the design – described by its programmatic brief, by its division into different components and their specific functional requirements and size in terms of surface area and height. The spatial program of an art institution with its offices, toilets, storage, gallery, auditorium, café, etc., usually forms a coherent unity, with one author. Our strategy breaks with this assumption and separates the building brief into independent components. Programmatic pieces such as galleries, offices, bookshops etc. will be planned by different authors (in fact, by artists) in a sequential time logic, by accumulation so to speak. It will be a time-based, growing institution, comparable to the logic of an *exquisite corpse*: an image or story that is built collectively from individual segments, a network of routes from one beginning (in our case, the office of the European Kunsthalle as an Ur-cell) to many possible endings.

NICOLAUS SCHAFHAUSEN What is the conceptual link between the programmatic components and the artists?

NIKOLAUS HIRSCH It is both a conceptual link and an empirical phenomenon. Today, you can observe that many artists are interested in infrastructures: think of the conference room that Liam Gillick did for you at the Frankfurter Kunstverein, or Monica Bonvicini's *Toilet*, Elmgreen & Dragset's galleries (better known as *Powerless Structures*), Anton Vidokle's and Julieta Aranda's *Martha Rosler Library* and many other archive and library projects. We use this phenomenon and push it further towards the construction of an accumulative Kunsthalle.

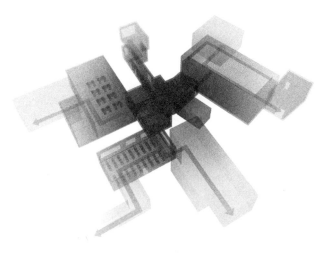

NICOLAUS SCHAFHAUSEN This appears to be the logical step in the post-Bilbao era: the architecture becomes the exhibition, but under conditions set by the curators and artists.

NIKOLAUS HIRSCH Absolutely. Every new piece of the building becomes a new piece of the art exhibition. Not ad hoc, but in the typical timescale of exhibitions, for example, three months. The architecture is curated. What we are aiming at is a direct, inseparable relation between the heavy luggage of architecture and the temporary structure of the exhibition, i.e., its timescales, funding policies, and programmatic volatility.

NICOLAUS SCHAFHAUSEN What happens is a hybridization of roles: the artist becomes the architect, the architecture of the building becomes the exhibition. Does your strategy imply a new understanding of your own role as an architect?

NIKOLAUS HIRSCH What is new is a radical questioning of authorship. Making architecture in this strategy might be closer to scripting than designing. In this case, i.e., in an international context in which spectacular museum architecture has become inflationary and tends to create an endless déjà vu, it might make sense to *not* define my role through designing. Yet, it is still planning: we define the rules of the evolution of the Kunsthalle. We plan the logics of connectivity between the different components, referring to the typologies of museal organization: linear and circular sequences like the classic *parcours*, continuous bifurcations or autonomous units.

NICOLAUS SCHAFHAUSEN If you question disciplinary boundaries and roles, do you still consider yourself an architect in the traditional sense?

NIKOLAUS HIRSCH It would be misleading to pretend that I am not following the role model of what is traditionally called *the architect*. Like it or not, my practice is part of a culture of planning that uses particular tools such as drawing to describe and prescribe a physical condition in the future. It is an extreme form of authorship if you think of it in terms of "authority." The construction of such a complex and slow phenomenon as a building requires an unavoidable, sometimes perverse control over time and space. But indeed, there seems to be a new notion of architectural practice in an expanded field, in which the material and its cultural references change more and more rapidly. The architect cannot count anymore on his "slow" medium and increasingly becomes a hybrid actor in the field between curators, artists, users, and the public. In this sense, the question of authoring space becomes more critical in my work.

NICOLAUS SCHAFHAUSEN Would you agree that contemporary architects work more in the field that lies between architecture and other disciplines? Is there more demand today for such trans-disciplinary practice in architecture?

NIKOLAUS HIRSCH Sometimes it is more efficient to work from the boundaries of a discipline. Yet this does not imply giving up the hard core of the profession. In fact, I do not believe in the complete dissolution of disciplines towards a smooth and gentle cross-over, but in a culture of collaboration that also includes "friendly fire" between the disciplines. In this sense, it is less a matter of "architecture & …," like architecture and dance, visual arts or theater, but a question of conjunction, a question of developing specific tools that could act as a common ground. What is necessary is physical material that can be negotiated and create a productive conflict.

NICOLAUS SCHAFHAUSEN This productive conflict and its reflection in the European Kunsthalle should also be seen in the context of previous collaborations. You have worked with choreographer William Forsythe and recently with visual artists Thomas Bayrle and Raqs Media Collective. How do collaborations between architects and artists work in practice?

NIKOLAUS HIRSCH Practice makes two things clear: the common and the different. These collaborations confronted me with very different artistic role models and, consequently, with diverse spatial strategies. My work with William Forsythe provoked a friendly fire between planning and improvisation, between a discipline that establishes control through a plan and one that achieves it through a body. The *Node House* for Raqs Media Collective was a rather free spatial translation of a narrative structure of 18 videos and ultimately had an enormous sculptural presence, whilst in the collaboration with Thomas Bayrle – the *Autobahn Tower* at the Museum of Modern Art in Frankfurt – I adopted the main parameters of Bayrle's *Autobahn* (a work previously shown at the Venice Biennale in 2003) - a specific grid, the weaving technique, the cardboard material – and made it "more three-dimensional," eventually turning it into a building. The degree of invention was quite minimal, as if my style, signature, and ego had disappeared in an increasingly complex *Autobahn* structure.

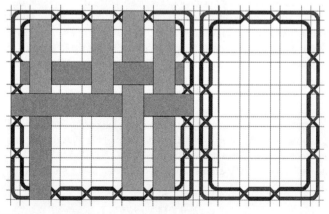

NICOLAUS SCHAFHAUSEN When we shift the discussion from collaborative projects to exhibition projects, we talk about a category of architecture in which the idea of "service" seems to be critical. Exhibition architecture is a phenomenon that is increasingly visible today. With its temporary spaces, design, layout, partitions, it often takes on a position of equal importance to the artworks. Do you see this as a positive development?

NIKOLAUS HIRSCH It is at least a critical development. To put it into general terms: architecture is not necessary for the display of art, but sometimes it contributes to an additional reflection on the exhibition itself. So one of the first things one should ask is: how much architecture is necessary? Each architectural intervention should have a certain necessity – and sometimes it is just not necessary. At the "Manifesta 4" I told the curators that they do not need an architect for the refurbishment of their old building. A paradoxical process: they did not believe me and I had to prove the dissolution of my own role by architectural drawings.

NICOLAUS SCHAFHAUSEN The nearly invisible position you took at the "Manifesta 4" is one extreme; the other is your work for "Frequencies-Hz" at the Schirn Kunsthalle in which your work was much more dominant, ultimately becoming a piece on its own within the exhibition.

NIKOLAUS HIRSCH You can understand the architecture for "Frequencies-Hz" as an adjustable superstructure that integrates different artistic positions as spatial variables of a group show. But this is just one side of the phenomenon "exhibition architecture." The other is that a number of artists explicitly refer to exhibition architecture and design in their work. The whole idea of display becomes part of an artistic practice too, for example Eran Schaerf's structure for "The Eighth Square" at Museum Ludwig in Cologne, or Michael Beutler's "exhibition architecture" for your "Don Quijote" show at the Witte de

With. It matters little if such a structure is conceived by an artist or by an architect. In the best case, it can produce a reflexivity upon exhibition-making itself.

NICOLAUS SCHAFHAUSEN In consequence, would you define architecture as a form of art, as an artistic discipline?

NIKOLAUS HIRSCH I think architecture is a form of art; one that is deeply and problematically involved in pragmatism. This means that the autonomy of architecture is constantly under threat. How can one react to this? My position is that architecture should not claim a degree of autonomy known in the visual and performing arts. On the contrary, the threat posed by other realities is what makes architecture so specific. You can either see this as a problem or as a potential. I see it as a potential.

FROM 2005 TO 2007 THE EUROPEAN KUNSTHALLE WAS LED BY ITS FOUNDING DIRECTOR NICOLAUS SCHAFHAUSEN. AS AN INTEGRAL PART OF THE EUROPEAN KUNSTHALLE, NIKOLAUS HIRSCH, MARKUS MIESSEN, PHILIPP MISSELWITZ, AND MATTHIAS GÖRLICH CREATED A SERIES OF INSTITUTIONAL MODELS AND DEVELOPED THE PROJECT "SPACES OF PRODUCTION."

THE ARCHITECTURAL THING
THE MAKING OF "MAKING THINGS PUBLIC"

If politics is about *things*, as Bruno Latour and Peter Weibel argue, what are then the politics of an exhibition space in which things are spatially organized? Who organizes the territory? How are decisions made? How is space shared, how is the proximity between things negotiated?

After a decade of intense critique on planning methods and their political territorialization, one might be tempted to answer: certainly not by handing the power over to architecture, the metaphor of state building par excellence. But the distribution of more than 700 pieces within 3,000 square meters is not a matter of self-organization. It seems as if a structuring principle combined with a certain authority has to be introduced, i.e., something that can be circumscribed with the Greek notion of *archè.* Eventually, cultural mechanisms direct this issue to a specialist: the *archi-tect*.

If the architect's position as such is already ambivalent – in an exhibition on *Dingpolitik* it is critical. How can I as an architect avoid the profession's problematic heritage, i.e., its tendency to predetermine a future end state, or *telos*? How can I counter the primacy of *telos* that is based on a procedure that determines and subordinates the place of the various parts? A contemporary attempt to investigate these issues might accept the authority, but instead of falling back on the traditional patterns of the discipline, a "thing" must be constructed that can be shared with other disciplines so that authority can be handed back.

Consequently, the architectural strategy developed for "Making Things Public" explores a material tool that can be negotiated between artists, scientists, curators: the wall as the most basic element of spatial differentiation. Neither the classical white museum wall, nor the transparent wall of modernist ideology, this new wall reflects its own ambiguity, thus, allowing different appropriations and changing environments. The wall is an appropriation of the existing wall system of the museum, using its naked aluminum structure as a visible element, but rejecting its notorious plaster cladding. The new surface, a soft translucent polycarbonate skin, is exposed to numerous manipulative processes: openings are cut, screening surfaces are painted, cables introduced, monitors and cases integrated, foils with slogans mounted and removed. As a basic instrument to negotiate different environments, these walls place the usually solid boundaries into an ambivalent and critical position, creating blurred transitions rather than rigid definitions, atmospheres rather than areas.

Through a simple yet flexible rule, the dominant industrial grid of the ZKM turns from a foreground to a background: every existing column is linked to a new wall element that can be positioned in every possible geometry – except at a 90 degree angle. The orthogonal grid of columns vanishes behind the 57 new translucent walls that change the geometry of the industrial space into variations of cells, agglomerations, and assemblies. One is left to ask: do these new configurations eventually become a work of participation? Or a work of self-organization? Neither nor. These notions present models that tend to romanticize the moment of decision-making and ignore the antagonistic character of the political in this process. It is rather a work that embodies the political in any work of architecture as a precondition for shared space.

FIRST PUBLISHED IN *MAKING THINGS PUBLIC*, EDS. BRUNO LATOUR, PETER WEIBEL, CAMBRIDGE, MA: MIT PRESS, 2005, PP. 536-539. THE EXHIBITION "MAKING THINGS PUBLIC: ATMOSPHERES OF DEMOCRACY" WAS CURATED BY BRUNO LATOUR AND PETER WEIBEL AND WAS SHOWN AT ZKM KARLSRUHE FROM 20 MARCH TO 7 AUGUST 2005. THE EXHIBITION ARCHITECTURE WAS DESIGNED BY NIKOLAUS HIRSCH AND MICHEL MÜLLER.

UNITEDNATIONSPLAZA: BUILDING KNOWLEDGE
MARKUS MIESSEN IN CONVERSATION WITH NIKOLAUS HIRSCH

MARKUS MIESSEN Does an architect always design? It seems to me that your involvement in unitednationsplaza proposes a new model of contemporary architectural practice that fuses allocating space, strategic spatial planning, designing physical matter, knowledge production, and teaching.

NIKOLAUS HIRSCH I am trying to connect what used to be separated parts of my work. This sounds rather simple, but actually it does create a conflict with the highly specialized discipline of architecture. In this respect the concept of unitednationsplaza questions the role of an architect in a particular way. To produce a building for an exhibition that actually is not an exhibition, but a school, inevitably implies an architectural practice that is more than design. The shift from exhibition to school emphasizes a social situation; a communal condition which changes the way things are manifested physically in space. The effect on myself was a constant negotiation between different role models: planner, craftsman, and teacher. On the one hand, I am organizing matter, inert matter that ultimately forms something like an institute. On the other hand, I am – invited by Anton Vidokle and together with Boris Groys, Martha Rosler, Walid Raad, Jalal Toufic, Liam Gillick, Natascha Sadr Haghighian, and Tirdad Zolghadr – part of an academic space. In a certain way this reflects an approach that understands a work of architecture as both a theoretical model and a physical space. unitednationsplaza is both a model and a real building in Berlin.

MARKUS MIESSEN What is your personal take on the current trend of institutionalizing future production, that is to say art institutions as places of knowledge production becoming, in the long term, initiators of actualities and matter. How would you describe the new relation between academies and exhibiting art institutions such as galleries and museums?

NIKOLAUS HIRSCH Undoubtedly, there is a new dynamic between museums and academies. This has to do with a critical understanding of knowledge production, and in a larger context, with the arts aiming for socio-political relevance. If you look back to the history of exhibitions in the past 15 years it becomes obvious that some of the most important shows defined their role as that of an initiator of an active social project. The aim was to reposition the exhibition as a project that would in some way be transformative on a social scale – something that, by the way, architecture even unintentionally always does. Yet, it becomes more and more clear that the problem might be that the exhibition deals with things on the level of representation and might just not be the right format to aim these ambitious goals. This limitation explains the recent interest of art institutions, such as museums and galleries, in academic structures. Museums are trying to legitimize and reinvent themselves by expanding to new audiences and – always in danger of political instrumentalization – by referring explicitly to their enlightening mission. In a way, unitednationsplaza is trying to start from the other side: from the school model.

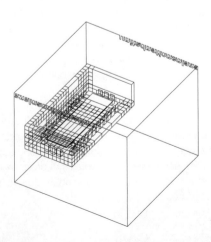

MARKUS MIESSEN The genealogy of unitednationsplaza can be traced back to the failure of the Manifesta School in Nicosia. Could you give us insight into how things moved from Nicosia to Berlin?

NIKOLAUS HIRSCH In 2005, I was asked by the curators Anton Vidokle, Mai Abu ElDahab, and Florian Waldvogel to develop a spatial strategy for the Manifesta 6 School in Nicosia, or more precisely, to plan a coherent structure for three different departments which were spread over the divided city. In 2006, the project was cancelled due to political conflicts between the Greek and Turkish sides. After the failure of the project, we received invitations from several art institutions in Europe to host the project, but in the end we decided against those "friendly takeovers" and opted to create an autonomous institute in Berlin instead.

MARKUS MIESSEN How would you summarize your experience in regards to the impact of the Cypriot site?

NIKOLAUS HIRSCH The critical factor was the friction between the theoretical and physical sides of the model. The concept of a "school as exhibition" in Nicosia was unusual because it did not operate with the more than obvious geopolitical clichés implied by the Cypriot context, but with a rather abstract format: the school. This approach was not site-specific. That's why – on a spatial level – I was trying to develop a rather neutral infrastructure. All the paradigmatic elements of a school such as the auditorium, seminar spaces, offices, kitchen, cafeteria, and dormitories were planned as logistic components, provided by "neutral" organizations like the United Nations' peacekeeping forces or less neutral, private service companies – an approach that Liam Gillick and I described as the *Halliburton Model*. In the end geopolitics had the last word: the attempt to install Anton Vidokle's department in an empty hotel on the Turkish side led to the cancellation of the Manifesta School by the Greek Cypriot authorities.

It was literally difficult to put things on the ground, to implement things physically.

MARKUS MIESSEN In such a context, what is the role of the architect in regards to the relationship with the participating artists, especially with Anton Vidokle? How has this influenced your spatial strategy in Berlin?

NIKOLAUS HIRSCH My relationship to Anton Vidokle, the founder and organizer of unitednationsplaza, was never an architect-client-relation, but much more of an open collaboration. Consequently, the built result is not the answer to a specific commission or brief, but rather the expression of an experimental constellation. What made the collaboration almost "natural" is something that one could describe as the architectural aspect in Vidokle's work: his interest in infrastructures such as e-flux, the *Martha Rosler Library*, the Agency for Unrealized Monuments or the e-flux Video Rental. In fact, the starting point of our project "school as exhibition" in Berlin was not a question of design. In the beginning, it was about the identification of a strategic site. We were on the search of a paradox: an *objet trouvé* that works as an infrastructure.

MARKUS MIESSEN I think what is particularly interesting here is that as soon as certain projects in the architecture world start to touch on the alternative issue of spatial strategy, people often seem to misunderstand it as an analogy to or methods derived from Situationism. What is your take on that?

NIKOLAUS HIRSCH Our working process is neither based on techniques of situationist dérive nor of a flaneur's technique of getting lost in the city. It avoids the – usually accurately hidden – romantic motivations of those approaches. On the contrary, during our three-day walk, Anton Vidokle and I developed a set of criteria for a space. Walking and looking was a means of reducing options; almost stochastically. Through a kind of spatial probability calculation we tried to reduce the possibilities in a city in which it is almost too easy to find vacant space – Berlin has more than one hundred thousand empty apartments and a similar number of unoccupied commercial spaces. After the second day and a beginning uneasiness on the amount of spatial "freedom," we found out that *economy*, the relation between rent and square meters, and *centrality*, the proximity to the cultural hubs of Berlin-Mitte, were no sufficient criteria. We needed another parameter.

MARKUS MIESSEN What do you mean exactly?

NIKOLAUS HIRSCH Reflecting more carefully on the aspect of autonomy within the concept, we realized that – in contrast to the common gallery typology which is incorporated in the spatial framework of a larger building – the autonomy of a building offers advantages: freestanding, visible, accessible. The dry typology of an institute. This third parameter reduced the options from several hundred spaces down to three autonomous buildings in Mitte. Beyond its intriguing address Platz der Vereinten Nationen (United Nations Plaza) and its reference to the former Cypriot context, the building that we finally selected had the advantage of lacking the notorious factor of site-specificity. This three-storey, cubic building neither speaks within the rhetoric of the Stalinist Karl Marx Allee nor the bohemian patina of Berlin-Mitte. It is rather about something generic, something whose age – even though obviously modern – is difficult to grasp. This quality makes people think of a building from the 1970s, but actually it was built in 1993 – a rare example of a post-1989 building that avoids the architectural language of reunification. For me, this process of investigation was another way of designing a piece of architecture.

MARKUS MIESSEN How did you intervene in the built structure?

NIKOLAUS HIRSCH The intervention was less a work of addition than of subtraction. We took several walls out, removed one layer of the floor and simplified the lighting system, and, on the façade, we developed the four-sided logic for the positioning of Liam Gillick's unitednationsplaza sign.

MARKUS MIESSEN You planned the conversion of the building and its main public venue, a kind of conference room. Which typologies of institutional practice, and indeed critique, do you play with?

NIKOLAUS HIRSCH The spatial concept of unitednationsplaza addresses the ambivalent character of the contemporary art institution. Is it a gallery, a theater, a cinema or an auditorium? Being interested in this hybrid condition, we developed a lightweight modular system – the material is a compressed white and yellowish foam – that can be reconfigured into different formats: from an exhibition into a seminar, from a video-screening into a performance, from a lecture into hybrid and unpredictable arrangements. Thus, unitednationsplaza is a space in which institutional models themselves are displayed.

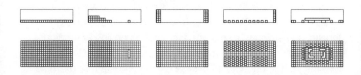

MARKUS MIESSEN Taking into consideration such a model of institution, how does one deal with display? In other words, how much display is still needed?

NIKOLAUS HIRSCH A model always works as a kind of display of itself. In this sense, display is unavoidable. You can hide it behind cleverly disguised strategies. You can pretend a non-plan or a self-organization of the audience – but even this is a specific decision and a form of display, or in other words, a spatial configuration whose quantitative logics and geometric patterns can be accurately described.

MARKUS MIESSEN How does the issue of exhibiting social processes relate to the work that you did with Bruno Latour for "Making Things Public" at ZKM in Karlsruhe?

NIKOLAUS HIRSCH unitednationsplaza could be seen as a reality check of what Bruno Latour describes as a *thing*, or more precisely of what he describes – extending the notion *Realpolitik* – with the German neologism *Dingpolitik*. It is about the potential of a physical thing becoming active in terms of sharing and assembling. Something that becomes public matter in the sense of a *res publica*. An architecture that attracts the various, often contradicting forms of togetherness.

MARKUS MIESSEN How do the seminars at unitednationsplaza assemble an audience?

NIKOLAUS HIRSCH The seminars are structured as both a seminar and residency program that – despite the small size of the building – involves a relatively large number of artists, writers and theorists. In the tradition of Free Universities, its events are open to anyone who is interested in participating. The seminars by Boris Groys, Martha Rosler, Walid Raad, Jalal Toufic, Liam Gillick, Natascha Sadr Haghighian, Tirdad Zolghadr and myself – imply very different settings. The crucial problem is the question of format: what is a seminar? What is a lecture? How does a speaker interfere with the audience? For Liam Gillick and his respondent Maria Lind, I displayed the formality of the seminar situation: a strict grid of benches and chairs and a frontal position between speaker and audience which emphasized the performativity of Liam Gillick's speech. On the next day of the opening conference "Histories of Productive Failures: from the French Revolution to Manifesta 6," for Diedrich Diederichsen's seminar session and his direct involvement of the participants, the space and its elements – like chairs, benches, and tables – were in a more accidental, half-circular and scattered geometry. In Martha Rosler's seminar "Art & Social Life: the Case of Video Art" and its focus on screening formats, the space turned into a hybrid of seminar and gallery space. In Tirdad Zolghadr's seminar, the wall that was previously a wall for screening moved from a vertical into a horizontal position and turned into a stage.

MARKUS MIESSEN What do you consider your site of knowledge production? You have been teaching at the Architectural Association in London, at Gießen University, HfG Karlsruhe and the University of Pennsylvania in Philadelphia. Now, it seems to me that you are developing an alternative approach here, one that fuses academic research and physical practice. From this perspective, unitednationsplaza could be seen as part of a trilogy together with your theater project for the Institute for Applied Theater Studies in Gießen and the Mohalla Lab with Sarai in Delhi.

NIKOLAUS HIRSCH Yes, there is an explicit attempt to extend the formats of what I was doing at the Architectural Association and other places. Now I am interested in a situation in which teaching becomes building and, vice versa, building becomes teaching. I am trying to connect knowledge production with the production of real building.

MARKUS MIESSEN How does this apply to your work with composer and director Heiner Goebbels for the Institute of Applied Theater Studies in Gießen?

NIKOLAUS HIRSCH We are aiming at a situation in which the learning environment and knowledge production become interdependent. A situation in which architecture becomes a self-reflexive tool for the institution. We developed a structure that allows for different performative typologies: from the black box theater to the seminar space, from artificial to natural light, from hermetic situations to open configurations with views to the outside and the potential to use this as a stage set. This approach is being pushed further for the Mohalla (the Hindu word for "neighborhood") Lab in Delhi, a project that we are about to develop with Delhi-based think tank Sarai, the NGO Ankur – Alternatives in Education, and a group of young media practitioners. Here the notion of cultural production is crucial. The production, display and archive of image libraries, texts, weblogs, and sound-work is not separated from the structure of the building. The building as permanent display.

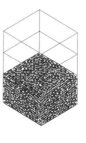

MARKUS MIESSEN How do you understand your role in this process?

NIKOLAUS HIRSCH The question is: am I a service provider or an author? Maybe I am always both of them. I am invited as an author and I provide a service. The resulting architecture has different authors. Me and others. Something like co-authorship.

MARKUS MIESSEN Would you agree if I said that the notion of collaboration, on the one hand, adds a critical dimension to a project, but, on the other hand, is also a means to outsource responsibility? Was there a moment within unitednationsplaza when you felt that some form of conflictual participation, a form of productive conflict that derived from a multitude of dissimilar voices, produced new forms of knowledge?

NIKOLAUS HIRSCH The work for unitednationsplaza suggests the contrary to outsourced responsibility: an increase of responsibility, a kind of liability on a personal level, between authors. This participation does not create a world of false compromises or hidden agendas, not even a rhetoric of conflict, but opens up the space to particular positions. The communal situation is part of that research and not an end in itself.

UNITEDNATIONSPLAZA IS ORGANIZED BY ANTON VIDOKLE IN COLLABORATION WITH LIAM GILLICK, BORIS GROYS, MARTHA ROSLER, NIKOLAUS HIRSCH, WALID RAAD, JALAL TOUFIC, NATASCHA SADR HAGHIGHIAN, AND TIRDAD ZOLGHADR. ITS ARCHITECTURE WAS DEVELOPED BY NIKOLAUS HIRSCH AND MICHEL MÜLLER.

ERSATZSTADT: REPRESENTATIONS OF THE URBAN

What is the "city" and why should this theme be dealt with in the theater? Perhaps because the theater is closely linked to the development of the city and the creation of an urban public. Yet the issue of how the city of today can be regarded as a public matter, a *res publica*, is cloudier than ever. As a consequence of the increasing mobilization of work and capital on a global scale, a crisis of representation has spread: the good old *res publica* of the city seems to be disappearing, for it is barely recognized any more as a political-aesthetic object. It has become imperceptible.

Ever since the development of Athenian democracy, there has been something – particularly in the European context – which used to present a discernable link between spatial parameters and forms of social organization, but this has given way to a ubiquitous, diffuse state of urbanity. The city is everywhere and nowhere. Deregulation and globalization have redrawn maps and established new conditions of space, radically altering the way society shapes and represents things. Parallel societies, ersatz models, countercultures, and shadow economies have been created in the much-praised homogenous "European city." They question the social-democratic, consensual model of the urban representative democracy, which is constantly involved in negotiating compromises, yet they might also function as potential counter models for social and spatial organization.

The city – as it once was, and in its continuation as a faked, imaginary "European city" – no longer exists. The traditional bourgeoisie, the basis of urban society, is dissolving into globalized space. However, the classic cultural institutions that assure the city of its identity have remained: the theater and the museum. They continue to exist and yet seem increasingly anachronistic. No wonder, then, that new topoi and formats are gradually making their way into those old buildings: the camp, the disturbingly beautiful slum in de Rijke/de Rooij's *Bantar Gebang*, the flea market, informal urban developments, anarchitecture (referring to a term Gordon Matta-Clark once appropriated from Robin Evans), Utopia Station, the state of emergency, the *ErsatzStadt* [ersatz city]. Yet what actually happens when urbanist and geopolitical discourse enter the theater? Will Soja, Davis, and Lefebvre be hysterically shouted down, as in René Pollesch's monologue, which updates fragments of text from his piece, "Stadt als Beute" [city as loot], to reference current debates in Berlin?

CRITICISM OR HYPOCRISY
Inversely proportional to the retreat of communal and state structures is the increasingly widespread urban discourse in art. How else can the inflated interest in urban interventions be explained, as theaters and museums go outside or bring the outdoors indoors? One theory might involve the interpretation of art as a space for criticism or even resistance, a strategic position taken by the Volksbühne in a reunited Berlin. In the attempt to discover themes and opportunities in the urban discourse through theater, visual art, music, and architecture, however, contradictions emerge. In the foreground is the ambivalence between urban intervention and the artistic means employed. In reference to Brian Holmes's *Reverse Imagineering* one might ask: what kinds of strategies can help art to avoid doing whatever modern city marketing expects it to do? For art is not really all that innocent in its urban practice. Regardless of whether they are in Berlin-Mitte, New York's Chelsea, or London's Shoreditch, artists are always agents of gentrification – whether they want to be or not. So if the avant-garde is actually the vanguard for wheelers and dealers in real estate, then the process of capitalist deregulation in the urban space is being promoted by those who criticize it the most. There's a thin line between criticism and hypocrisy.

THE STABLE HOUSE
Analogous to the "white cube" of visual art, the "black box" of the performing arts is an architectural paradigm that is constructed for

total control: it is an autonomous, neutral, stable space with even light and a steady climate. Unlike the museums of modern art, the classic "city theater" is a "stable house" with a basically secure social structure that usually includes a permanently employed ensemble and unionized stage technicians.

The stable house and its structural engineering are therefore almost forced into the center of contemporary cultural debates: is the stable house a model of a protected space in times of economic and social deregulation, and therefore a necessary oppositional model? Or should the theater rid itself of its static structures and promote the development of more flexible models that will ultimately be more in accordance with changing artistic strategies and productions? Strategically opening up the theater affects the immediate physical space, as well as those involved in the process. Wherever light, sound, and space must be produced in a theater, an obvious tendency emerges: technicians, who have up till now been strictly unionized, are increasingly being turned into flexible, freelance production units. On the artistic side, the permanent ensemble is faced not only with the specter of limited engagements, but also with an increasing number of strategies that integrate amateur performers or experts from other disciplines as an element of the work, as *Rimini Protokoll* did. The exterior relationships of the stable house are being renegotiated. Boundaries are shifting. Yet the question of whether expansion of boundaries occurs under the premises of the theater or the city remains controversial.

HOT AIR

When talking about boundaries, they must be regarded as directly physical. Every building – the theater in particular – creates specific boundaries. Wall, floor, and ceiling act as the material bounds separating the internal system of the "theater" from its environment. They are responsible for environmental control, that is, they absorb, protect, and store. Their materials specify different perceptions and negotiate the instability of external environments: degrees of visual protection and exposure, acoustic conditions ranging from noise to quiet, and climate factors, from climates that remain steady and even regardless of the season to those influenced by seasonal fluctuations in temperature.

The building itself and its environmental determinants become performative, and the British artist pair Lone Twin have made this the subject of their performance "Clouds over Volksbühne." The physical antagonism between internal stability and external instability is converted into hot air, hence, the theater's protected interior is explicitly related to conditions of the world outside. The performer's body brings the climate from the outside indoors, and takes it back again: i.e., the body of the performer mediates a relationship between interior and exterior. Warmly dressed and heavily equipped from their rigorous urban peregrinations, Gregg Whelan and Gary Winters make their rounds on the stage of the protected, warm interior of the theater. The body here is not only a storage of narratives, but also of temperature. They tell stories, jokes, and anecdotes from the city. At the end – heated from walking and back on the cold streets – they leave the theater and produce an enormous cloud of condensation.

HOW DANGEROUS IS THE STREET?
In total contrast to a building containing the established theatrical house with its secure formats, the street – according to popular rumor, at least – seems to offer a potential Other: a site of unpredictable conflicts, interactions, situationism, and dérive. It is the space of Poe's "Man in the Crowd," of Benjamin's flaneur. A person can remain anonymous, get lost in the masses. Swallowed up by the city, like the legendary jazz musician and bassist Henry Grimes, who pawned his instrument and first resurfaced three decades later.

From the protected house to the street: the dangers of the street exist today in what Eyal Weizman describes as "urban conflict as spatial practice." The description of the city as a homogenous, social, spatial entity gives way to analyses and theories that emphasize the loss of coherence. It is about disintegration, overlapping, and the creation of new spatial structures. Urban protagonists accordingly become "builders and warriors."

Where the political conflict is less obvious than it is in the West Bank, where the political conflict is planted instead in the boredom of social-democratic welfare states, then the dangers of the street have to be staged. They are reintegrated into the system and ultimately become entertainment. Anyone who is bored enough to want to break out, however, can, at best, still seek danger in illegal high-speed driving, as Matias Faldbakken's *Getaway* documents the urban expressways of Scandinavian countries.

A LICENSE TO ECONOMY

The old situationist spectacle has become part of a neoliberal, event economy. Everything is turned into a product. Every little gesture, every apparently insignificant object. Commodification continues unchecked. Operating outside this logic is becoming increasingly difficult. Resistance, itself now a paradigm of the cultural industry, seems futile. It could be more relevant to dive into the world of products and inquire into the genealogy of a product. Where does it come from? How is it marketed? Who made it? Who owns it?

The Danish artist group Superflex, which has been exploring the development of alternative production models for radio stations, energy production, and media pirating since the mid-1990s, developed a specific infrastructure that was set up in the Volksbühne for the three days of *ErsatzStadt*: the *Free Beergarden*. It not only functioned as an intervention in the space, but was primarily an economic model based on the production of one's own beer. *Free Beer* is an open source project and can be interpreted as a model that opposes the practices of multinational companies. The recipe is available to everyone. It can be used or even modified by anyone through a Creative Commons license, and commercially implemented, with the publication of the original product and its specific composition. This approach is not devoted to the socialist-romantic belief in subversion or illegal economies, but shifts the parameters of the economic system. Licenses, intellectual property, and authorship become the parameters of the artistic practice.

URBAN MUSIC OR ONOMATOPOEIA

When, in their *ErsatzStadt* workshop "Der letzte Metro," Diedrich Diederichsen, Björn Gottstein, Christian von Borries, and Ekkehard Ehlers ask how raw concrete could be mutated into a guitar riff – or what the squeaking of the streetcars has to do with the high-pitched string instruments of an orchestra – then they are dealing with more than just translation problems. The question is how much of an active part music itself takes in the creation of a city, and even ultimately if music produces the urban or simply reflects it.

As Christoph Gurk writes about Diedrich Diederichsen's lecture, "Keine Sorge wegen der Regierung" [Don't worry about the government], the city in popular music until 1950 was a code for the Promised Land, adventure, and the Vale of Tears; the city was, however, usually as passively described as nature. "It was pop music that produced answers to the question of how one could appropriate the city for oneself, from street fighting to 'Dancing in the Streets.' Here, the city burns more frequently than anything else: 'London's Burning,' 'Motor City is Burning'…" As time goes by, however, it seems as if pop music since the 1980s has been more about self-reflection. Those now making a reflective sort of pop music seem to want to interpret cities rather than occupy or possess them. The time of fighting for the city appears to be over for now.

CITY AS ERSATZ

It must be asked if *ErsatzStadt* is about a theatrical strategy that uses the political vacuum, and if – at the point where political and artistic discourses intersect – it will itself become an urban ersatz protagonist, or, if it is a kind of legitimizing strategy, if not another trick of contextualization.

Meanwhile, the dangers of the street have been turned into entertainment. The situationist spectacle, with its political implications, has become part of the event-culture of neoliberal strategies. The streetfights of the 1980s that Heiner Goebbels turned into the audio piece, *Berlin Q-Damm 12.4.81* have become "Surrogate Cities," as Goebbels titled his play that premiered in 1998. What meaning does *ErsatzStadt* have now? Ersatz as a site of political opposition, or ersatz as a manipulated surrogate?

What was once known as "city" has been dissolved in countless levels of administration and sovereign proceedings – a permanent leap in scale, from micro to macro, from the citizens' committee to the supranational entity. Imperceptible and dull. Where is the political here? Anri Sala's video work *Dammi i Colori* presents an excessive illustration of city politics as he documents an urbanist project in his hometown of Tirana. A concept of color on an urban scale turns the re-appropriation of the city into the theme. The work was created during a drive with the initiator of the project, former artist-turned-mayor Edi Rama, and it questions the active role of artists and politicians in contemporary urbanism. A rare case of the realization of an old dream (or nightmare?): the artist and politician united in one person.

In Berlin this functions through a greater division of labor. Yet here, too, it is possible to see the problems of a cultural policy, which, confronted by the disappearance of cohesive forces, threatens to become a type of compensation that will use the "city," including its architecture, as an ersatz in the crisis of representation. It brings up a discussion concerning a concept of the urban that, faced with an increasingly complex situation, promises a little bit of visibility in the service of a mimetic longing for a concretization of politics and society.

This not only refers to the traditional, apologetic representational policies of a disappearing bourgeoisie, but also to a critique of representational policy that continues to think in categories of the oeuvre, and therefore still supports the unity of the work and the community. According to Henri Lefebvre's theories, the city is a collective, living work of art. This interpretation of the city and its inhabitants creates a welcome legitimation of the artist. However, after a decade of intensive debate, there are increasing doubts: is there a silent agreement between politicians and artists? Is it a case of mutual instrumentalization as the urban conflict degenerates into a pretext? A quandary for both representation and translation: not to think of the city as a work of art.

THIS TEXT IS BASED ON NIKOLAUS HIRSCH'S KEYNOTE ADDRESS TO "ERSATZSTADT: REPRÄSENTATIONEN DES URBANEN" HELD AT THE VOLKSBÜHNE AM ROSA LUXEMBURG PLATZ FROM MAY 20-22, 2005. NIKOLAUS HIRSCH WAS THE CURATOR, SUPPORTED BY A TEAM OF ADVISORS – DIEDRICH DIEDERICHSEN, EKKEHARD EHLERS, NICOLAUS SCHAFHAUSEN – ADDITIONALLY SUPPORTED BY CHRISTOPH GURK (DRAMATURGY) AND CELINA NICOLAY (PRODUCTION DIRECTOR). THE EVENT INCLUDED PERFORMANCES, PANELS, INSTALLATIONS, LECTURES, WORKSHOPS, CONCERTS, AND FILMS BY FATMA AKINÇI, MARYANNE AMACHER, JAKOB BOESKOV, CHRISTIAN VON BORRIES, ALICE CREISCHER, FRIEDRICH DIECKMANN, DIEDRICH DIEDERICHSEN, DE RIJKE/DE ROOIJ, EKKEHARD EHLERS, HEINZ EMIGHOLZ, MATIAS FALDBAKKEN, HARUN FAROCKI, GANG GANG DANCE, GOB SQUAD, HEINER GOEBBELS, HENRY GRIMES, BJÖRN GOTTSTEIN, CARL HEGEMANN, BRIAN

HOLMES, HANS-THIES LEHMANN, LONE TWIN, BART LOOTSMA, OLAF METZEL, ASTRID MEYERFELDT, MARKUS MÜLLER, BERT NEUMANN, PHILIPP OSWALT, RENÉ POLLESCH, JULIANE REBENTISCH, RECHENZENTRUM, ANRI SALA, SABINE SANIO, WERNER SEWING, ANDREAS SIECKMANN, SUPERFLEX, ALBRECHT WELLMER, AND EYAL WEIZMAN.

THE ARCHITECT AND HIS BOUNDARIES
DAVID ADJAYE IN CONVERSATION WITH NIKOLAUS HIRSCH

DAVID ADJAYE Visiting your first work I was struck both by the scale and the ambition of an architect's beginning. The project of the Jewish cemetery in Frankfurt opens up a comprehensive discourse about the nature of the profession: the role of an architect and of architecture in the city.

NIKOLAUS HIRSCH Contrary to the traditional assumption that architects should start with a small house or apartment, our first realized project – the Jewish cemetery at the Börneplatz in Frankfurt – was a monument on a large urban scale. Both aspects are unusual: the urban impact and the notion of the *monument* as such. The project was extremely instructive about the role of the architect and his boundaries in contemporary society. It gave us the potential to work in an expanded field, but with the limitations that make this discipline so specific. In other words, we had to bridge two aspects: an increasingly complex field of interrelated disciplines which ultimately raises the question of the cultural relevance of architectural work; second, the architectural tradition of planning, i.e., the architect's culture of control that tends to predetermine physical condition in the future. In fact, I think that both aspects are still relevant in our work: on the one hand the freedom to work in a larger social and political context, on the other hand the precision of an engineer. The result in Frankfurt was similarly wide-ranging: not an autonomous, isolated object, but a 300m-long wall, based on a small-scale material element, producing a piece of urbanism.

DAVID ADJAYE What fascinates me is the representational quality of the project. Its "monumentality" operates within a frame of contemporary art and architecture, as well as within an idea of a critical construction of history. How did you – as an architect - bring these conditions under one umbrella?

NIKOLAUS HIRSCH These conditions are not separate issues for me. They are both part of the same problem: how to define my role in a given site? I am careful with narrative, but interested in the potential that lies in the material of big and small histories, of sites and clients. They offer contradictions and problems. In fact, what was required in Frankfurt was a certain ability to find a problem. We questioned the competition brief and expanded the site, linking it to the old cemetery, thus creating the physical resistance that was necessary for such a project.

DAVID ADJAYE Traditionally an architect is meant to find the solution to a problem given by the client. The idea of the architect "finding a problem" seems like an inversion of that role. It presents a new paradigm, not just about the client understanding what it requires, but about the architect uncovering the latent potential of the context. I like the way you phrase this, it gives it a certain poetry. The problem is stated by you as the architect and in a way the solution then becomes, what it has to become. There is an incredible elegance to the idea of authoring. You seem to be seeking a different model of the architect as author.

NIKOLAUS HIRSCH At least, I see "authorship" as one of the hidden but crucial problems of architecture.

DAVID ADJAYE There is a coherent idea of questioning perception and meaning that runs through all your projects in a coherent way. How would you describe the role of material in this process? Looking at your projects, for instance the Dresden Synagogue, the material approach absolutely underscores the meaning.

NIKOLAUS HIRSCH The architectural operation starts with a search for material, in fact with a confrontation with the politics of architecture. The material condition of Dresden is characterized by two traumatic destructions: that of Gottfried Semper's synagogue in the *Kristallnacht* in 1938 by Germans, and of the entire historical city in 1945 by allied bombing. The two destructions are historically linked, yet the architectural consequences couldn't be more different. In one instance, Dresden reconstructs its historical monuments, establishing a false continuity and a problematic pretension of architectural stability. In the other, the new synagogue is an attempt to investigate the conflict between stability and fragility, between the permanent and the temporary, or – if you want to refer to its historical typologies – between temple and tabernacle. This became the starting point of the material strategy. Exploring the implications of stability and fragility, the architecture of the synagogue is characterized by a dualism: a monolithic structure of precast concrete stones and an interior structure of a soft brass textile that we developed over two years with a clothing manufacturer.

DAVID ADJAYE How did you then translate the material strategy into a volumetric logic?

NIKOLAUS HIRSCH The question was: how to develop a building that is specific, not just a generic reproduction of existing typologies and patterns? The project consists – in contrast to the competition brief and the other entries – of two distinct buildings: one a religious space, the other containing spaces for different social functions. Based on the orthogonality of the site, the volume of the synagogue twists towards the religiously symbolic eastern direction in a rotation of masonry layers, producing positive and negative cantilevers. We were interested in developing a complex, curvilinear geometry that is based on the simple principle: only one stone, one mould for the whole building. The effect is striking: the perception of the volume changes dramatically from one perspective to the other. In the end the process of perception goes far beyond any operational planning logic.

DAVID ADJAYE Traditionally one thinks of *materiality* in the sense of elemental building materials. What's striking about the Dresden project is that one first perceives it as a stone building, but actually it is a concrete building. So there is a kind of switching of meaning that is not romantic at all, but a way of substantiating reality.

NIKOLAUS HIRSCH The material discourse you mention has different aspects: structure, perception and urbanism. The project is situated in a critical urban position between the historic part of the city, made of local sandstone, and the enormous prefab concrete housing projects of the socialist modernity. In that sense the material strategy was a critical rethinking of the question "what is the site?" We were interested in negotiating between two problematic tendencies: the contextual or regionalist approach of the sandstone, and the industrialized and globalized logic of prefabricated concrete. The result of this material negotiation is a specifically developed artificial stone – a fusion of prefabricated concrete with natural local aggregates.

DAVID ADJAYE Your intensity of material research in this project and others is impressive. The development of the artificial stone and the brass textile are just a few examples in your work. How would youdescribe the impact of this approach on the working process in your practice?

NIKOLAUS HIRSCH Our design process is non-linear, continuously producing reiterative feedbacks between small and large scale. Unlike the usual linearity of design phases, we start with tests in a 1:1 scale at a very early stage. As a tectonic detail, the material has the capacity to conceptualize an approach.

DAVID ADJAYE There is another phenomenon that occurs in the Dresden Synagogue and relates to your new project, the document center in Hinzert. In a way I see a link between the material strategies and an environmental agenda that is starting to develop in the work.

NIKOLAUS HIRSCH In our work we are investigating an expanded idea of the notion "environment" that includes different perceptive criteria: visual, acoustical, climatic. We are trying to develop specific environmental systems for each building, i.e., an approach that turns the specificities and even contradictions of a program to its advantage. In the case of the synagogue in Dresden we developed a system based on the inertia of a monolithic building. In our new project, the document center in Hinzert, the situation is fundamentally different because it is located in a remote landscape: 4 km away from the next village and its technical infrastructure. That's why this project deals with autonomous environmental strategies such as geothermal techniques.

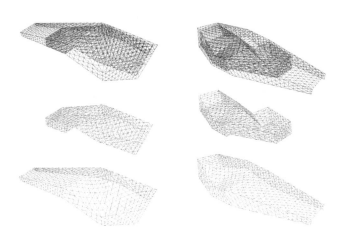

DAVID ADJAYE Could you describe the building itself and the impact of a shift of site from the city to the landscape? In Frankfurt and in Dresden you had been working within historic urban conditions, and suddenly you have to work within an extreme landscape.

NIKOLAUS HIRSCH In contrast to the precise spatial limitations in dense urban contexts, the project in the landscape around Hinzert has no particular limitation. We did not work from the perimeters to the inside, but from the inside to the outside, continuously adapting the program and pushing the geometry into the surrounding landscape. Around the main exhibition space we developed a series of pockets of small libraries, archives, research studios, and three-dimensional exhibits which manipulate the profile of the outer shell, creating a complex geometry of triangulated surfaces.

DAVID ADJAYE I would like to discuss another side of your work, where you are collaborating with artists in the field of theater, music, visual art, and ballet. Some of these are temporary projects: buildings which happen for a moment and disappear. Can you elaborate on the role of these works in the practice of architecture which generally is very slow?

NIKOLAUS HIRSCH You are right, the relation between planning and different rhythms or time-scales has an enormous, often underestimated effect on architectural practice. But to be honest, I need this tension of different time-scales in my work. There are buildings like the synagogue in Dresden that have to deal with criteria of duration, and there are buildings that disappear after an intense public use. What is important to understand is that the idea of time scale itself has to become an integral parameter of the planning process *and* of the built result.

DAVID ADJAYE How does the idea of time manifest itself in your collaborations? How do you negotiate time?

NIKOLAUS HIRSCH There seems to exist an assumption that in collaborations, as we practice them, boundaries between the disciplines blur. My romantic side tends to support this idea, but at the same time the most productive outcomes are often a result of a difference or even of a conflict between the disciplines. A critical difference is the rhythm of production. For example, in our collaboration with choreographer William Forsythe in converting a depot into a theater in Frankfurt, two fundamentally different rhythms were at work: the architect's tendency to predetermine a future status, and Forsythe's dance strategy based on improvisation techniques in real time.

DAVID ADJAYE Coming back to the impact of the physical, it seems that in all these works you have developed a very strong material strategy. How do you relate this to the idea of "boundary" as one of key spatial notions?

NIKOLAUS HIRSCH One needs physical material as a kind of resistance that can be shared and negotiated. A strong material strategy can become the common ground for a collaboration, like in our acoustically performing foam structure for "Frequencies-Hz", or our music pavilion at the Museu Serralves in Porto. In this sense the notion of *boundary* operates in a double way. On the one hand, it describes an increasingly complex collaboration with specific planning experts. On the other hand, I use the notion of boundary in a literal sense: as a material element – like wall, ceiling, and floor – that is interpreted as an interface between an architectural system and its environment, as a tectonic boundary that negotiates opening and closure.

DAVID ADJAYE'S INTERVIEW WITH NIKOLAUS HIRSCH TOOK PLACE AT THE VOLKSBÜHNE BERLIN AND WAS FIRST PUBLISHED IN *BUILDING DESIGN*, **15 JULY 2005.**

GEOPOLITICAL TECTONICS
TBILISI OR HOW TO FIND A CONTEXT
FOR YOUR ARCHITECTURE

Searching for the local. A context for my work. Or is it a pretext? The spatial facts are straight forward: designing a 35,000 square-meter building in Tbilisi, integrating a complex programme of offices, shops, conference areas, and apartments, finishing the construction by 2008. Less clear is the political space: post-revolutionary Georgia – with its strategic position between oil-supplying and oil-buying countries – is exposed to the imperial ambitions of both the United States and Russia. Do geopolitics affect architecture? It certainly does on a large territorial scale. But what about the scale of a single building? How to develop a material strategy, to bring the material from A to B, to assemble it according to a territorial logic? Can we invent something like geopolitical tectonics?

Of course, the discipline of architecture provides us with diverse contextual instruments (or ruses?) to find and appropriate the local: typologies, heights, roof shapes, and a material strategy with local references. After all the ignorant destructions of modernist planning, we prefer to pretend an architecture of respect. Yet, is this possible: polite architecture? Maybe it is just a contradiction per se. A day with our Georgian clients proved that contextualization might have its good intentions, but is in the best case romantic, in the worst case patronizing. Curious about this new land on my architectural map, I asked questions. A lot of questions – call it research. Though, after continuous interrogations about local materials, patterns, stones, timber, and carpets, the client realized what I was after and stated quite bluntly: "Do not patronize us. You do not have to explain to us what Georgian culture is – you are here because we want internationally compatible architecture." Such as it is: the limits of contextualization. I have finally reached the dead end of a culture of good intentions.

Thrown back to my status of "international architect," I have to search for something beyond the references to Old Tbilisi and its wooden balconies. The question is: how can the ever-expanding world of construction be re-territorialized? What is local? For now, I am tempted to answer: first of all, rules and standards. Beyond the picturesque discourse about context, it is the law that defines what is specifically local. A legal paper whose paragraphs define data, not style: maximum density, volume, height or minimum insulation, fire protection, health, and safety parameters. In a world in which the standards are approaching "a standard," the little differences in a boring text define the local. Unspectacular, small paragraphs on the natural lighting of workspace can have spectacular effects on the volume of a building. The distance from a window to a work desk becomes a defining parameter of local difference: whilst German codes in their obsession with natural light allow work desks a maximum distance of 4.50 meters from a window (which explains the endless repetition of thin office buildings throughout the country), Georgian building regulations offer particular opportunities: deep buildings. Our project tests the limits of the law: a depth of more than 20 meters (the building width is 48 meters), based on a porous sponge-like system of deep light holes and modulated façade elements. Is this a new version of "site-specificity," driven by rules and laws?

Today the old problem of site-specificity might be extended to a logistical question: how does a material come to a site and where does it come from? These banal questions become architectural questions. They determine design decisions. What happens is a territorialization of material and tectonics. Details, joints, surfaces – every piece of the building is checked against the instability of geopolitical environments (getting worse since Russia's embargo) and evaluated according to the geo-economical logics. Hence, the building can be described as a genealogy of construction. It can be understood as a geopolitical and geo-economical materialization that offers the potential of architectural manipulation. We can draw something that we did not know before: a diagram of the building as a map of the world, indicating the origin of each building component. The world in a building.

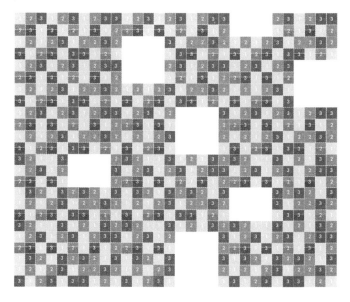

Playing and subverting this new toolbox of geopolitical tectonics means: what is underground, i.e., the dirt of the earthwork and the rough concrete substructure becomes a local affair, whereas the material decision for the superstructure follows a strategy of forced import. Afraid of the uncertainties of local concrete, we decided on a steel structure that – because of the total lack of Georgian steel – out of necessity, had to be imported from Turkey (i.e. from the west). With the façade – the most sensitive, specifically developed part of the building – the geo-material system expands even further west.

The mock up of a façade fragment stands far away in a little village in Germany. In its perverse logic, the coherence of the work seems to depend on the level of autonomy away from the local. In other words, the coherence of my work increases with the distance from the local. Welcome to the uncanny world of planning. A world in which control is everything and the loss of control appears as the last taboo of architecture.

FIRST PUBLISHED IN *ICON* (OCTOBER 2006), P. 75.

GROUNDED TOWERS

"In a building, pride is supposed to render itself visible, victory over gravity, the will to power; architecture is a kind of oratory of power in forms, at times persuading or even flattering, at times simply commanding. The highest feeling of power and certainty finds its expression in a *grand style*. Power which needs no additional proof; which disdains to please; which does not answer lightly; which is unaware of any witnesses to it; which lives in oblivion to all opposition to it; which reposes within *itself* [*in sich ruht*], fatalistically, a law among laws. Buildings are supposed to render pride visible, and the victory over gravity, the will to power. Architecture is a kind of eloquence of power in forms – now persuading, even flattering, now only commanding. The highest feeling of power and sureness finds expression in a *grand style*. The power which no longer needs any proof, which spurns pleasing, which does not answer lightly, which feels no witness near, which lives oblivious of all opposition to it, which reposes within itself, fatalistically, a law among laws."[01]

It seems as if the age of the "autistic" building is over. Those "witnesses" of whom Nietzsche speaks have reported in with objections, above all, to buildings that have dared to go further than others. In particular, the high-rise has been handed a polite request of being "city friendly."

This paradigm shift to contextualism is literally based at the base of the high-rise. For it is less the defining quality of the high-rise – its height – that is called into question than its being "grounded" on the city's land. This points to the place where a worldwide concentration of services collides with local traditions, where a property designed to be seen from afar and shape the skyline meets the

---

[01] FRIEDRICH NIETZSCHE, *TWILIGHT OF THE IDOLS*, TRANS. R. J. HOLLINGDALE (IN 1968) (INDIANAPOLIS: HACKETT PUBLISHING, 1997), P. 57. HERE SLIGHTLY MODIFIED BY THE EDITOR.

perspective from the street. With this in mind, the base of the high-rise, indeed its roots, appears to be its soft spot.

CLOSING

In Frankfurt in the 1960s and 1970s, the self-referential "autistic" high-rise was the rule. Among the buildings that earned the city the – at the time – not very flattering name "Mainhattan," the high-rise of the Dresdner Bank, built by ABB Architekten between 1971 and 1980, is an instructive example. This is true not only of the design logic and its implementation but also of the dramaturgy of its site. The building volumes tower above the Wilhelmine-era buildings in the vicinity of the main train station. One looks in vain here for any connection to the context in the spirit of today's "compatibility with the city." Anyone approaching the high-rise from the train station will notice from quite a distance a highly reflective vertical service core on the corner of the property that sharply contrasts with the small-scale stone block structure. Abruptly, without any superfluous differentiation, full-story aluminum panels extend from the ground to a height of 166 meters.

The choice to use flat-fitted materials such as aluminum and glass for the service cores and of prefabricated façade elements for the office floors is at variance with any kind of depth. The façade is not articulated by any protrusions or indentations, and no aging process has given it any additional meaning, or semantic surplus value, so to speak. Indeed, the building radiates the relations of material to time that Robert Smithson, one of the protagonists of Minimal Art, characterized in his essay "Entropy and the New Monuments" as characteristic of the art and architecture of the 1970s: "Instead of being made of natural materials, such as marble, granite, or other kinds of rock, the new monuments are made of artificial materials, plastic,

[02] ROBERT SMITHSON, "ENTROPY AND THE NEW MONUMENTS," *ARTFORUM* (JUNE 1966), P. 26.

chrome, and electric light. They are not built for the ages, but rather against the ages."[02]

The interface between the "self-referential time" of the Dresdner Bank high-rise and the "process-based" time of the surroundings is exemplified by the entrance area. It is here that the uniformity of the aluminum-clad building is broken. Projecting far behind the office floors, the building withdraws into its function of providing access and makes use of only a third of the site's area. Every day, around two thousand employees approach the entry hall, which is enclosed in brown-tinted glass, passing one by one – each recorded by a surveillance camera – through one of five revolving doors. Once the first barrier between outside and inside has been crossed, they cross the foyer with just a few steps and arrive at security gates in front of the elevators where their ID cards are read. The turnstiles mark the inner area, which need not be exited again even for lunch, since there is a large cafeteria on the third floor. Visitors with appointments are issued magnetic cards at the reception desk. With its round protective glass, the counter picks up the motif of the omnipresent rounded corners, which recurs in the void of the foyer as brown anodized space capsules. Protected by a higher level of security, this is the central administrative office, the building's brain.

Down to its last detail, the Dresdner Bank high-rise reveals itself to be a closed system that obeys only its own laws. Following Niklas Luhmann's theory of self-referential systems, one might say that the decoupling from its urban surroundings is made possible by functional and formal closing and represents a condition of its functioning. It is only logical that the building is literally closed at closing time. A grate is rolled down between the free-standing, aluminum-clad supports. The entrance area disappears. The forecourt of the bank – by day, the transitory space of the money traders – belongs at night to the red-light district around the train station.

MIRRORING

When Heinrich Klotz proclaimed the "Revision of Modernism" in the newly opened German Architecture Museum in Frankfurt, the highrise of the Deutsche Bank was being completed on the other side of the Main River. Into the 1990s, the 155-meter-high, mirror-glass twin towers dominated the panorama of the city, but its architectural presence stood in strange contrast to the attention paid to it in discussions of architecture, which at the time was primarily concerned with museums and "town houses." One reason for this disregard may have been that the building consciously eludes legibility. The polygonal towers are related in such a way that it is impossible to attribute definite form to them. Moreover, the mirror-glass shell is one of constant change, depending on the weather, to the massive tube-in-tube concrete building. The gaze seeking articulations and transitions finds no footing; on the contrary, the mirror glass rejects it. It almost seems as if it is not the city observing the building but the building observing the city.

The logic of the visible, public space, on the one side, and an invisible, private space, on the other, tilts on the building's base, a broad four-story base that, while vaguely reminiscent of a city block, primarily follows the formal and – with the exception of a steakhouse – mono-functional logic of the high-rise. As one approaches, the mirroring effect recedes. The gaze begins to penetrate. In order to prevent unwelcome views into the office spaces, even on the ground floor, behind the façade there is a second layer, consisting of cloth venetian blinds. The closing of the blinds remains as a last retreat.

Although it was originally employed to unify the building complex, the mirror glass cannot prevent the whole from disintegrating into its component parts. Things become visible: for example, the mirror-glass gates, which only close at the end of the workday, cannot conceal the dark chasm of the underground garage. And even the mirror-glass apron that runs diagonally over the main entrance is nothing other than a canopy. Despite all the talk of "high-rise sculpture," there is an irreconcilable difference between a high-rise intended as large-scale sculpture and a sculpture as a work of art. The latter doesn't have to concern itself with the problem of an entrance.

OPENING

In the 1990s, the high-rise increasingly began to be seen less as a solitary object in an indifferent spatial continuum than as integral element of an urban ensemble. Hence, the relationship of private to public space became a crucial criterion for the acceptance of high-rises. Corporate cultures opened up to the city. The bank's own brochure on the DG-Bank on Westendstraße states: "The building complex belongs to a new generation of high-rises that put into practice visionary concepts such as the integration of working, dwelling, and living. Its design is contextual – that is to say, it relates to its surroundings – taking into account the diversity of human needs." This "people-friendly" high-rise by the architects Kohn Pedersen Fox was completed in 1993. It can be read as a blueprint of contextualism: a 20-meter-high outlying building mediates between the interior and the Wilhelmine-era residential district of the Westend; a 50-meter-high wing adopts the scale of office buildings from the 1960s; a 150-meter-high square tower adopts the familiar height of the previous generation of high-rises, and finally another volume, rounded on one side, soars up to a height of 200 meters. An essential aspect of integrating the high-rise into its context was apparently the form of the base. According to Christian Norberg-Schulz, this presented nothing less than a reconciliation of (architectural) independence and (urban-planning) dependence.[03]

---

[03] CHRISTIAN NORBERG-SCHULZ, "THE HIGH-RISE CITY," IN *KOHN PEDERSEN FOX: ARCHITECTURE AND URBANISM, 1986–1992*, ED. WARREN A. JAMES (NEW YORK: RIZZOLI, 1992), P. 9.

The "reconciliation" between the new building for the DG-Bank and the City of Frankfurt began with the way the high-rise is "grounded." Whereas fifteen years earlier artificial material was drawn over the entire façade in deliberate indifference, now historical typologies for articulation have been reactivated, as a way of stabilizing a connection to the surrounding built structures. The cold, artificial material has given way to "natural" material. A dark-gray granite expresses the transition from the city's ground to the bright granite of the façade. This differentiation does not mean that the different uses have been accorded to the different logics of materials, as is clear from the south side of the block. There the scale of the contextually rationalized articulation meets the immense infrastructure of the high-rise. Emergency exits, building services, and entrances to the underground garage are squeezed into the predetermined stone framework.

The hope of enlivening the base was not fulfilled. One essential reason for this may be the orientation of the complex around its center, the Winter Garden. Accessed by two arcades and a temple-like portal, which makes the adjacent investors' entrance seem almost modest by comparison, the 27-meter-high, palm-lined hall was conceived as a "link between the business district and the residential district." Wooden benches in colonial style are intended as invitations to linger. The noises of the air-conditioning system are gently drowned out by the flowing water of a water wall integrated into the stone façade. A Chinese restaurant, a parfumerie, a florist, a hair salon, and a cocktail bar are meant to breathe life into a place that bears all the signs of a privatized public sphere. Instead, the bank employees and customers remain among themselves. The place – which is intended for events spanning the gamut "from classical concerts to fashion shows" – is the site of an automobile show on the day that I pass by. A new model is being presented. The Winter Garden has become the stage for an automobile with gleaming chrome beneath the glare of theatrical lights. Between them are discretely located sales desks.

INDIFFERENCE

For Leon Battista Alberti, the house was a small city and the city a large house. This dictum seems to come to mind in times of increasing segregation. Is it possible, one is tempted to ask, for the high-rise to be a "micro-city"? Is it open to processes that are not predetermined from the outset? Experience thus far would suggest that economic logic largely determines the building. The public sphere becomes public relations. Against that backdrop, the contextual high-rise appears to be no more than a more subtly differentiated autistic high-rise, one that rolls out the grating at closing time. Because differentiation always relates to a boundary, the incorporation of mixed uses is in no small measure also an extension of the boundary between inside and outside. A building in this sense would be open to influences from the environment, but these influences are merely external stimuli that remain subject to internal criteria for selection. The secret plan is the construction of its own context.

WALDSTADT
A DIALOGUE BETWEEN MICHAEL HIRSCH
AND NIKOLAUS HIRSCH

MICHAEL HIRSCH Föhrenwald. Starting with the name, it reminds one of Buchenwald. …

NIKOLAUS HIRSCH … or not so much big history as our own small history: Waldstadt, the suburban West German idyll near Karlsruhe where we grew up. In both cases, it is uncanny.

MICHAEL HIRSCH Yes, the place is uncanny, somehow eerie. At the same time I see a similarity to other suburban row house tracts and garden cities; and then there are different layers of meaning. We are dealing with a profound transformation of political and historical contexts and population structures. It begins with a plan for a very concrete goal: building homes for the workers of an armaments factory deep in the Upper Bavarian landscape in a pine forest [Ger. *Föhrenwald* means "pine forest" – Trans.] on the Isar River. It was originally planned as a National Socialist model housing estate, then converted into a camp for forced labor, then in 1945 into a camp for Jewish displaced persons ("Government Camp for Stateless Foreigners"), and then, after it was purchased by the Catholic Church, into a settlement for expellees from former German territories. And today it is home to their descendents.

NIKOLAUS HIRSCH What I find interesting about that is the constant transformation of the built space by the new residents. The characteristic aspect of the history of Föhrenwald, now known as Waldram, is the inertia of the architecture. Physically, it hardly seems to change at all. It permits everything.

MICHAEL HIRSCH In fact, we only see what we already know. This idea opens the door to the contingency of all judgments and meanings. And contingency means dependence on the observer's point of view, which can always differ.

NIKOLAUS HIRSCH I think that we are faced with a problem of representation. In two senses. First, in relation to the concrete object of our observation. But also – and this is perhaps the main motif of this dialogue – in terms of the relationship between architecture and political philosophy understood as a problem of the body or of mimesis. The problem of making something readable is a difficulty that was already unsettling for the fathers of contemporary urbanism debates: namely, Lefebvre, de Certeau, and Soja. They saw a precarious relationship between physical and mental space. Although Lefebvre insisted on the complex relationships between these two spheres on the basis of everyday social praxis, he was nonetheless unsettled by the "dominance of the readable and visible" in the interpretation of space. Interpretation, according to Lefebvre, comes later, as an afterthought of the production of social space, so to speak. "Reading" follows production in every case except where space is produced in order to be read (which applies in the case of Föhrenwald). So the question is: does architecture make politics visible? Does architecture shape politics? The current fascination with urbanism and architecture in art is based in part on a certain overburdening of the built. It is as if buildings were the ultimate opportunity to make politics visible, without being obscured by the largely abstract and opaque processes that usually characterize politics but instead as an immediate expression of society.

MICHAEL HIRSCH That is an important idea for political theory. Particularly in the context of the more advanced French theory, there is a concept of the political that is, so to speak, autotelic – that is, it has no object outside itself: the political as an ontological ur-phenomenon. Although most of these authors come from a rather leftist spectrum of theory – like Jacques Rancière, Chantal Mouffe and Ernesto Laclau, Alain Badiou, Giorgio Agamben, Claude Lefort – they are adopting a central theorem of the conservatives: the political as a form that constitutes and represents community; as a form of identification. Whereas the right-wing model of this sort of conception of the political indulges in a mythology of unity – as it were, a mythology of the homogeneous body of the people that is aimed against strangers and enemies – the leftist models develop a sort of mythology of conflict. That is a kind of aestheticism, an aestheticizing of politics from the left. This model of the political is agonistic or antagonistic, oriented not around unity but around difference, around conflict. The focus is on the idea of debating various positions in the public space: that is, a metaphysics of the vacant space of power; an aesthetic of the representation of conflicts. The unity or form of community is not embodied but instead remains vacant, in motion. It is no coincidence that culture, and especially contemporary art and urbanism, has taken over the task of representing this contradictory society in a "documentary" way.

NIKOLAUS HIRSCH But is the left-right scheme really so sharply divisible?

MICHAEL HIRSCH The seemingly clear distinction between left and right blurs as soon as we look at Hannah Arendt, who was perhaps the one who worked out this "aestheticist" paradigm of the political most clearly. By her definition, politics has no object outside of its own manifestation or outside the space where it manifests itself. Her theme is not *society*, the distribution of positions of social and economic power and rights. This realm is – in her rather conservative approach – excluded from political discourse. Arendt's theme is *community*, the ritual articulation of the gestalt of the polity, the struggle for recognition in public space. It is no coincidence that, faced with today's political resignation in relation to a progressive, egalitarian transformation of society, these kinds of structurally conservative ontological models of the political are playing an ever greater role: if the structure of society is not going to be transformed politically, the least one can do is articulate critically the contradictions of society. The *city* and the *urban* become metaphors of this new political culture of conflict. In contrast to fascist forms, this culture of conflict does not lead to a unified body of the people, a unified picture of community. It is more an aesthetic of discourse than of image. In a certain way this new political culture produces "monuments" not of a community conceived of as organic but of a critical public sphere: discoursive monuments to civil society.

NIKOLAUS HIRSCH Constructing *discourse* is not simple, and it may even be a contradiction that an architect cannot resolve. The particularity of the architectonic lies in the organization of order, whether one wants to or not, and even more in predicting and predetermining a future final state.

MICHAEL HIRSCH A *telos*. An intersection of architecture and politics. In a process in which each side gets its object from the other side.

NIKOLAUS HIRSCH Hence it is no surprise that architects have always been accused of standing on the side of authority, on the side of a system that organizes society and gives it form. They are, if one follows the etymology, "architects." This verbal compound suggests that there is more to it than just producing a building, more than just the pragmatic activity of a *tektonikos* who satisfies the needs of users and then becomes invisible again. *Archè* implies a coordinating authority and a principle that determines the end in advance. One approach to overcoming this dilemma is the *organic*. And the concept of the organic does indeed appear in various and often contradictory forms over the course of modernism, always with the goal of overcoming the tendency to alienation that is inherent in the architectonic. It starts with Louis Sullivan's dictum "form follows function," which he understood as organic, not as functional, evolved by way of the garden city movement, Jugendstil, and Hugo Häring's organic architecture from which Mies van der Rohe distanced himself and even extends, to some degree, to the complex geometries of the diagram architecture of the 1990s which were based on theories of natural growth. The genealogy of the term also includes parallel strands of development that lead us from ambivalent figures like Heinrich Tessenow directly to the architect of Föhrenwald. The planning of this housing estate in the late 1930s was an attempt to build an artificial village or, in the words of the architect, an attempt to produce a "picture of an organically grown place."

MICHAEL HIRSCH An artificial *Heimat* [homeland], so to speak. When I read Heidegger's "Homelessness is coming to be the destiny of the world," I automatically imagine him in front of his cabin in Todtnauberg. The one who is truly still dwelling, in an emphatic sense, tells us that we no longer dwell. Applied to the problem of architecture and its concept, it means that the *archè*, the reason or principle of architecture, is disappearing and all that remains is the *tectonic*, the usable floor space and the shell of the building.

NIKOLAUS HIRSCH Houses become empty vessels, containers. That is the current criticism of twentieth-century modernism. Boxy row houses have repeatedly been used, even in the visual arts, as symbols of a general cultural criticism of modernism. Dan Graham's *Homes for America*, produced from 1965 onward, is one example. The houses depicted in it, partly in an ironic criticism of the parameters of Minimalist Art, were, characteristically, also built for workers in an armaments factory. They are signs of the interchangeability of habitation, of the loss of homeland, and of a lack of connection to landscape. The Föhrenwald housing estate – which, paradoxically, was built at a site dedicated to producing the means to destroy people, landscape, and houses – appears to show exactly the reverse: the will to visual idealization and design, to the artificial production of *Heimat*.

MICHAEL HIRSCH This reveals a fundamental paradox of National Socialism, and to some degree of modern conservatism generally. Moeller van den Bruck, a spokesman for the conservative revolution and an influence on the so-called *Heimatschutzbewegung* [movement for the protection of *Heimat*] wrote: "Being conservative means creating things that are worth preserving." For this kind of modern conservatism, architecture is an attempt to build the places of *Heimat* and community; an attempt to produce artificially the organic and grown. They wanted to make solid things and houses that looked like they had always been there. If High Modernism emphasized the constructive and abstract, the transparent and, thus, the contingency of construction, fascist modernism was concerned with faking a legacy and thus with creating something that could be referred back to in the future. All of the conservative and counter-Enlightenment concepts of modernism are structured on the paradoxical model of a conservative revolution: creating an artificial *Heimat*, values that can be believed, forms and shapes that look like they had always been there. The epitome of this fundamental paradox is the modern concept of the nation. It refers to the natural, to something that emerged on its own. But in the modern age the natural and organic have to be created artificially; they have to be faked. They are, in other words, a myth.

NIKOLAUS HIRSCH That is why politicians or legislators like to refer to themselves as architects. Architecture as the classic metaphor for politics. And architecture as structures of thought: the Tower of Babel, the pyramids, the labyrinth, the network.

MICHAEL HIRSCH Yes. Philippe Lacoue-Labarthe referred to National Socialism in this sense as *national aestheticism*. The program of politically and intellectually relevant conservatism is always at its heart an aesthetic one. Its protagonists are always the architects of the people, to whom they are supposed to give an identity and form. As Goebbels put it, politics is the *bildende Kunst* [visual art, but literally "shaping art" – Trans.] of the people. For this entire world of ideas the only thing that is *organic* is the vision of the people as form or body. The vision of people and community as a work and a shared political task. The people as a *Gesamtkunstwerk* [total work of art].

NIKOLAUS HIRSCH The interesting thing about this is that the tendency to represent the people or a community spatially is much more difficult to categorize in terms of ideology and iconology than you might at first think. The label "Nazi architecture" is problematic here, and it is motivated more by a friend-foe schema that serves more to legitimize other positions. The efforts to escape the alienated existence of the modern age can be traced back to the garden city and even beyond to the communal architecture of early socialism. The principle of the organic is closely linked with the principle of *community*. The remarkable thing about Föhrenwald is the large number of communal buildings. The proportion of communal buildings to residences is strange. There is a surplus of community. They are typologically related to the residences, with their steeply sloping roofs, but they are scaled up, crudely enlarged to large scale. The residences are deprived of essential functions that normally define a house and the life of its inhabitants. The kitchen becomes a communal kitchen.

MICHAEL HIRSCH Communal life wasn't organized into households, into the "private" sphere of the bourgeois nuclear family, but rather sourced out to a public structure for nutrition and for cultural and political leisure time. There were no households in the true sense of the word *oikos*. For there was no kitchen – that is, no "homey hearth" – they lacked the true center of every house. The ideal, homey world in miniature – the basic ideology of National Socialism – was not able to develop because the other side of this ideology – "total mobilization" (Ernst Jünger) – destroyed the foundations of bourgeois society – namely, the household and the family. The dominance of the communal buildings here shows the profoundly collectivist approach of this model housing estate: collective organization of work, of board an lodging, and of leisure time. The ideological influence and spatial surveillance are almost absolute in this structure. It is a radical form of compulsory community.

NIKOLAUS HIRSCH That is what makes it so depressing. Uncanny. And it is strange that it is only the world of home improvement centers slowly covering up the old façades that gives me any hope at all: the false, purchased individuality of entrances, carports, skylights, and garden fences. But even so, at least it does something to counter the surplus of communal architecture.

MICHAEL HIRSCH The casualness of the current residents about the historical legacy of their housing estate is primarily the result of the concrete needs of the people. They are looking for affordable residences in quiet surroundings. They are the first people to live here voluntarily. In some sense they occupy a monument, but they are probably largely indifferent to the significance of that monument.

NIKOLAUS HIRSCH The traces of praxis – or, as de Certeau would put it, the *ruses* of the users in dealing with the monument – can certainly be interpreted as something positive, as something subversive that inverts the planning and the place that resulted from it. All the little details seem like an ironic commentary on the history of the place – even if it is perhaps unintentional. The positive reading would be to see it as *an-archic*. Another reading is that it is not a matter of small-scale, individual ruses but rather of a new homogenous layer that is embedded in the landscape of a seemingly natural capitalism and its fetishism of the commodity. The communal would thus remain behind as discredited.

MICHAEL HIRSCH If we look at the enormous communal buildings that dominate the entire site (the canteen, the assembly rooms, the cinema, and so on), it is clear that they are no longer used as originally planned. Instead they are used for education facilities by the Catholic Church. The communal buildings are simply left standing in the middle of the complex, as a center that the residents have abandoned. The particular history and political significance of the place have been partially extinguished or at least covered over by its present use. The petit bourgeois idyll of the tract of row houses is, after all, a common topos in the political iconography of the progressive critique of society in the twentieth century.

NIKOLAUS HIRSCH But the relationships have become more complex.

MICHAEL HIRSCH Right, such housing estates no longer simply symbolize the petit bourgeois ideology of property and an ideal world among like-minded people – the ideology of a certain sociocultural homogeneity that has taken the place of the totalitarian ideal of homogeneity. Owning one's own home at the edge of the city or in the country has long since become an icon of pragmatism in present-day capitalism. Especially in cities with expensive rents, like Munich or Frankfurt, owning one's own home outside the city gates has spread into leftist milieus as a way of life. Because the social context has since become characterized by social insecurity and an increasingly precarious existence, suddenly the *security* and *immobility* of a dwelling have become a plausible option even for those who explicitly define themselves in opposition to petit bourgeois philistines.

NIKOLAUS HIRSCH And this is where it – the historical comparison – becomes interesting. Götz Aly's book *Hitlers Volksstaat* made us aware of the extent to which National Socialism was also a welfare state that enticed the socially weaker strata of the population with all kinds of social services. Home ownership supported by tax breaks is not just an ideology but also a concrete way of life that is supported by our political system through massive economic and tax subsidies. It is a way of life that in turn generates other ways of life – concrete lifestyles and dependencies, soil sealing, the destruction of the landscape, automobile traffic flows …

MICHAEL HIRSCH It is a matter of a practical ideology with a use value that is evidently real. Like all other ideologies, this ideology of the home has a real function in our life, as long as other ways of living and dwelling are not found. I would say that today, after an explicitly antibourgeois intermezzo, the political search for other ways of urban life has largely been abandoned. For lack of realistic alternatives, the seemingly obsolete bourgeois forms have again become plausible as an option. The so-called ideology of the family that was embodied in such tracts of row houses – and in the associated models and ideas of living based on gender and the division of professional labor – may have been attacked on a cultural and ideological level but never in terms of its real function within the social structure (as a means of obtaining security, inclusion, and acceptances for all involved). That is why today, after the failure of all the egalitarian utopias of High Modernism, they can be restored without any problems. Today we are living, as Alain Badiou wrote recently in *Le siècle*, in an age of restoration. The family is not alone in this: all the other "authoritarian" institutions of bourgeois society are also experiencing a triumphal resurrection today: the state, justice, elites, experts, corporations, "permanent positions," and so on.

NIKOLAUS HIRSCH "Government camp for stateless foreigners" – from 1945 on that was what the sign read that stood on the perimeter of this camp for displaced persons. That sign, and all the forms of demarcation from the outside, are important. This was an exterritorial space. Not only was it an artificial village for Jewish refugees with a completely autarkic infrastructure (police, legal jurisdiction, food stores, synagogues, schools, library, cinema, assembly rooms, bathhouses, and so on). In this camp, the Jewish so-called stateless foreigners established an artificial *Heimat* that was provisional. Later it was inhabited by expellees from former German territories and more recently by migrants of German ancestry from Eastern Europe. The connection to territories conquered by National Socialist Germany had been established before that. The architect's own text reads: "The streets and plazas have been named with an eye to history after regions that have been reconquered." Here too one recognizes a will to represent the historical and political situation in the architecture.

MICHAEL HIRSCH Hence Föhrenwald becomes a place with many superimposed historical references. The current residents are appropriating the site according to their own needs. Additions to entrances, individually designed garden fences, and so on. They are covering up more and more traces of the original architectonic condition. In other words, they are increasingly transforming their housing estate from a historical monument to a "normal" tract of row houses. The architectonic form, per se, is secondary in the eyes of the residents/users. They are pragmatic, and their horizon is at cross-purposes to the horizon of the observer/theoretician. They neutralize the historical-political-aesthetic context. The whole place lives from this neutralization and repression of the historical layer of meaning – from a forgetting in the service of life. But the forgetting is still present. The whole semantic field of habitation [*Wohnen*], habituation [*Gewöhnung*], and ordinariness [*Gewöhnlichkeit*], of homeland [*Heimat*], the cozy [*heimelig*], the homey [*heimlich*] and the uncanny [*unheimlich*] is significant here. The ordinary is superimposed on the monstrous and vice versa.

NIKOLAUS HIRSCH "Habituation," a concept that Walter Benjamin used in relation to the reception of architecture, illustrates the whole dilemma. The reception of architecture takes place in a process of habituation, in a process of perception that is distracted, not the concentrated attentiveness that is shaped by the very object encountered that occurs in the reception of an art object. The problem, however, is that as an architect or philosopher one finds oneself in a situation more like that of art. It is difficult, if not impossible, to step outside of systemic orders. For both the architect and the philosopher it is difficult to do what the residents do: to allow the architecture to become unfocused, to let the hard lines go soft.

THE DIALOGUE BETWEEN PHILOSOPHER MICHAEL HIRSCH AND NIKOLAUS HIRSCH TOOK PLACE ON THE OCCASION OF MICHAELA MELIÁN'S WORK "FÖHRENWALD" AND WAS FIRST PUBLISHED IN *FÖHRENWALD*, EDS. HEIKE ANDER, MICHAELA MELIÁN, FRANKFURT AM MAIN 2005, PP. 129-144.

PERMANENCE AND SUCCESSION
MONUMENTAL QUESTIONS REGARDING TRACK 17, BERLIN-GRUNEWALD TRAIN STATION

After profound historical disruptions, oblivion was once decreed. Nothing less than "eternal oblivion and amnesty" – or *perpetua oblivio et amnestia*[01], as it said in the Westphalian Peace Treaty of 1648 – would be in force. To form the basis for an everlasting peace, there were to be no assignations of guilt, no punishments imposed. However, events in the twentieth century fundamentally altered this practice. "Crimes against humanity," especially genocide, have been excluded from amnesty since the Nuremburg Trials. On a cultural level, oblivion by decree becomes an obligation to remember. This reversal is well-intended, but it opens up a few questions: can memory be permanently established? Is it possible to maintain it, as time marches on? And how does this happen?

Memory relies upon mnemotechnics: the spoken or written word, rituals, monuments. The difficulty, however, is that the very mnemonics which guarantee recollection also contain the potential for forgetting. Memory props are unreliable. They can be frozen or take on forms empty of content. They can become random, interchangeable. With this in mind, in *Being and Time* Heidegger describes an ordinary mnemonic: a knot in a handkerchief.[02] The knot is supposed to remind one of an event one is afraid to forget. As a pure signifier, it can represent an endless number of things to be remembered. But what is it, exactly, which has to be remembered? Under these circumstances, it is quite possible to become confused. So the trouble is not merely that the knot can only be understood by the initiated, but also that other signs are required in order to understand it. In these circumstances, therefore, another knot has to be added to the first. Yet even though this does not cause the *monumentum* to lose

---

[01] SEE HARALD WEINRICH, *LETHE. KUNST UND KRITIK DES VERGESSENS* (MUNICH: C.H. BECK, 1997), P. 217.

[02] SEE MARTIN HEIDEGGER, *SEIN UND ZEIT* (TÜBINGEN: MAX NIEMEYER VERLAG, 1986), P. 81

its character as a sign, it does give it the replaceability of a dispensable object.

A FLEETING OBSERVATION

One way to oppose the tendency of detaching monuments from the signified event is to create a relationship between a monument and its site. Of course, site specificity as such is also a construction, one that creates a context. However, unlike the *tabula rasa* of an empty lot, a site offers a different way of solving the problem of remembering: instead of isolating the memory, it can be confronted with other parameters; furthermore, it gives one the opportunity to reflect upon one's own role as a constructor of memory. Put cautiously, exact observation has at least one particular advantage: namely, anything can be found on site and left as it is. It has less to do with reshaping a site than adding to it or integrating something in it. While autonomous parcels of land, such as the historically imprecise site of the Holocaust Memorial in Berlin, tend to strengthen the lack of association between the signifier and the signified (and this, using the logic of Eisenman's formalism, is even interpreted as a special quality), a connection between deed and site offers a possible structural link.

The Berlin-Grunewald train station is the scene of a crime, and yet it is still a completely ordinary place. Hardly anything there refers to the fact that the deportation of Berlin Jews began here in October 1941. Today, as then, Track 17 is embedded in a context of ordinary parallel uses. Commuters from the wealthy suburb ride the S-Bahn to work. Others travel to the suburb to wander around the woods. High-speed trains rush by. On Track 16 is a railroad caravan for the employees of the rail company: curtains at the windows, satellite dishes on roofs; a few chairs and a barbecue in front of the railway cars during the summer. On the ramp leading to Track 17, this time it is the vacationers who await to board an *Autozug* [the car-train].

Track 17 has not been used much since the end of the war and is now overgrown, but it is not isolated. It is not an autonomous place excluded from the everyday. Rather, it is a linear element among others, an ordinary place in a context made up of parallel, transitory phenomena. The very ordinariness of the place calls attention to a mode of perception that Walter Benjamin described as being characteristic of architecture: "… [it] occurs much less through rapt attention than by noticing the object in incidental fashion. This mode of appropriation, developed with reference to architecture, in certain circumstances acquires canonical value. For the tasks which face the human apparatus of perception at the turning points of history cannot be solved by optical means, that is, by contemplation, alone. They are mastered gradually by habit, under the guidance of tactile appropriation."[03] It is precisely in places of transition – like train stations – where perception is indeed fleeting. Applied to the question of the monument, perception is not really about an observer standing opposite a monumental object in order to view it in a state of stasis, but rather more about perceiving things in passing: literally, things directly associated with motion and walking.

OVER TIME
How can the ambivalence between lasting memory and oblivion be understood as a question of materials? Can ambivalence be constructed? Is it possible to build a fleeting quality or even doubt into a monument? Nothing would be simpler than to distance oneself from the *monere* of the monument, that is, from well-intended warnings and didacticism, and to come down entirely on the side of the fleeting, as well as of the processual. Thus, the memory that aims for duration, which seems increasingly suspect, would then give way to a kind of memory that is part of everyday practice, always in motion,

---

[03] WALTER BENJAMIN, "THE WORK OF ART IN THE AGE OF MECHANICAL REPRODUCTION," IN *ILLUMINATIONS*, ED. HANNAH ARENDT, TRANS. HARRY ZOHN (NEW YORK: SCHOCKEN, 1968), P. 240.

constantly being changed by the interaction of individuals. Jochen Gerz, for instance, used this approach for his "Monument Against Fascism" in Harburg, which has thousands of comments from private parties etched into it; and as an approach, it is certainly the easiest way to uncouple the question of the monument from the state-supported, politicized culture of memory, and yet still to document, almost incidentally, that one "is on the right side."

A less comfortable procedure, on the other hand, but therefore probably all the more relevant, is to take on the problem of the monument (including the questionable, long-term expectations of the state's politics of memory) by allocating it to an area of conflict, and, at the same time, subject it to essentially uncontrollable processes. It's about exposing the parameters of permanence to everyday changes, creating a relationship between what is fleeting and what lasts. Not deciding. Perhaps that is the impenetrable quality underlying "doubt."

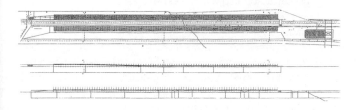

What is the meaning of permanence as a material strategy here? First, that Track 17 does not have to be discovered or reconstructed. It already exists. The intervention, therefore, is limited to defining a horizontal structure that makes it possible to see and access the site. This structure does not seal anything off, but with its open pattern, settles on top of the existing area, following its slightly crooked course and oddly distorted topography. The number and order of the horizontal elements is determined by the numerical logic of the 186 transports. Horizontal components, each 1.42 x 3.12 meters, form two platforms, each 132 meters long, which makes it possible to walk around Track 17. In passing – that is, while walking – the chronology of a schedule is revealed whose coordinates are embedded on the platform: date of the transport, number of deportees, destination.

When duration is an essential parameter of a monument, the material acquires special significance. It has to be constructed so that the data remain inscribed on site for as long as possible. With the unforgiving precision of the engineer, time-related factors can be researched through construction physics and then further developed. Material strategy can also be contextually based – after all, the history of train stations is closely connected to the invention of cast iron. The material becomes a reference to traveling and the distribution of commodities. Yet how transitory or durable is the material? To what extent is one responsible for the implications inherent in a type of material? And to what degree are these discourses linked to time? Even an apparently transitory material like iron is subject to discursive transformation, as Walter Benjamin remarked: "The first iron structures served transitory purposes, as market halls, train stations, exhibition halls. Hence, iron is immediately connected to functional aspects of economic life. Yet what was in those days functional and transitory is beginning to appear formal and stable, due to the changing pace of the present day."[04] As material, cast iron can be even more stable. Made to fit the intervention at Track 17, its durability can be strengthened by adding lamellar graphite. Ultimately, however, the answer to the question of the material is a contingent decision. In reference to the event that is to be remembered, it is not a counter-

04 WALTER BENJAMIN, *DAS PASSAGEN-WERK*, VOL. 1, ED. ROLF TIEDEMANN (FRANKFURT AM MAIN: SUHRKAMP, 1983), P. 216. (TRANS. FROM THE GERMAN HERE BY ALLISON PLATH-MOSELEY.)

part, a translation, an imitation, or even a type of constructed pity. At the end, it is a decision to use corrosion-resistant cast iron GG 30.

STABILITY AND INSTABILITY

The issue of how materials can be linked to historical-political discourse is marked by "stable" and "instable" strategies. Two competing concepts of the monument, developed around 1900 by Alois Riegl and Georg Dehio, are open to debate. The question is: should we let things happen, or place the monument in a state of stasis? These inventors of modern historical preservation agreed that relicts of the past should be maintained and protected by law. However, they disagreed fundamentally about how to deal with a specific material and its parameters of durability.

Georg Dehio demanded nothing less than the interruption of the material process.[05] Time should be stopped. The material should be preserved in its historical condition. However, in order to even come close to stabilizing the material, monuments have to be actively preserved through repairs, restoration, and, in extreme cases, reconstruction.

For Alois Riegl and his "modern cult of monuments,"[06] on the other hand, there was a crucial "aging value" that was not legitimized by the past, but solely by the present alone. Consequently, the task is not to preserve the condition of the material as it was in the past, but to allow it to decay. This concept explicitly refers to the natural

[05] SEE GEORG DEHIO, "DENKMALSCHUTZ UND DENKMALPFLEGE IM 19. JAHRHUNDERT. FESTREDE AN DER KAISER-WILHELM-UNIVERSITÄT ZU STRASSBURG, DEN 27. JANUAR 1905" (1988), IN *KONSERVIEREN, NICHT RESTAURIEREN. STREITSCHRIFTEN ZUR DENKMALPFLEGE UM 1900*, EDS. GEORG DEHIO, ALOIS RIEGL (WIESBADEN: VIEWEG VERLAG, 1988), PP. 88-103.

[06] SEE ALOIS RIEGL, "DER MODERNE DENKMALKULTUS, SEIN WESEN UND SEINE ENTSTEHUNG," IN DEHIO/RIEGL, OP.CIT., 1988, PP. 43-87.

process of decay that any ruin is subject to. Arresting time is not the goal: letting things happen is.

Which strategy is now the correct one? In all likelihood, it is not about choosing one or the other, but about criticizing a dichotomy that has always had more to do with ideological battles than with real material conditions. Seen this way, the work on Track 17 is based on an approach that seeks to orient itself somewhere in the conflict zone between the founders of modern historical preservation – between Riegl's aesthetic of natural disappearance, on the one hand, and Dehio's idea of stabilizing the material, on the other.

MEMORY AND OBLIVION

Track 17 is marked by a historical event that should be firmly inscribed (quite literally, into the landscape) and, therefore, remain in stasis. But other things have simply happened. A single phenomenon distinguishes Track 17 from all of the other tracks at the train station: succession. Despite all appearances to the contrary, this is not a historical-philosophical theory, but an ecological concept, which creates a relationship between vegetation and the parameters of time. Over the past sixty years, a forest has grown up between the rails of Track 17. A line of trees spontaneously grew in an area about half the length of the track, which has not been used since the end of the war. There, different types of vegetation appeared successively, marking periods of time and even total overall change. In the initial phase, pioneering plants like short herbs and grasses sprung up. Next, a dense forest of birch trees rose up from the inhospitable, gravel-covered ground between the rails and ties. This phase of vegetation remained stable until enough humus had formed to enable the present-day state of beeches and oaks.

This self-organized process of succession will inevitably continue. It will probably take over and develop within the framework of the 186 elements comprising the platform itself. Here, the perforations in the individual cast iron components function as a pattern open to changes. In the future, a layer of vegetation might grow over the platform, dependent upon how much the platform is used. Visitor access will then become a parameter that regulates if and how much grass will grow over the whole thing.

Maybe this is an attempt to take seriously the monument and its parameters of duration, but also to build-in a kind of doubt at the same time. An attempt to develop a structural association between memory and oblivion. The uncertain status of memory would then become the focus of the intervention at Track 17: on one side, the determinateness of the data, and, on the other side, the indeterminateness of time; for one thing, the lasting definition of the area through a framework that encloses it as one walks around it; for another, the successive changes caused by vegetation. The structures undertake the futile attempt of arresting time. The processes go over them, marking the irreversibility of time.

TRACK 17 AT BERLIN-GRUNEWALD TRAIN STATION IS A MEMORIAL OF DEPORTATION BUILT BY NIKOLAUS HIRSCH, WOLFGANG LORCH, AND ANDREA WANDEL IN 1998.

ARCHITECTURAL WORKS BUILT FOR NATIONAL UNIFICATION

The reconstruction of Berlin's *Schloss* – literally "castle" – would be a gift to the soul of the nation. Or so says the head of government of a united Germany. When a nation is to find itself in a work of architecture, then the architectural figure of thought – once developed by Hegel in his lectures on aesthetics – has unexpectedly reared its head at the beginning of the 21st century again: "Architectural works built for national unification." In the Hegelian system, symbolic and independent architecture stands at the beginning of all art. "Independent architecture," unlike the house and the temple – that is, housing for men and for God – requires no external purpose. It comprises the architectural works by means of which society constructs itself in, as it were, a mimetic process. Architecture becomes a political-ontological project.

If pursued to its logical conclusion, the "independence" of a work of architecture must have structural consequences for Berlin's Schloss. Assuming that the supporters of the Schloss reconstruction are right, and the question of its inner function is indeed irrelevant – what would be more obvious than following the structural principles of the tower of Babel and the other examples adduced by Hegel, and to say without a bad conscience: the Schloss must be massive; ergo, inaccessible.

A MONUMENTAL FUNCTIONALIZATION

The alternative to the reconstruction of the Schloss is to keep and re-use the existing structure: the Palast der Republik [Palace of the Republic].

If a lack of function is the prerequisite for the independence of the Schloss, then conversely a monumental functionalization is essential to the interpretation of the Palace as a "fun palace." This approach, it seems at first, is no longer about establishing a mimetic shortcut between society and the architectural work but rather about a structural openness of the building for external purposes and functions. Unpredictable processes could lead to ever-new modifications, ways of being colonized, and further adaptations. Architecture would be a background rather than a foreground. In analogy to Cedric Price's "Fun Palace," a strategy of instability could be developed: a building as a framework for diverse forms of appropriations, a process-oriented structure, a site for the culture of the "non-plan."

The novel aspect of this approach would be a concept of the monument that differs fundamentally from the purified, quasi-ahistorical state to which many monuments have been converted in the late nineteenth century and primarily over the course of the twentieth century. Allegedly, aesthetic pollutants were eliminated, banal functions of buildings – such as living and working – were removed, monuments like the cathedral of Paris were set free through the demolition of the adjacent buildings. Today, it might be possible to invert this logic. Processes – like those that the Colosseum underwent as a result of complex functional modifications that lasted until the architectonic-political "cleansing" under Mussolini – would now proceed in the opposite direction. The aim would be permanent change – until the original monument becomes unrecognizable.

NON-PLAN TODAY: A CRITIQUE OR AN AFFIRMATION OF THE CIRCUMSTANCES?

The approach of a seemingly organic non-plan must take into consideration two problematic aspects: first, we have to ask critically whether it is not simply a desire for an embodiment of society and, hence, ultimately – in parallel with the Schloss but from another perspective – not simply a project of political ontology. The second concern is the increasingly obvious proximity of Situationist and neoliberal strategies. The Situationist and process-based approaches that were developed in the 1950s and 1960s have since been adapted and perfected by neoliberal market strategies. Non-plan is, thus, not a value in itself. Rather, the term embodies, in the meanwhile, not so much a critique as an affirmation of the deregulated global economy. The "fun" of the Fun Palace has become an industry, perfectly integrated into the mechanisms of the market. In this sense, a strategy that relies above all on the supposed counter-economy of temporary events increasingly runs the risk of becoming part of the general "event culture" and, thus, even strengthens the trend toward plasticity or even eliminating, "stable houses" (e.g., theaters in Berlin). As a perpetual event machine, one supposes, the Palace would share the absurd fate of the erstwhile department store, now artist squat Tacheles where sub- and counterculture has become a protected landmark.

BACK TO PLANNING
It is striking that the discourse on architecture over the past ten years has focused largely on terms like "time" and "process" but, at the same time, it has remained ignorant of historical time and the phenomenon of the monument. What is the basis of this ignorance? On the one hand, it can be traced back to a nearly unbroken faith in the omnipotence of "design" and its ability to integrate incommensurable processes in the form of diagrams; on the other, the theoretical tools for grappling with the question of "palace or castle" as one of contemporary architecture seem to be lacking. What is necessary is a strategy capable of coupling questions of political history and current architectural discourse. In this context, it might be helpful to recur to Alois Riegl, the founder of the Modern Cult of Monuments. Riegl's theory of the monument, which is based on a memory-value (i.e., age-value and historical value) and a current value (i.e., art-value and use-value) comes closer to the actual problem. Yet, in order to engage in the contemporary debate and to be able to develop a viable design option, the theory would have to radically expand its scope of duty. Not only the existing, authentic substance of the past should be part of the agenda but also new and virtual material. Hence, the

concept of historic preservation could adopt the paradox of a new avant-garde that looks both backwards and forwards.

CASTLE *AND* PALACE

If judged by a concept of the monument based exclusively on existing material, the preservation Palace of the Republic would have to be given preference over the reconstruction of the Schloss, if only because it physically exists in the here and now. The Palace of the Republic, a historical document of the German Democratic Republic and symbolic of the upheaval of 1989, would be thought of as part of an urban-planning ensemble that extends to Hermann Henselmann's 1969 TV Tower to Alexanderplatz, and it would have to be reprogrammed. But is there enough of a programme? Would the architecture go beyond a harmless retro-design of socialist modernism or, at best, a nostalgia for the appropriation strategies of the 1990s?

Maybe the hyperbolic alternatives "palace or castle" are too simplistic, even trapped, in a shoe-box mentality that is largely satisfied with identifying the enemy and, thus, avoids any risk that is beyond its own protected boundaries. The real challenge for Berlin's center may thus lie in a programmatic approach that considers palace and castle as inseparable counter-buildings to each other and condemns both to a forced architectural marriage. This is not to create an "either/or" situation, which would perpetuate the comfortable friend-enemy scheme, but rather a strategy merging the physical ruins of the palace with the virtual ruins of the castle. Conservation *and* reconstruction. The socialist People's Court *and* the Royal Court [*Volkskammer and Schlüterhof*[01]]. The result would be a hybrid construction that is reconfigured by contradicting components. The volume of the east-west aligned Palace would be fused with the north-south orientation

---

[01] THE IMPLICATION HERE BEING A REFERENCE ALSO TO THE BAROQUE CASTLE'S ORIGINAL ARCHITECT, ANDREAS SCHLÜTER.

of the Castle, nearly identical in its size and cubature. An architectural mutant that turns Palace and Castle into something new.

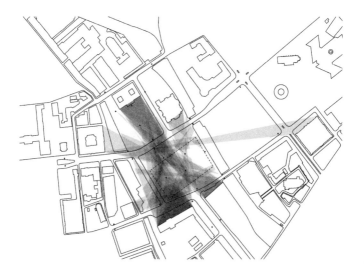

THE ORIGINAL GERMAN VERSION OF THIS TEXT WAS FIRST PUBLISHED IN *FUN PALACE 200X. DER BERLINER SCHLOSSPLATZ*, EDS. PHILIPP MISSELWITZ, HANS ULRICH OBRIST, PHILIPP OSWALT, BERLIN 2005, PP. 166-169.

MATERIAL TIME
NOTES ON THE DRESDEN SYNAGOGUE

The design of a synagogue primarily raises questions on the relationship between the building materials and the parameters of time. How does architecture react to a culture that has maintained a coherent written tradition over thousands of years, but whose architectural tradition tends to be incoherent, in essence, and characterized by unstable spatial conditions? How does a contemporary synagogue react to an urban context whose mission is determined by the notion of reconstructing "Dresden as it used to be"? And finally, how do the repercussions of time affect the building's materials and its tectonics?

STABLE AND UNSTABLE CONDITIONS
Even the attempt to glean a contemporary synagogue's design from historical or traditional typology will inevitably land at a dead end: in other words, it stops with the realization that no specific "synagogue" typology exists. The architectural history of the synagogue is, to a great extent, dependent upon changing, often precarious local conditions. Sometimes the synagogue slips into the guise of a house; sometimes into that of a pseudo-church. A more direct way to formulate a material strategy, on the other hand, would be to begin with the conditions of what could be called the founding architectural experiences of Judaism: the temple and the tabernacle. As early as the 1920s, during a competition for a synagogue in Vienna-Hietzing, Viennese art historian Max Eisler suggested that the "tabernacle" would be an appropriate architectural form for "a wandering people."[01] Most recently, Salomon Korn[02] referred to the significance of the opposites "temple" and "tabernacle." The advantage of this approach is

---

[01] MAX EISLER, "DER WETTBEWERB UM EINE WIENER SYNAGOGE," IN ÖSTERREICHISCHE BAU- UND WERKKUNST, VOL. 2 (1925/26), PP. 1-7, QUOTED BY RUTH HANISCH, OTTO KAPFINGER IN "DER WETTBEWERB UM EINE SYNAGOGE IN WIEN-HIETZING," IN VISIONÄRE & VERTRIEBENE. ÖSTERREICHISCHE SPUREN IN DER MODERNEN AMERIKANISCHEN ARCHITEKTUR, ED. MATTHIAS BOECKL (BERLIN: ERNST & SOHN, 1995), PP. 249FF.

that these opposites link material conditions to the social context, and, therefore, create a specific – though always precarious – relationship to a place.

TEMPLE AND TABERNACLE

The first Jewish house of worship was provisory: the tabernacle was a tent that could be taken down and moved at any time, acting as an ephemeral shell for the portable Ark of the Covenant. In contrast to this mobile holy shrine, the second Jewish house of worship was a stable one: Solomon's Temple. Tightly bound to the Holy Land and the topography of Mount Zion, and supported by enormous substructures, the temple was a massive assertion of permanence. In general, it can be said that the synagogue displays a variety of different elements from the temple and the tabernacle. Depending on interior conditions and exterior contexts, the architecture of the synagogue is either more or less permanent – or else temporary. Until the early nineteenth century, external conditions in Germany were so precarious that the synagogues, which were built on the peripheries of societies and towns, tended to have the provisory character of the tabernacle. When emancipation occurred in the nineteenth century, the architectural paradigm also changed: the model was no longer the portable house of worship, but the permanent temple with its promise of a homeland. That is, political emancipation was more firmly established through architecture. Emancipation and assimilation found their manifest forms. Christian typologies of sacred architecture were adopted. The Semper Synagogue, whose interior oriental motifs allude to a "foreign" ancestry, is completely neo-romanesque on the outside. In this way, the

---

02 SALOMON KORN, "SYNAGOGENARCHITEKTUR IN DEUTSCHLAND NACH 1945," IN *DIE ARCHITEKTUR DER SYNAGOGE*, ED. HANS-PETER SCHWARZ (STUTTGART: KLETT-COTTA, 1988), PP. 287FF. REVISED EDITION IN SALOMON KORN, *GETEILTE ERINNERUNG* (BERLIN: PHILO VERLAG, 1999), PP. 35FF.

"German-romanesque style"[03] symbolized a patriotic commitment within the public space – although ultimately, this architectural commitment could not protect synagogues in Germany from destruction.

THE SEARCH FOR MATERIAL

What does it mean to build something anew, anyway? Before we invent new material, we look for old material, which is often in ruins or has vanished. "Dresden" is a code word for "destruction." Less firmly anchored in public awareness, however, is the fact that Dresden was the site of a "double destruction": the destruction of old Dresden by Allied bombers on 13 and 14 February 1945 – which seems to have cast the city in the role of victim once and for all – and the repressed destruction of the Semper Synagogue on 9 November 1938. Although the two destructive occurrences are connected in terms of space and history, reactions to the disappearance of the buildings could hardly be more different. The reconstruction of the Frauenkirche and other buildings deeply rooted in the collective memory represented the attempt, over fifty years later, to heal the architectural phantom pain and restore continuity between the past and the present. Destruction's spatial caesuras – which make history visible – are gradually disappearing. In the age of reconstruction, a new kind of urban architecture that needs no planning has arisen. The unofficial master plan for present-day Dresden is an aerial photograph taken in the late 1930s. Plastered all over the city by the thousands, a poster of this photograph shows the intact world of old Dresden – or, as the title says, *Dresden wie es einmal war* [Dresden as it used to be]. My gaze wanders to the upper right of the photo, to the eastern edge of the old city, to the spot where the Semper Synagogue should be visible. It is not there. Vanished. Deleted from *Dresden as it used to be*, which was, even in those days, not really

[03] EDWIN OPPLER, "REPORT ON THE SYNAGOGUE IN HANOVER, DATED 5 AUGUST 1863,"

IN *DIE ARCHITEKTUR DER SYNAGOGE* (STUTTGART: KLETT-COTTA, 1988), P. 221.

as intact as it now insists. The desired image, the unofficial master plan for today's reconstruction, was photographed after the destruction that occurred on 9 November 1938, and, hence, does not include the synagogue.

RECYCLING

The history of reconstruction is more complex than an architect would like it to be, especially if the architect believes himself to be part of a contemporary architectural discourse that is always on the lookout for the "new." In Dresden, this history begins with the reconstruction of the Zwinger, which was not so much an act of restoration as it was an act of resistance toward the Socialist party's policies of demolition and modernization. It continued with a copy of the Semperoper [Semper Opera House], which was not an exact copy, due to new fire prevention regulations, and carried on with the Frauenkirche [the Church of Our Lady], whose ruins served as an anti-fascist, anti-war memorial until 1989, when the process of rebuilding was instigated. The insistence on unbroken continuity – already ambivalent in these cases – is more than questionable in the case of the synagogue. As the desired image of a supposedly intact Dresden also shows, the synagogue is not part of the history of the city's reconstruction. In contrast to the Frauenkirche, no ruins of the synagogue remained. An instructional film made in late 1938 by the Technische Hilfswerk uses the Dresden synagogue as an example of how to correctly demolish ruins. It's like an obscene case of "applied ecological fascism": the ruins of the burned-out synagogue were carted away after the *Kristallnacht*, and these were shred and recycled into road-building material.

FROM SITE TO EMBANKMENT AND BACK AGAIN

The material was gone. The site was there, available to fulfill the ambitions of post-war modernism. Assuming that a synagogue would never be built there again, plans were made for the land to accommodate the infrastructure of a new society. Conduits for water, gas, and electricity were laid. An enormous new bridge spilling into a six-lane highway was constructed, radically altering the site's geometry and topography. At the spot where old Dresden met the huge apartment blocks of socialist post-war modernism situated to the east, a bit of land was leftover – not much more than a long embankment. Decades later, what can be done with it? Is it possible to build here? The "invention" of a new configuration must at first proceed without regard to the outlines of historical buildings; instead, it needs to be based on what we find: the vague, somewhat accidentally created site; its measurements, and its topography of complex slopes, into which the new synagogue has to be squeezed. In a series of layered models, we smooth out the different heights and inclines to form a pedestal, which then joins with the topography that slopes down toward the Elbe, creating a variety of ways to enter the new public space between the synagogue and the community house: a place that is both exposed and protected. Yet what do we mean by "public" here, anyway? How public can (others would say "may") a synagogue be?

VISIBILITY
The public and the visible used to be related concepts in the politics of urban space. Anything that was public was also visible and vice-versa. This has drastically changed and not just because of television and the Internet. We distrust the physically visible city – the public always seems to be elsewhere.

Architecture as a medium for making public affairs visible seems to be yesterday's news. Yet what actually happens when a social or religious group becomes visible to the public, when it becomes a tangible *res publica*? After decades in a hidden, peripheral position in new Dresden, the rapidly growing community, now made up mostly of immigrants from the former Soviet Union, is returning to the historical site of the Semper Synagogue – to the center of the city, that is. The criticism of this return comes all too soon: too big, too central, nothing more than spatial reparations.[04] But what is the alternative: a fragmented community in backyard spaces scattered across the city? However, it is not just the continuing discussions about the construction of mosques in German suburbs which demonstrate how the strategies of fragmentation, invisibility, and periphery are contradictory. Ultimately, perhaps, they create no more than subtle new forms of exclusion carried out under altered – even well-meaning – political auspices.

Why not go to the center? To the place where it hurts? Confront the hegemonial powers and take up the architectural problem of visibility. What can be seen is the return of a community to the center of the city, to the immediate context of the city's monumental buildings and hot spots of identity, lined up along the panorama of the Elbe, next to the Albertinum, the Frauenkirche, the Kunstakademie [art academy], the Schloss [castle], the Hofkirche [court church], and the Semperoper. What becomes visible is the critical moment in which a community manifests itself in architecture and becomes hard, solid material. The material publicly carries out the political-cultural discourse – and yet obeys the law of its own inertia.

CLEAR GEOMETRY AND UNCLEAR PERCEPTION
In designing the Dresden synagogue, geometrical and perceptive processes are in a consciously ambiguous relationship. What is clear in the geometrical construction seems to be unclear in its spatial perception. Out of the narrow, orthogonal geometry of the site, the massive structure of the synagogue is continually turning eastward. The complex shape of the curvilinear wall is based here on the simple geometric operation of a successive rotation of orthogonal layers,

[04] SEE MARK JARZOMBEK, "DISGUISED VISIBILITIES: DRESDEN/'DRESDEN'," IN *LOG* (FALL 2005), PP. 73-82.

which in turn are made of monolithic concrete blocks, each measuring 120 x 60 x 60 centimeters. Despite the simple geometric operation, curvilinear surfaces are created; depending on the point of view, these are perceived in different ways, and, hence, it is not possible for the eye to reconstruct them in terms of clear geometry. An optical hint is offered by the structure and the shadows it casts. Due to the rotation of the individual layers of masonry around the central point of the building, cantilevers of 55 millimeters are created in the corners of the building, and their shadows make it possible to see the geometric operation. The shadows begin at the corners of the building and run to the zero crossing of the rotating structure. Beyond the center of the wall, the logic of the shadows is inverted.

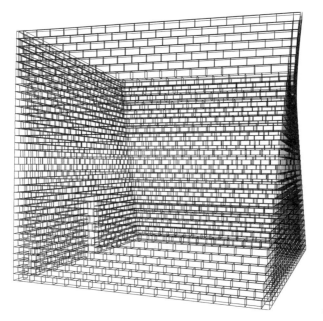

MASSIVE PROBLEMS OR WHAT IS A STONE?

In the context of an architectural culture that considers the "stone" to be nothing more than a surface phenomenon – and, therefore, produces increasingly large quantities of stone-patterned wallpaper – planning a massive, monolithic building also means getting rid of a few familiar prejudices: first of all, the one that tells us that a stone has to be natural. "Our" stone *should* – for reasons of personal preference – and *must* – for structural reasons – be artificial. The term "artificial stone" describes the subject matter: a material that explores the area between the living mineral quality of natural stone and the standardized, industrial neutrality of prefabricated stone; a material that takes a critical position between the sandstone bliss of reconstructed old Dresden and the technocratic fantasies of the socialist prefabricated housing blocks, thus, reflecting the synagogue's situation at the intersection of old and new Dresden.

CLOTHING

Architecture and clothing are usually thought of as opposites: hard versus soft, cold versus warm, permanent versus temporary. The more unusual in this context is the approach that Gottfried Semper developed in his 1860 treatise "Der Stil," a theory of *Bekleidung* [clothing], which relates the origins of architecture to textiles. According to Semper's theory, the wall, the essential element in creating boundaries of space, can be traced back to felt robes, braided and woven materials. The history of architecture could then be read as a history of the increasing solidification of "clothing."

While Semper, our predecessor, as the architect of the Dresden Synagogue, alluded to the massive wall as a kind of clothing, our approach again dissected the elements. Fabric should not be used in a mimetic way, as a visual reproduction; it should become soft again, and its visual and tactile qualities should be shown to advantage: wrapping, flowing, altering colors, and reflecting light. Brass fabric hangs from the ceiling scaffolding into the ritual space inside the synagogue. An apparent contradiction is created: building clothes.

SPATIAL CONFLICTS

According to Bruno Latour, people gather around *things*.[05] They are not mere objects, but things, which are themselves active and mark the political, social, and religious behavior of gatherings. So the spatial disposition of the synagogue is unusual: things act in opposition to each other. Wooden furnishings of various sizes are placed in the textile space: the gallery, the benches, the *bima* (the central lectern from which the Torah is read), and the Torah shrine. The organization of the essential ritual elements makes it clear that there is a "synagogal conflict of space."[06] On the one hand, the movement toward the Torah shrine at the eastern end of the room makes it a longitudinal space; on the other, the placement of the bima focuses on a centralized space. The direction of prayer becomes ambivalent. The space moves in opposing, confusing directions.

To a certain extent, the central position of the bima returns to the spatial disposition preceding that of the Reform synagogues, such as the Semper Synagogue in Dresden, when assimilation in the nineteenth century led to the introduction of altar-like arrangements in the chancel. While these architectural ideas conformed to the model of the Christian church and also created new hierarchies of space and ritual, positioning the bima in the middle creates a non-hierarchical movement in the space, oscillating, as it does, between the central and longitudinal directions. There is a shift from an

[05] SEE BRUNO LATOUR, *DAS PARLAMENT DER DINGE. FÜR EINE POLITISCHE ÖKOLOGIE* (FRANKFURT AM MAIN: SUHRKAMP, 2001).

[06] SALOMON KORN, "SYNAGOGENARCHITEKTUR IN DEUTSCHLAND NACH 1945," OP.CIT., P. 292.

architecturally unambiguous, defined situation to a condition of spatial indeterminacy.

BETWEEN TAUTOLOGY AND NARRATIVE

In the attempt to connect material conditions to political, social, and historical periods of time, and to make this the launching pad for the design strategy, we enter a gray zone. The parameters of the design become ambiguous. It is a tricky thing to enter this zone between the parametrical design and something that might be circumscribed as narrative. We leave the safe foundation of translation techniques, the spatialization of programme and the answers to technical problems. Undoubtedly, we are concerned about the consistent organization of material but not with tautology or a simple comparison in mind. As much as architects pain themselves to declare their work to be parametrically developed products, thus, avoiding the responsibility of "authorship" through what seems to be an unintentional "no style" – something like "added value" still arises. A surplus that is indeed problematic, yet indispensable for every form of architecture. In the 1990s, the most advanced forms of architectural practice concentrated on an architecture of emergence and "parametrical design." However, after a decade of emergence and the denial of narrative that accompanied it, a deep gap has opened up between the seemingly endless variations of formal, material, and organizational possibilities, and their specific use in political, social, and economic contexts. It might now become necessary for a concept of architectural practice that ultimately becomes specific in the conflict between the internal physical possibilities of the autonomous discipline and the external, political, cultural narratives. The material of architecture would then become both: handwork and politics.

THIS TEXT IS BASED ON A LECTURE HELD AT THE FRAUENKIRCHE IN DRESDEN IN 2001. THE DRESDEN SYNAGOGUE, BUILT IN 2001, WAS DESIGNED BY NIKOLAUS HIRSCH, WOLFGANG LORCH, AND ANDREA WANDEL.

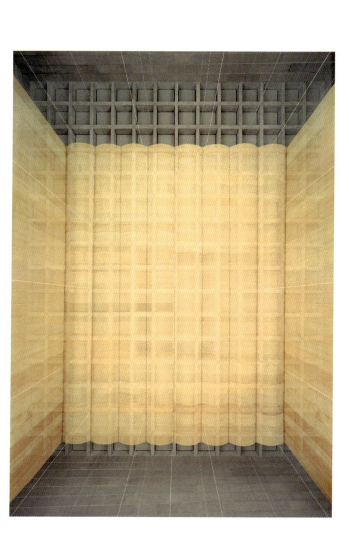

GRENZEN
ODER ÜBER DIE SCHWIERIGKEIT, DIE KONTROLLE ZU VERLIEREN

Einst galt die Architektur als die Mutter der Künste. Heutzutage mag die Architektur zwar noch immer zur Familie der Künste dazugehören, doch haben sich die alten Hierarchien grundlegend verändert. Die anderen Künste sind erwachsen geworden und die Architektur ist zum Kontrollfreak der Familie geworden, der vor allem mit seinem obsessiven Ordnungssinn beschäftigt ist: Stabilität, Kontrolle, Sicherheit, Gewissheit, Autorität, Institutionalisierung, Hermetik. Diese beruhigenden, wenn auch unplausiblen Schutzfantasien delegieren eine entscheidende Rolle an die Grenzen, die zwischen Phänomenen des Innen und des Außen vermitteln. Tatsächlich haben architektonische Grenzen eine doppelte Natur: die fachlichen Grenzen der Disziplin und die physischen Begrenzungen eines *shelter*, eines Schutzraums. In extremen Architekturmodellen wie dem White Cube und der Black Box verschmelzen die disziplinären und physischen Grenzen zu *einem* Zustand.

Der Schutzraum für Kunst verkörpert den protektionistischen Charakter der Architektur und verstärkt gleichzeitig den kreativen Widerstand anderer Disziplinen. Es ist kein Zufall, dass die bildende und darstellende Kunst in ihrer Selbstbeschreibung auf architektonische Modelle rekurrieren. Über die Jahre hinweg hat die zunehmende Autonomie der Kunst zur Konstruktion von Paradigmen der Umweltkontrolle geführt, die den Zustand der zeitgenössischen Institutionen und deren physische Bedingungen umfassend kontrollieren. So fungiert der schützende Raum sowohl als systemische Selbstreflexion als auch als materialer Zustand.

Die sicheren Grenzen des selbstreferenziellen Raums werden heute jedoch in Frage gestellt: von Außen durch soziale und ökonomische Kräfte, welche die Grundbedingungen für Kunst verändern; von Innen durch künstlerische Strategien, die sich in zunehmendem Maße in äußere Wirklichkeiten einklinken. Die Konflikte des Innen und

Außen, die dem hermetischen Modell eines Museums oder Theaters eingeschrieben sind, erzeugen eine Situation, in der Architektur und Architekt zwangsläufig eine kritische Rolle einnehmen.

EINEN PLAN HABEN

Was ist *Protection* [Schutz] in der Architektur? Vielleicht geht es immer mehr um eine doppelte Logik: einerseits um den physikalischen Zustand architektonischer Tektonik, andererseits um einen Diskurs, bei dem die Rolle des Architekten selbst zum Gegenstand wird. Diese Dopplung steht für einen kritischen Moment in der Architektur. Die materialen Zustände eines Gebäudes werden im Zeitalter des Spätkapitalismus in zunehmendem Maße beliebig, austauschbar und zufällig. Die Frage ist: wie kann heute jemand, der Materie gestaltet – man ist versucht, „bloß träges Material" zu sagen – noch kulturelle Relevanz haben?

Die Disziplin der Architektur hat ohnehin schon einen zweideutigen Ruf. Nach Aristoteles beruht die Essenz dieser Disziplin auf der Voraussicht und Vorherbestimmung eines zukünftigen Endzustands, eines *telos*. Das Primat des *telos* basiert auf einer Methode, anhand derer die verschiedenen Elemente eines Gebäudes vorausbestimmt und untergeordnet werden. Der Architekt ist mehr als nur ein Techniker, ein *tektonikos*. Folgt man der Etymologie, ist er ein *archi-tect,* der sich sowohl mit *archè* als auch mit *technè* befasst. Er etabliert *archè*, seine stärkste Waffe: ein Prinzip, eine Autorität, die untrennbar mit dem Begriff des Politischen verbunden ist.

Das grundlegende Instrument des Architekten ist der Plan. Er ist sowohl exakte Beschreibung der räumlichen Anordnung eines Gebäudes als auch ein Mittel zur Kontrolle von Zukunft. Dies wohnt allen architektonischen Handlungen inne. Der Plan gestaltet ein Objekt, fasst unterschiedlichste, oft widersprüchliche Faktoren in einer Sprache zusammen und stellt Kontrolle über die Zeit her.

Das Projekt wird zu einer Projektion, geworfen in die Zukunft.

Doch als Behauptung stabiler Zustände wirkt die Architektur immer mehr wie ein baulicher Anachronismus, wie ein träges Objekt mit schwerwiegenden Anpassungsproblemen an eine immer unvorhersehbarer werdende Zukunft. Die Frage lautet: Wie baut man in einer Zeit ohne *telos*? Wenn man solche Überlegungen anstellt, ersetzt man *die* Architektur durch Architekturen. Dies impliziert die Transformation einer Tradition in einen Ort der Übersetzung. Die potenzielle Universalität eines Projekts wird den spezifischen Gegebenheiten angepasst: wo das Bauen den Menschen nicht bloß eine Vision oktroyiert, sondern einen Lebensraum situativ gestaltet. Diese Herausforderung ist heute eines der drängenden Themen der Architektur: im Sinne einer Architektur, die nicht das Produkt eines hermetischen Systems, einer Signatur oder Urheberschaft ist, sondern vielmehr eine Reterritorialisierung in spezifische Situationen und kulturelle Phänomene.

DIE KONTROLLE VERLIEREN

Das Problem des – gewollten oder ungewollten – Lesbarmachens stellt eine Schwierigkeit dar, die schon Henri Lefebvre, dem Vater der aktuellen urbanistischen Debatten, Kopfzerbrechen bereitete. Er insistierte auf den komplexen Beziehungen zwischen den Sphären des physikalischen und des mentalen Raumes auf der Basis einer sozialen Praxis des Alltagslebens. Die „Dominanz des Lesbaren und Sichtbaren" in der Interpretation des Raumes irritierte ihn hingegen. Die Interpretation soll, so Lefebvre, später kommen, sozusagen als Hintergedanke in der Produktion von sozialem Raum. Das „Lesen" hat in dieser Logik Nachrang gegenüber der Produktion; allerdings mit Ausnahme jener Fälle, in denen der Raum explizit geschaffen wird, um gelesen zu werden.[01] Genau diese Ausnahme beschreibt

---

[01] HENRI LEFEBVRE, *THE PRODUCTION OF SPACE*, OXFORD 1991, S. 141-147.

jedoch präzise die problematische Lage des Architekten. Er liest die ganze Zeit. Er konstruiert räumliche Produkte, damit sie gelesen werden: ein Spekulieren über die Welt in Form von Gebäuden. Wie könnte der Architekt das räumliche Lesen und Spekulieren überwinden? Wie entledigt er sich seiner wirksamsten Waffe: einer Autorität, die letztlich seine Urheberschaft garantiert? Wie lässt sich Zweifel bauen? Wie verliert man die Kontrolle?

In den vergangenen Jahrzehnten war der *Non-Plan* eine der geläufigsten, wenn auch problematischsten Antworten auf diese Fragen. Als Alternative zu den klassischen Kontrollmechanismen architektonischer Systeme bietet er einen scheinbar privilegierten Zugang zu einer Realität, die als heterogen, offen und ungeplant verstanden wird. In diesem Ansatz verwandeln sich die Stadt und ihre Straßen in ein Arsenal von Metaphern des Konkreten und Realen. Temporäre Strategien in der Tradition des Situationismus verlassen den engen Käfig kultureller Institutionen und eignen sich urbane Territorien an, laufen dabei jedoch Gefahr, einer Festivalisierung unter den Prämissen der neoliberalen Deregulierung in die Falle zu gehen. Der euphemistische Non-Plan verwandelt sich in eine neue Version des kapitalistischen *Laissez-faire*.[02] So ist es ungeklärter denn je, ob die Versuche, die Idee der Institution an sich zu verwerfen – häufig ein Reflex auf Foucaults genealogisches Werk über institutionelle Körperschaften wie Irrenhaus, Krankenhaus und Gefängnis – erfolgreich gewesen sind. Auf Dauer neigen die antiinstitutionellen Off- und Subkulturen dazu, genauso stabil und beschützend zu agieren wie ihre ideologischen Antipoden.

---

[02] JONATHAN HUGHES, „AFTER NON-PLAN: RETRENCHMENT & REASSERTATION", IN JONATHAN HUGHES, SIMON SADLER (HRSG.), *NON-PLAN. ESSAYS ON FREEDOM, PARTICIPATION AND CHANGE IN MODERN ARCHITECTURE AND URBANISM*, OXFORD 2000, S. 175-178.

[03] SIEHE NICOLAS BOURRIAUD, *POSTPRODUCTION. CULTURE AS SCREENPLAY: HOW ART REPROGRAMS THE WORLD*, NEW YORK 2002, S. 22.

Die umgekehrte Strategie setzt im Inneren des hermetischen Schutzraums an. Seit den 1990er Jahren saugen Kunstinstitutionen die Phänomene der Straße und andere informelle Organisationsformen in sich auf. Räumliche Modelle wie der Flohmarkt[03], das Camp, die Schule und der Workshop haben in Nicolas Bourriauds und Jérôme Sans' Palais de Tokyo in Paris, die *ErsatzStadt* an der Volksbühne Berlin, den Umbau des Bockenheimer Depots in Frankfurt und die abgesagte Manifesta 6 School in Nikosia Einzug gehalten. Jedoch hat die Arbeit im *expanded field* zwei Seiten: Was sich optimistisch betrachtet als eine Strategie der Öffnung und der Risikobereitschaft sehen ließe, präsentiert sich von einer eher pessimistischen Warte aus betrachtet als eine weitere Wendung in der anhaltenden Ausdifferenzierung systemischer Grenzen. Was subversive Infiltration oder ein Prozess des „Schmuggelns"[04] sein will, könnte sich am Ende als raffinierte Form der Integration erweisen. Eine mehr oder weniger unbewusste Ausweitung auf das, was einst außer Reichweite und außer Kontrolle gewesen ist.

Problematisch ist heute, dass die Öffnung des hermetischen Käfigs „Kulturinstitution" und die Entwicklung konkreter sozialer Projekte nicht die exklusive Idee von Kuratoren ist, sondern zu einem ausdrücklichen Bestandteil staatlicher Politik geworden ist. Als Tony Blair in seinem Vorwort zu *Because Britain Deserves Better*, dem Manifest der New Labour, feststellte, dass „die Kunst eine zentrale Rolle bei der Aufgabe, die Gemeinschaft wiederherzustellen" einnehme, wurde offensichtlich, dass der avantgardistische Kampf um eine radikale Verknüpfung von Kunst und Leben inzwischen von anderen Akteuren angeeignet wurde und nun Gefahr läuft, als utilitaristische Vorgabe an die Kultur zu dienen. Fast scheint es, als habe

[04] IRIT ROGOFF, „SCHMUGGELN. EIN KURATORISCHES MODELL", IN VANESSA JOAN MÜLLER, NICOLAUS SCHAFHAUSEN (HRSG.), *UNDER CONSTRUCTION. PERSPEKTIVEN INSTITUTIONELLEN HANDELNS*, KÖLN 2006, S. 130-133.

die Kunstinstitution eine historische Entwicklung von harten zu weichen Grenzen vollzogen: vom *Museum*, das als Begriff im späten 16. Jahrhundert aufkam und eine strikte Trennung zwischen dem Alltagsleben und den Kunstwerken einführte, über die Einrichtung der öffentlichen Institution (als drei Jahre nach der Revolution von 1789 die *Assemblée Nationale* beschloss, den Louvre in eine öffentlich zugängliche Galerie umzuwandeln) zum Museum, das die Auflösung der Grenzen zwischen Kunst und Leben behauptet. Letztendlich läuft die Kritik hermetischer Modelle Gefahr, zu einer heuchlerischen Architektur der weichen Grenzen zu führen. Und schlimmer noch: Diese Politik der Barrierefreiheit erzeugt eine neue Form des *Social Engineering*.

PLANUNG ALS KONFLIKT
Die professionellen Grenzen stehen auf dem Spiel, wenn die Konstrukteure des Kunstraums zusammenarbeiten. Die in Hassliebe verbundenen Künstler, Kuratoren und Architekten bilden einen explosiven (und manchmal auch produktiven) Mix, wenn sie um die Kontrolle über denselben Raum und damit letztlich um ihre Autorschaft kämpfen. Die Grenzen der Disziplinen werden hinterfragt und neu verhandelt. Was als Zusammenarbeit beginnt, kann mit einem *friendly fire* enden. Doch wie lassen sich die Beziehungen auf systemischer Ebene definieren? Wie viel Distanz und wie viel Nähe sind möglich?

Aus einer historischen Perspektive heraus betrachtet, weisen die Grenzen zwischen den Disziplinen eher unscharfe Konturen auf. Kunst und Architektur waren einstmals keine eigenständigen Berufe, sondern über Jahrhunderte eng miteinander verflochten. So war die Architektur der Renaissance das Produkt von multidisziplinären Autoren: Michelangelo, Leonardo und Alberti waren Architekten, Maler, Bildhauer und Schriftsteller. Heute ist die Kunst noch immer eine offene, ungeschützte Disziplin, wohingegen die Architektur ein rechtlich geschützter Beruf geworden ist – wohl in der Annahme, dass Architekten ähnlich wie Ärzte und Juristen den Menschen Schutz bieten; keinen rechtlichen oder körperlichen, sondern einen räumlichen Schutz.

Als ab Mitte des neunzehnten Jahrhunderts die Architekten begannen, sich als klar definierte Berufsgruppe zu organisieren, entwickelten sie eine Doppelstrategie zur Legitimierung ihrer sozialen und kulturellen Position: eine starke Strategie und eine schwache. Einerseits rühmten sich die Architekten ihrer fachlichen Kenntnis der Raumorganisation und -konstruktion sowie ihrer Fähigkeit, den Bauprozess zu leiten und zu überwachen. Auf der anderen Seite verwiesen sie auf den künstlerischen und kreativen Aspekt ihrer Arbeit, ein Element, das die Einzigartigkeit ihrer Arbeit seit alters her definiert hatte. Als sie erkannten, dass die stärkere ihrer Legitimierungsstrategien durch die Konkurrenz der Ingenieure und die Modernisierung der Bauindustrie unter Druck geriet, ordneten die Architekten der modernistischen Avantgarde ihre schwache *Raison d'être* einer starken Strategie mit einem völlig neuen Dreh unter: mithilfe effizienter Bautechnologie und Produktionsmethodik waren die Architekten in der Lage, die Grenzen ihrer Profession neu zu gestalten und bis in die 1970er Jahre unentbehrlich zu werden. Ein Erfolg zu einem hohen Preis: die Nähe zu den Interessen der Industrie und der staatlichen Politik hat die Legitimität des Architekten ernsthaft beschädigt. Mit dem gesteigerten Status von Kunst in der zeitgenössischen Kultur wird heute die künstlerische Seite der Architektur wieder entdeckt. Die schwache Strategie wird wieder stärker.

Die Architekten realisieren allmählich, dass der Raum zwischen Kunst und *Engineering* eng wird. Ingenieure wie Cecil Balmond treiben die Entwicklung der Architektur weiter voran als jeder Star-Architekt, während Künstler wie Olafur Eliasson, deren Ateliers immer mehr Architekturbüros gleichen, eine Phänomenologie des Raums konstruieren, die selbst für den sensibelsten Architekten kaum erreichbar ist. In dieser schwierigen Dreiecksbeziehung sucht der Architekt, der traditionelle Spezialist für die Konstruktion von geschützten Räumen, nach seinem eigenen Refugium. Doch der alte Protektionismus funktioniert nicht mehr. Dasselbe gilt für den interdisziplinären Charakter des Architekten, den ersten Aspekt, den Vitruv beschrieb, als er die abendländische Architekturtheorie aus der Taufe hob. Höchstwahrscheinlich bleiben dem Architekten zwei Optionen: Entweder wartet er auf den Zusammenbruch der disziplinären Grenzen zugunsten einer allumfassenden *Baukunst* oder er verschiebt die Kategorie des Grenzkonflikts auf den ausdifferenzierten Maßstab eines Gebäudes und die Mikropolitik des Planungsprozesses.

VERHANDELTES MATERIAL: PROTEKTION UND EXPOSITION
Die architektonischen Implikationen von Grenzkonflikten evozieren unterschiedliche Modelle der räumlichen Trennung und Durchlässigkeit, d.h. Strategien, die Umweltbedingungen der Öffnung und der Schließung definieren. In diesem Zusammenhang arbeitet der Begriff der Umwelt in unmittelbarer Weise mit der Konkretheit des architektonischen Materials, seiner inhärenten Fähigkeit, die Instabilität der physikalischen Umwelt zu vermitteln. Elemente wie Decke, Boden oder Wand lassen sich als materiale Übergänge zwischen System und Umwelt definieren, als Grenzen, die Öffnung und Schließung definieren. Durch Gebrauch und Missbrauch des Widerspruchs zwischen der Instabilität externer Fluktuation und der Stabilität internen Stillstands, erzeugt die Materialstrategie eine Architektur, die auf unterschiedlichen Rhythmen und graduellen Phänomenen beruht. Als tektonisches Detail konkretisiert das Material unterschiedliche Wahrnehmungsmodi: verschiedene Abstufungen visueller Protektion und Exposition, Rhythmen von Geschwindigkeit und Langsamkeit, Lärm und Stille.

Zur Bewahrung von Kunstgegenständen hat das Museum üblicherweise die Aufgabe, die Alltagsbedingungen der externen Umwelt zum Stillstand zu bringen. Es friert einen Idealzustand des Objekts ein. Für alle Ewigkeit. Im Gegensatz dazu würde die Fortsetzung des „Lebens" eines Objekts durch Verlängerung der ursprünglichen Umweltbedingungen langfristig zu seinem Verfall führen. Diese Stabilität war einstmals der wichtigste Parameter eines Kunstraums, heute jedoch gewinnt der Begriff der Instabilität angesichts der Zunahme von partizipativer und interaktiver Kunst zusehends an Relevanz.

Wenn jedoch die Verhandlung von Parametern der Protektion und Exposition – oder drastisch formuliert: der Konflikt zwischen Objekten und Nutzern – letzten Endes zu einer gefährdeten Kunstinstitution führen sollte, muss man sich fragen: Wie verhandeln wir das physikalische Material in der architektonischen Praxis? Welchen Status hat das Material? Die Behauptung, dass Bautechniken und Materialien wie Glas, Stahl und Beton der Entwicklung der Architektur den Takt geschlagen haben, ist trivial. Weniger banal ist der Verdacht, dass neuere Entwicklungen weniger Wert auf die Technologie von Werkstoffen legen als auf die Bauorganisation an sich. Die Bauindustrie hat den Ehrgeiz abgelegt, den Rohbau zu revolutionieren, der sein archaisches Schicksal nun schon seit dreißig Jahren erträgt. Die wesentlichsten Veränderungen vollziehen sich stattdessen im Bereich der Materialanwendungen, insbesondere bei Fassaden, Oberflächen- und Sicherheitstechnologien. Diese neuen Systeme haben mit traditioneller Tektonik nichts gemein. Zumeist sind sie vielschichtige hybride Konglomerate aus Werkstoffen mit genau definierten Anwendungsbereichen. Die Schnittstelle zum Rohbau wird über hoch entwickelte Technologien gesteuert, die einen Werkstoff mit dem anderen verbinden. Letzten Endes wird das Bauen zu einem Problem der Schnittstelle. Diese Situation trifft den Architekten, den traditionellen Spezialisten für Tektonik, also dem Zusammenfügen von Material. Weit weg von den Produktionsprozessen der neuen

Konglomerate, die sich seiner tektonischen Kontrolle entziehen, wird er zum bloßen Moderator der Systeme.

MODELLWELT

Wie weich oder wie hart sind die Grenzen der Architektur? Seit den 1990er Jahren verschieben die avanciertesten Formen der Architekturpraxis ihren Fokus von den Themen der Repräsentation, der Bedeutung und der Sprache in Richtung jener der Organisation, der Produktion und der Technik als potenzielle Formenerzeuger. Das Einfließen von computergestützten Tools in die Planungspraxis hat durch das Postulat einer *Architecture of Emergence* einen wesentlichen Teil der Architekturdebatten in den Bereich des „parametrischen Designs" verschoben. Doch in gleichem Maße wie das Produktionspotenzial exponentiell wächst, tut sich nun eine Kluft zwischen den scheinbar unendlichen Möglichkeiten an formalen, materialen und organisatorischen Möglichkeiten und deren konkreter Umsetzung im Rahmen politischer, sozialer und ökonomischer Zusammenhänge auf. Sie manifestieren einen reinen Planungsprozess, in dem der kritische Moment der „Entscheidung" ausgeblendet ist. Heute kommt die alte Frage, ob Gebäude rein materiale Erscheinungsformen der Disziplin „Architektur" seien oder ob sie sich über ihre bloße organisatorische Beschaffenheit hinaus auf externe Systeme beziehen sollten, mit neuer Virulenz auf.

Wir werden Zeugen einer weichen Sprache. Einer Politik der Barrierefreiheit. Einer Architektur der weichen Grenze. Die freundlich daherkommende Gefahr geht nun von einer neuen Form des *Social Engineering* aus. Um dem zu begegnen, müsste klar werden, dass es weder Aufgabe der Architektur ist, die Trennung zwischen Kunst und Leben zu bewahren, noch, sie zu überwinden. Sie ist weder reiner Ausschluss noch reiner Einschluss. Es wäre naiv, den protektionistischen Charakter von Architektur zu ignorieren, um einen grenzenlosen Zugang zu räumlicher Produktion zu propagieren. Vielleicht ist es eher an der Zeit, den perversen Charakter des Architekten kritisch zu würdigen. Gewiss kann er seine Beteiligung an all den modernen Bautypen kritisch untersuchen, die einst Foucault als Modell gedient haben: das Hospital, das Gefängnis, die Psychiatrie – hinzuzufügen wäre noch Krankheitsbild des Museums. Doch es überwinden? Sich seiner entledigen?

Vielleicht stimmen ja alle Klischees über die Architektur: Ordnung, Stabilität, Kontrolle, Sicherheit, Gewissheit, Autorität, Hermetik, Institutionalisierung. Doch genau diese Klischees sind der Grund, warum die Architektur für die Kunst relevant ist und auf eine unheimliche Weise anziehend wirkt. Sie erzeugt Widerstand und kritischen Diskurs. Den protektionistischen Charakter der Architektur zu überwinden, würde diese auflösen. Sie würde unkritisch. Es könnte sinnvoller sein, die kritische, oft unbequeme Position eines Spezialisten für räumliche Kontrolle und Sicherung aufrechtzuerhalten. Eines Erbauers von Schutzräumen, der sich auf dem schmalen Grat zwischen buchstäblichem physischem Schutz und der Modellwelt der Metaphern bewegt. In der Uneindeutigkeit der Kategorie könnte sein größtes Potenzial liegen: architektonische Metaphern und ihre physische Manifestierung sind eins. Letzten Endes ist es dieser doppelte Charakter, der den Architekten zu einer politischen Figur macht – ob gewollt oder ungewollt. Der Architekt verfügt über die Instrumente, Ordnung zu simulieren und Modelle zu entwickeln. Diese Modelle müssen sowohl utopisch als auch bewohnbar sein.

ERSTVERÖFFENTLICHUNG IN *PROTECTIONS*, HRSG. VON ADAM BUDAK, CHRISTINE PETERS, KUNSTHAUS GRAZ, KÖLN 2006, S. 186-203.

DIE PLANUNG DES UNVORHERSEHBAREN
EIN DIALOG ZWISCHEN NIKOLAUS HIRSCH UND WILLIAM FORSYTHE

NIKOLAUS HIRSCH Im Bockenheimer Depot arbeiteten wir an einem Zustand, der zwischen Determiniertheit und Indeterminiertheit oszilliert. Ich bin immer noch nicht ganz sicher, wie unsere Rolle zu beschreiben ist: Haben wir den Raum designt, also im wörtlichen Sinn des Prädeterminierens und Designierens?

WILLIAM FORSYTHE Ist es Design? Noch nicht ganz. Es ist möglicherweise etwas, das man mit „Protodesign" umschreiben könnte. Eine erste Entscheidung betraf den Boden: Die Nutzer sollten zurück zum Boden. Deshalb ist der Raum sehr stark auf den Boden hin orientiert.

NIKOLAUS HIRSCH Der Boden, der ebenso wie die anderen Raummodule aus Filz gefertigt wurde, machte den Raum zu einem weichen Raum. Dies hatte einerseits eine Verbesserung der akustischen Bedingungen im Raum zur Folge, andererseits entwickelte sich dadurch ein enormer Einfluss auf menschliche Positionen und Haltungen.

WILLIAM FORSYTHE Dies ist verknüpft mit Größen und Proportionen, die sich nicht an spezifischen Altersgruppen orientieren. Mit anderen Worten: die Elemente funktionieren für große Menschen, kleine Menschen, Babys, junge Menschen, alte Menschen. Sie gestalten ihr eigenes Wohlbefinden. Was also haben wir gemacht? Falls überhaupt, haben wir Möglichkeiten für Nutzer entworfen.

NIKOLAUS HIRSCH Das „Machen" dieser Möglichkeiten war, von einem architektonischen Standpunkt aus gesehen, ein Prozess des Planens, des Anfertigen von Zeichnungen. Und doch scheint mir im Vergleich mit anderen Projekten, dass unsere Zusammenarbeit, d.h. der Dialog zwischen Architekt und Choreograph, völlig anders war.

WILLIAM FORSYTHE Ich würde nicht „völlig" sagen, dies ist möglicherweise zu absolut. Architekten schaffen ja immer Räume für menschliche

Körper. In diesem Fall konzentrierten wir uns auf Körper im öffentlichen Raum. Sogar in Industriearchitekturen geht es ja um den Zusammenhang zwischen Maschinen und Körpern. Wie sind Menschen üblicherweise durch den öffentlichen Raum konstruiert? Sie sind standardisiert. Ihre Bewegungen sind determiniert. Die Herausforderung für uns war zu sagen: „Dies ist ein nicht-standardisierter Raum".

NIKOLAUS HIRSCH Ich denke, dieser Ansatz ist selbst im Detail ersichtlich. Zum Beispiel, als wir Diskussionen führten über Bänke, Dimensionen …

WILLIAM FORSYTHE … die Kanten von Dingen …

NIKOLAUS HIRSCH … und Proportionen. Ich erinnere mich an ein Treffen im Ballettsaal, als wir die Verhältnisse zwischen Körper und modularen Elementen probten. In dieser direkten Arbeit im Maßstab 1:1 ging es darum, räumliche Proportionen und Größen zu entwickeln, die nicht spezifische Positionen determinieren, sondern unvorhersehbare Körperhaltungen erlauben.

WILLIAM FORSYTHE Wir haben die Nähe zum Boden gesucht, weil es sich um einen Tanzraum handelt. Die Frage war also: Wie können wir etwas schaffen, das die Benutzer unterschiedlich auf den Raum reagieren lässt? Eine Antwort, Ansatz war, dass sie ihren Körper nicht in Bezug auf die Situation arrangieren, sondern dass sie die Situation in Bezug auf ihren Körper arrangieren. So sind beispielsweise alle Bänke ein bisschen zu breit – sie sind breit genug, um andere Dinge zu tun als nur darauf zu sitzen. Sie definieren nicht nur *eine* spezifische Position oder Funktion. Man sieht, wie sich die Körper der Besucher ausstrecken, spreizen und dehnen. Sie nehmen eher Positionen ein, die in ihrer Geometrie zweifach gekrümmt sind. Zur Statik ihrer Körper nutzen sie mehr als nur ihr Rückgrat. Die Körper sind ausgebreitet, ihr Gewicht wird unterschiedlich verteilt. Verschiedene Muskel werden eingesetzt.

NIKOLAUS HIRSCH Durch diese Art der Benutzung tendieren die modularen Elemente dazu, allmählich zu verschwinden: Sie werden weich. Sie werden in unvorhersehbaren Konstellationen neu konfiguriert. Was man „Architektur" nennen könnte, ist ein permanenter Prozess. Das räumliche Konzept ist ein Zustand, in dem Stabilität und Instabilität immer wieder neu verhandelt werden. Wie beurteilst du das Verhältnis zwischen Architektur und Tanz? Grob vereinfachend könnte man sagen, dass es bei der Architektur eher um Statik geht, während es beim Tanz eher um Bewegung geht. Diese beiden Disziplinen scheinen gegensätzlich zu sein.

WILLIAM FORSYTHE Für mich ist eher schwirig, Architektur als etwas zu denken, das nicht für Körper gemacht ist. Tanz ist nur eine andere Art, Körper zu sein. Wir sind immer Körper, Tag und Nacht. Wir haben Betten, Bettdecken. Es gibt bequeme Körper, bestrafte Körper, Körper in Fitness-Studios, Körper in der Rehabilitation. Was wir im Raum des Bockenheimer Depots vorschlagen, ist die These, dass es mehr als eine Art gibt, Körper zu sein. Die Frage lautet dann: Was ist ein Körper im öffentlichen Raum? Und was könnte ein Körper in einem kaum definierten Raum sein? Architektur macht uns immer in einer bestimmten Art und Weise zum Körper. Allein die Entscheidung für Treppen, Aufzüge oder Rampen ist eine autoritäre Art zu sagen: „Sei Körper auf diese Weise, sei Körper auf jene Weise".

NIKOLAUS HIRSCH Wir haben einen Raum entwickelt, bei dem es weniger um eine endfixierte Form, weniger um das determinieren spezifischer Positionen als vielmehr um einen indeterminierten Prozess geht. Wie lässt sich dies auf deine Arbeit als Choreograph beziehen?

WILLIAM FORSYTHE Jede Choreographie etabliert eine Reihe von Parametern. Gewöhnlich versucht man nicht, jede mögliche Bewegung, deren der menschliche Körper fähig ist, zu verwirklichen. Man muss eine Reihe von diskursiven Kategorien wählen. Diese Bewegungskategorien sind die Ressourcen für eine bestimmte Arbeit. Ziel im Bockenheimer Depot war es, den Raum als Ressource zu präsentieren.

NIKOLAUS HIRSCH Das Konzept eines Raums als Ressource ist in Zeiten zunehmender Privatisierung des öffentlichen Raumes eine politische Fragestellung.

WILLIAM FORSYTHE Wenn wir es uns leisten können, hier Theater zu machen, so dachte ich, könnten wir uns hier vielleicht auch öffentliches Leben leisten. Das zeitgenössische Alltagsleben ist mehr und mehr konsumorientiert. Hier haben wir einen Raum, in dem man nicht gezwungen ist zu konsumieren.

NIKOLAUS HIRSCH Die Leute kommen mit ihren Kindern und bringen ihr eigenes Essen, ihr eigenes Trinken, ihre Fahrräder mit.

WILLIAM FORSYTHE Üblicherweise denken wir nicht über öffentliches Leben nach. Das Projekt ist ein Versuch, dies umzudrehen. Weg vom privaten Körper, hin zum öffentlichen Körper. Das physische Verhalten von Körpern ist meist reguliert. Wir wollten dagegen einen Raum schaffen, der es erlaubt, einfach nur Körper zu sein. Der Körper ist nicht nur physisch, sondern auch zeitlich. Ziel war daher die Schaffung eines Raums von unregulierter Zeit. Was wir mit unserem Körper machen, was wir mit ihm zeitlich machen, ist ein sehr wichtiger Aspekt. Und das ist vielleicht das, was man „choreographisch" nennen könnte.

NIKOLAUS HIRSCH Dieser Gebrauch von zeitlichen Parametern reflektiert den architektonischen Ansatz unseres Konzeptes: Auf der einen

Seite der Halle befindet sich ein eher formaler Raum (Auditorium und Bühne) mit einer regulierten und programmierten Zeit, auf der anderen Seite ein informaler Raum mit unregulierter Zeit. Das Verhältnis zwischen diesen unterschiedlichen Sphären wird durch ein großmaßstäbliches vertikales Element aus Filz verhandelt – ein ambivalentes Element zwischen Wand und Vorhang, das sowohl Autonomie als auch Austausch schafft. Das Element ist flexibel in der Längsachse des Gebäudes, so dass formale und informale Räume in ihrer Größe veränderlich sind, d.h. sie können proportional schrumpfen und expandieren. Hinsichtlich der zeitlichen Logik ergeben sich daher starke Rückwirkungen zwischen den Zonen. So breiten sich die Ballett-Aufführungen von Mitgliedern des Ballettfrankfurt von einem Bereich in den anderen aus, Louise Neris Kunst-Programm „Public Life" benutzt beide Sphären, Ekkehard Ehlers' und Olaf Karniks Musikprogramm „Under Construction" gebraucht und missbraucht die Filzmodule des indeterminierten Raums. Diese Phänomene treten auch in kleinerem Maßstab auf, wenn die Besucher die architektonischen Elemente gemäß ihrer eigenen zeitlichen Rhythmen manipulieren.

WILLIAM FORSYTHE Sie können ein Nickerchen machen, faul sein, nichts tun.

NIKOLAUS HIRSCH Es ist aufschlussreich wie die Module in einer unvorhersehbaren Weise zu Betten, Decken und Kissen immer wieder neu konfiguriert werden. Das ist ein Aspekt, der mich sehr interessiert: Wie etwas, das wir geplant haben, die Fähigkeit hat, als Design zu verschwinden. Ein Oszillieren zwischen etwas Geplantem und etwas sich Entwickelndem. Etwas scheinbar Widersprüchliches: die Planung des Unvorhersehbaren.

WILLIAM FORSYTHE Du beschreibst ein Paradox.

NIKOLAUS HIRSCH Das Paradox zwischen Planung und Evolution ist ein wichtiges Element in unserem Projekt. Die traditionelle Essenz von Architektur ist „Planung". In dieser Hinsicht war die Arbeit im Depot eine extreme Herausforderung: Wir mussten eine Strategie entwickeln, die auf höchst unterschiedliche Rhythmen der Produktion und des Machens reagieren konnte. Die Arbeit in einem theatralen Kontext – und hier insbesondere dein künstlerischer Ansatz – ist stark durch prozessuale Strategien geprägt. Diese unterscheiden sich erheblich von dem, was in der aktuellen Architekturdiskussion unter „Prozess" oder „prozessuales Planen" verstanden wird. Die Arbeit mit dir hatte eine Art von Direktheit, eine Suche mit allen Konsequenzen: ein iterativer Prozess des Vor und Zurück, der neuen Anfänge im Maßstab 1:1. Ich erinnere mich an Momente, in denen wir Architekten ein gravierendes Problem der Kontrolle hatten (oder zu haben glaubten), in denen wir formale, finanzielle und terminliche Kohärenz herstellten mussten. In diesen seltenen Momenten wurden wir zurückgeworfen in die klassische Rolle der Architektur: nicht Improvisation, sondern eine determinierende Strategie in Richtung Zukunft.

WILLIAM FORSYTHE Ja, völlig teleologisch.

NIKOLAUS HIRSCH Im Gegensatz dazu stand die Zusammenarbeit mit dir. Mir scheint, als gehe es bei deinem Ansatz darum, im Prozess des Machens Offenheit zu erhalten. Spielt der Begriff der Offenheit eine Rolle in deiner Arbeit als Choreograph?

WILLIAM FORSYTHE In Bezug auf Strategien und Organisationsstrukturen ist das „Staging" von öffentlichem Raum nicht grundsätzlich anders als das, was ich auf der theatralen Bühne tue. Akteur ist die Öffentlichkeit, die Bühne ist der öffentliche Raum. Wenn ich ein Stück für die Bühne entwickle, will ich wissen, wie groß die Bühne ist, wie hoch, wie tief. Man muss die Regeln des Raums kennen. Als ich in Groningen mit Daniel Libeskind arbeitete, wurde es für mich offensichtlich, dass es einen Unterschied gibt zwischen Dingen, die eine lange Dauer haben und jenen, die eine kurze Dauer haben, also jenen Phänomenen, die lebendig sind im Moment ihres Erscheinens und im nächsten Moment wieder verschwinden.

NIKOLAUS HIRSCH Die Performanz eines Gebäudes ist in ihrer Dauer verschieden von der Performanz eines Aktes oder einer Bewegung.

WILLIAM FORSYTHE Wie sieht die Performanz der Gegenwart aus? Zunächst stellen wir unsere Ressourcen fest und fragen dann: Was sind die Eigenschaften dieser Gegenwart? Unter Gegenwart verstehe ich eine politische Gegenwart, eine ökonomische Gegenwart, eine soziale und psychologische Gegenwart. Die Frage lautet: Wie kann ich am besten der Situation dienen? Wie kann etwas erscheinen, das eine andere Art von Wert hat; nicht einen monetären Wert, sondern einen rein ontologischen Wert, eine Art des Seins.

NIKOLAUS HIRSCH Ich bin – möglicherweise aufgrund der Prägung meiner Disziplin – interessiert am Prozess des Stückemachens vom Anfang bis zum Ende. Gibt es einen „Plan"? Wie schaffst du Kohärenz? Es scheint, als sei der Begriff des Gedächtnisses in dieser Hinsicht wichtig. In der Architektur spielt hierbei die Zeichnung eine entscheidende Rolle. Sie ist das Medium, das Erinnerung garantiert und stabilisiert, was wichtig ist in der Übersetzung vom Zeichnen zum Bauen. Beim Tanz scheint es dagegen um eine Erinnerung zu gehen, die nicht von anderen Medien wie Zeichnungen abhängt. Es ist eine andere Art räumliche Phänomene zu kommunizieren.

WILLIAM FORSYTHE Das gemeinsame Element ist die *Schwelle.* Architekten machen Pläne, sie müssen eine Richtung haben. Unsere Schwelle in der Choreografie ist viel weicher. Du als Architekt hast diese zweidimensionale Version. Es ist interessant, wie viele Dinge durch Flächen bestimmt sind. Ein Großteil der industriellen Welt ist an der Idee der Fläche orientiert. Die einzige Fläche, die wir haben, ist der Boden. Wir haben nicht die gleiche linguistische Logik: wir haben eine koordinatorische und physikalische Logik. Aber dies ist kein „Plan". Die Materialisierung einer Idee funktioniert nicht in der gleichen Weise. Wir gehen geradewegs von der Idee in die Struktur. Es geschieht im Prozess. Deshalb spreche ich von einer weichen Schwelle – es ist schwer zu sagen, wann du von einem Zustand zum nächsten übergegangen bist.

NIKOLAUS HIRSCH Ist die Übersetzung von der Zeichnung zur Choreographie (oder umgekehrt) ein Werkzeug, das du benutzt?

WILLIAM FORSYTHE Nein, Choreographie ist selbst eine „Graphie", eine Zeichnung. Wir zeichnen nicht, wir werden gezeichnet.

NIKOLAUS HIRSCH Es gibt keinen Zwischenzustand, keinen Mittler. Diese direkte Prozedur, die eine der Charakteristika des Tanzes zu sein scheint, wurde Teil des architektonischen Ansatzes.

WILLIAM FORSYTHE Die Idee der Prozedur kann umgekehrt werden. Wenn die Lobby des Depots nun eine Choreographie geworden ist, hat die Öffentlichkeit die Prozedur übernommen. Ob die Öffentlichkeit sich dessen bewusst ist, ist dabei nicht wesentlich. In anderen Worten: Das Bewusstsein muss nicht immer fokussiert sein, um die Bedeutung einer Choreographie präsent werden zu lassen. Sie kann in der Organisation der Architektur selbst liegen.

NIKOLAUS HIRSCH Im Depot rekonfigurieren die Nutzer das, was man Architektur nennen könnte.

WILLIAM FORSYTHE Was sie zurücklassen, hat eine interessante Organisationsstruktur. Wenn man am Ende des Tages den Raum verlässt, ergibt sich eine spektakuläre Situation.

NIKOLAUS HIRSCH Und es ist interessant, den Effekt am nächsten Morgen zu beobachten. Da ist eine Lücke, als ob die Gegenstände ihr Leben ausgehaucht hätten.

WILLIAM FORSYTHE Das ist möglicherweise die Differenz zwischen Raum und Ort. Was passiert ist, ist, dass Menschen in den Raum kommen und ihn in einen Ort verwandeln. Ein Ort hat eine Bedeutung, er ist personalisiert, wogegen der Raum abstrakt bleibt.

NIKOLAUS HIRSCH Die Unterscheidung zwischen Raum und Ort ist möglicherweise aufschlussreich, wenn wir uns auf die aktuelle Diskussion utopischer Räume beziehen, wie dies einige Kritiker und Kommentatoren in Bezug auf unsere Arbeit getan haben. Ist es ein utopischer Raum? Die Idee der Utopie ist in hohem Maße eine Frage des Raums und seiner idealen Organisation. Ich denke, dass die inhärente Tendenz zur Abstraktion innerhalb der klassischen Utopien autoritäre Züge trägt.

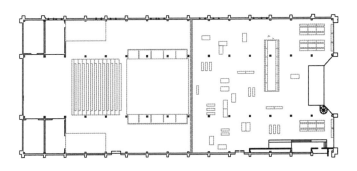

WILLIAM FORSYTHE Das denke ich auch. Die klassischen Utopien waren höchst determiniert. Im Depot schafft der Mangel an Determiniertheit einen Ort. Der Raum wird nicht zum Ort, bevor die Nutzer einen Effekt auf ihn haben.

DIE ERSTVERÖFFENTLICHUNG DES DIALOGS ZWISCHEN NIKOLAUS HIRSCH UND WILLIAM FORSYTHE ERSCHIEN ANLÄSSLICH VON *UTOPIA STATION* (BIENNALE VENEDIG, 2003) IN DEM BELGISCHEN KUNSTMAGAZIN *JANUS* 14 (2003), S. 64–68. DER UMBAU DES BOCKENHEIMER DEPOTS WURDE VON NIKOLAUS HIRSCH UND MICHEL MÜLLER IN ZUSAMMENARBEIT MIT WILLIAM FORSYTHE GESTALTET.

OBJEKTE GEGEN MENSCHEN

Wenn ein Objekt ins Museum kommt, ändern sich die Grundlagen seiner Existenz. Einem neuen und möglicherweise feindlichen Kontext ausgesetzt, wechseln die ursprünglichen Bedingungen, oder sie gehen sogar verloren im neuen Kontext. Wie gut, dass es einen Imperativ für Objekte unabhängig von Alter, Komposition und Zustand gibt: Konservierung. Das Museum übernimmt die Verantwortung für die physische Stabilität des Objekts oder zumindest für die Verlangsamung des Zerfalls.

Wenn die Umweltbedingungen des Museums allein auf die Bedürfnisse der Sammlung ausgerichtet wären, so wäre der Zerfall der Objekte langsam und alles in bester Ordnung. Doch Museen werden nicht nur von Objekten behaust, sondern temporär auch von menschlichen Wesen – Angestellte und in wesentlich größerer Zahl Besucher. Sowohl Menschen als auch Objekte sind sensibel in Bezug auf ihre Umwelt. Sie reagieren sogar auf die gleichen physikalischen Variablen von Umweltveränderungen. Das Problem ist, dass sie dies auf unterschiedliche Weise tun: Menschen sind vor allem temperaturempfindlich, während die meisten Museumsobjekte sensibel auf Feuchtigkeit reagieren. Eine Veränderung von 4% relativer Luftfeuchtigkeit (RH) hat auf Objekte den gleichen Effekt wie ein zehnprozentiger Temperatursturz oder -anstieg. Umgekehrt hat der gleiche Wechsel an Luftfeuchtigkeit auf Menschen einen Effekt wie gerade einmal 0,1 Grad Temperaturunterschied. Das bedeutet, dass Objekte hundertmal feuchtigkeitsempfindlicher als Menschen sind.

Museumsbesucher können aktiv werden, um ihre Umwelt zu beeinflussen; sie können sich anpassen, sie können sich von einem feindlichen Kontext erholen, indem sie ihre Verhaltensmuster ändern oder sich von einem Ort entfernen, an dem sie sich unwohl fühlen. Sie können sogar Art oder Anzahl von Kleidung vermindern. Von draußen kommend, tragen die Besucher schwere Kleidung, die zwangsläufig zu Überhitzung und Transpiration führt, wenn sie durch einen Ausstellungsraum laufen, der gerade warm genug ist, um einen thermischen Komfort für einen eher leicht angezogenen Museumswächter zu garantieren. An regnerischen Tagen tragen die Besucher feuchte Regenmäntel, die weiteren Feuchtigkeitsanstieg zur Folge haben. Die Lösung des Problems ist einfach: Sie können ihre Kleider an der Garderobe abgeben. Objekte haben jedoch keine solche Kontrolle über ihre Umwelt. Sie sind eher passive Rezipienten der durch Menschen geschaffenen Umweltbedingungen und können sich selten vollständig erholen, wenn sie einmal unter einer feindlichen Umwelt gelitten haben.

Der Konflikt ist fundamental: durch ihr schieres Da-Sein verursachen menschliche Wesen Veränderungen in ihrer Umwelt. Metabolistische Funktionen wie Atmen und physische Aktivitäten wie Gehen beeinflussen die Bedingungen von Temperatur und Feuchtigkeit in der Luft und verändern damit die Objekte. Ein Besucher setzt 60 Gramm Wasserdampf pro Stunde frei und mindestens 60 Watt als Wärme pro Quadratmeter Körperoberfläche. Kann er das je vermeiden?

Merke: Es gibt keine verlässliche Beziehung zwischen menschlichem Wohlbefinden und der adäquaten Umwelt für ein Kunstwerk.

„OBJECTS VS PEOPLE" IST EIN BEITRAG ZU HANS ULRICH OBRISTS PROJEKT „OUT OF EQUATION".

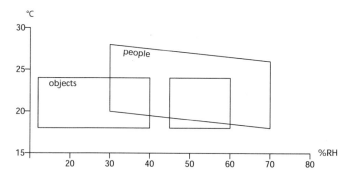

RH in the museum: objects vs people

EUROPEAN KUNSTHALLE
NICOLAUS SCHAFHAUSEN BEFRAGT NIKOLAUS HIRSCH ZUM VERHÄLTNIS ZWISCHEN KUNST UND ARCHITEKTUR

NICOLAUS SCHAFHAUSEN Architektur spielt eine zunehmend hypertrophe Rolle in zeitgenössischen Kunstinstitutionen. Du hast zu diesem Thema über einige Jahre hinweg an der Architectural Association und anderen akademischen Kontexten geforscht. In der Praxis hast du räumliche Modelle entwickelt für Institutionen wie das Bockenheimer Depot Theater in Frankfurt, ein Experimentaltheater an der Universität Gießen, die Manifesta School in Nikosia, unitednationsplaza und derzeit ein Kulturlabor in Delhi und – nicht zu vergessen – unser gemeinsames Projekt, die European Kunsthalle. Wie würdest Du die Rolle von Architektur in Kunstinstitutionen definieren?

NIKOLAUS HIRSCH Der Einfluss von räumlichen Strategien auf institutionelle Debatten ist entscheidend. Ein Grund dafür ist eine Entwicklung, die Kunstinstitutionen immer mehr zu strategischen Instrumenten der Stadtplanung und des City-Marketings macht, die ganze Regionen und Städte reaktivieren sollen. Dieses Phänomen, auch bekannt als „Bilbao-Effekt", weist der Architektur eine dominante Rolle zu. Die alternative Position wird von Strategien übernommen, die sich – in einer mehr oder weniger expliziten Tradition des Situationismus – existierende Territorien der Stadt temporär aneignen; Architektur wird dabei geradezu vermieden. In den institutionellen Debatten trifft man daher auf eine schizophrene Situation, in der Architektur entweder die Lösung oder das Problem ist. Dieses Schwarz-Weiß-Denken reflektiert eine Fetischisierung von Architektur auf beiden Seiten: Architektur als das absolut Gute oder das absolut Böse der institutionellen Kritik.

NICOLAUS SCHAFHAUSEN Als wir mit der European Kunsthalle begannen, habe ich dir kein spezifisches Programm gegeben, sei es nun der Entwurf eines neuen Gebäudes, eine Intervention in bereits existierende Räume oder eine temporäre Infrastruktur für Ausstellungen. Der Auftrag bestand allein darin, eine räumliche Strategie für die

European Kunsthalle zu entwickeln, also für eine Institution ohne Gebäude. Wie bist du an die Arbeit herangegangen und wie war sie strukturiert?

NIKOLAUS HIRSCH Auf Grundlage unserer Forschungen an der Architectural Association in London und eines Workshops an der RWTH Aachen habe ich gemeinsam mit Philipp Misselwitz, Markus Miessen und Matthias Görlich die Studie „Spaces of Production" erarbeitet. In deren Fokus steht nicht nur die offensichtliche Frage, wie Kunstwerke in einem Ausstellungsraum präsentiert werden, sondern vielmehr das Konzept einer Kunsthalle als Ort der Produktion. *Case Studies* zu so unterschiedlichen Institutionen wie Witte de With, Iaspis und Artangel wurden auf verschiedene Parameter hin untersucht: räumliche Konfiguration und Materialien, Organisations- und Finanzierungsmodelle, Kooperationsnetzwerke, zeitliche Struktur und programmatische Zielstellung. Das wichtigste Resultat der Forschung war das Herausarbeiten einer kritischen Proportion zwischen dem schweren Gepäck der Architektur und dem leichten Gepäck der Ausstellungen.

NICOLAUS SCHAFHAUSEN Dieses Proportionsproblem wird durch die beiden Schlüsselbegriffe deiner Arbeit für die European Kunsthalle reflektiert: Stabilität und Instabilität. Kannst Du dies ausführen?

NIKOLAUS HIRSCH Das Dilemma zwischen architektonischer Stabilität und Instabilität ist in der Tat wesentlich für *Spaces of Production*. Stabilität versus Instabilität – oder anders gesagt: die Frage architektonischer Dauerhaftigkeit – öffnet verschiedene Aktionsfelder und setzt doch Grenzen. Die Frage ist: Wie viel Kohärenz braucht eine Institution? Was bedeutet „Stabilität" in Bezug auf die physischen Bedingungen des Ausstellens von Kunst, d.h. die Kontrolle von Licht, Luft und anderer Umwelteinflüsse? Da gibt es zum einen die Institutionen, die ein perfekt kontrolliertes, abgekoppeltes Umwelt-system schaffen: ein neutraler und unveränderbarer Innenraum innerhalb eines stabilen Gebäudes. Auf der anderen Seite stehen Kunsträume, die mit dem Alltag der Stadt verschmelzen. Institutionen mit veränderbaren, dynamischen Grenzen, deren Ausstellungsräume explizit nicht sichtbar werden. Beide Konzepte haben ihre eigene Geschichte und Traditionen, doch heute können sie neu gedacht werden. Sie können neu kombiniert werden zu einem Modell, das sowohl Schutz als auch Exposition bietet. Tatsächlich haben unsere Forschungen gezeigt, dass sich die Rhythmen der beiden so konträr scheinenden Modelle zunehmend angleichen. Die Trennlinie ist häufig eher ideologischer Natur: instabile Modelle sind weder so ephemer wie sie behaupten, noch sind stabile Modelle unbewegliche Bollwerke der Hochkultur. Die instabilen Typologien benötigen immer mehr Stabilität hinsichtlich technischer und personeller Infrastruktur, während die scheinbar stabile Kunsthalle zunehmend destabilisiert wird durch die immer kürzere Lebenszeit von Gebäuden, durch immer häufigere Umbauten (u.a. ausgelöst durch den zunehmend raschen Wechsel in der künstlerischen Leitung und deren räumlicher Konzepte), durch einen immer schnelleren Rhythmus von künstlerischen Formaten wie Ausstellungen, Vorträge und Performances und deren räumliche Anforderungen. Unser Konzept zielt daher auf ein Modell der Kunsthalle, deren Architektur als Materialzyklus interpretiert wird.

NICOLAUS SCHAFHAUSEN Von der Forschung zum Programm der European Kunsthalle wechselnd: kannst du deine Rolle als Architekt in unserem diskursiven Programm *Under Construction* und der Ausstellung *Modelle für Morgen* beschreiben? Wie habt ihr diese temporären Formate einer Institution ohne festen Raum interpretiert?

NIKOLAUS HIRSCH Wir haben diese Formate als angewandte Forschung verstanden. Sie sind also weder reine Praxis, noch reine Forschung. Wir haben sie gewissermaßen als Test unter realen Bedingungen für eine instabile Kunsthalle benutzt. Beide Formate wurden temporär über die Stadt verstreut, dennoch hatten sie eine präzise zeitlich-räumliche Struktur. Für *Modelle für Morgen* haben wir auf der Basis dessen, was du als „nachöffentlichen Raum" bezeichnet hast, zunächst ein räumliches Inventar von Call Shops, Banken, Fitness-Studios und anderen Orten erarbeitet. All diese 22 Ausstellungsräume waren unterschiedlich in Bezug auf ihre Organisationsstrukturen, Öffnungszeiten und Logik von Inklusion und Exklusion. Das unscharfe Terrain – also das, was einst säuberlich in „privat" und „öffentlich" getrennt war – wurde immer wieder neu verhandelt. Zugänglichkeit wurde zu einem wesentlichen Kriterium; ein Kriterium, so unsere Schlussfolgerung, das essentiell für jede zukünftige Kunstinstitution ist.

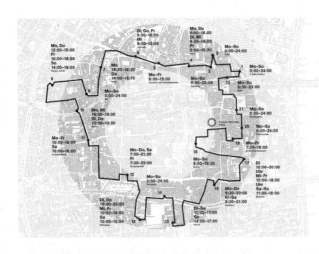

NICOLAUS SCHAFHAUSEN Die urbane Figur, die diese Räume zusammen bildeten, schuf kein zufälliges oder improvisiertes Muster, sondern eine spezifische Form. In gewisser Weise hast du auf den formalen Charakter jeglicher Institution insistiert.

NIKOLAUS HIRSCH Die räumliche Strategie war darauf angelegt, Kohärenz innerhalb eines temporären und fragmentarischen Konzepts zu schaffen. Wir wollten deutlich machen, dass eine Ausstellung kein improvisiertes Ereignis ist, sondern eine geplante Struktur, die eine Architektur im großen, urbanen Maßstab darstellt und als Modell für eine Institution ohne Gebäude funktioniert. Aus diesem Grund rekurrierten wir auf den Parcours als einer charakteristischen Logik des Museums. Wir schufen einen Loop, ganz wörtlich verstanden als einen kreisförmigen Rundgang mit einem Durchmesser von exakt einem Kilometer.

NICOLAUS SCHAFHAUSEN In der abschließenden Phase hast du ein neues Modell für eine Kunsthalle entwickelt, das sowohl stabile als auch instabile Parameter umfasst. Inwiefern stellt dein Ansatz eine neue Typologie der Kunsthalle dar? Wie reagiert es auf eine kulturelle Situation, die geprägt ist durch den zunehmenden Rückzug des Staats und volatile Privatinteressen?

NIKOLAUS HIRSCH Instabile und stabile Parameter werden so kombiniert, als würde sich etwas Provisorisches über die Zeit verfestigen. Die Kunsthalle entsteht durch Akkumulation. Uns geht es nicht darum, die ideale Kunsthalle zu erfinden oder zu entwerfen. Es geht nicht um den absoluten Masterplan (der dann in der Praxis scheitert), sondern um die Strategie eines konzeptuellen Pragmatismus – wenn nicht sogar um radikalen Opportunismus. Hierbei beziehen wir uns auf das übliche Prozedere bei der Planung eines Projekts. Jedes Gebäude kann – bevor überhaupt von Entwurf die Rede ist – durch sein Raumprogramm beschrieben werden. Es kann in seine verschieden Komponenten und deren funktionale und quantitative Parameter in Bezug auf Fläche und Höhe zerlegt werden. Das

Raumprogramm einer Kunstinstitution mit ihren Ausstellungsräumen, Büros, Lager, Toiletten, Auditorium, Café etc. formt üblicherweise eine kohärente Einheit, mit einem einzigen Autor. Unsere Strategie bricht mit dieser Annahme und löst das Raumprogramm in unabhängige, autonome Komponenten auf. Programmatische Teile wie Ausstellungsräume, Büros, Buchhandlungen usw. werden durch unterschiedliche Autoren (vor allem Künstler) geplant und in zeitlicher Abfolge, durch Akkumulation realisiert. Es wird eine zeitlich basierte, wachsende Institution sein, vergleichbar mit der Logik von *Corps Exquisite*: ein Bild oder eine Geschichte, die kollektiv aus individuellen Segmenten zusammengefügt wird. Ein Netzwerk von möglichen Wegen, die von einem Anfang ausgehen (in unserem Fall von dem Büro der European Kunsthalle als Ur-Zelle) und zu vielen möglichen Verzweigungen führen.

NICOLAUS SCHAFHAUSEN Was ist die konzeptuelle Verbindung zwischen den programmatischen Komponenten und den Künstlern?

NIKOLAUS HIRSCH Es ist sowohl eine konzeptuelle Kopplung als auch ein empirisches Phänomen, das uns aufgefallen ist. Heute kann man beobachten, dass viele Künstler an Infrastrukturen interessiert sind: man denke nur an den Konferenzraum, den Liam Gillick für dich im Frankfurter Kunstverein gemacht hat oder Monica Bonvicinis Toilette, Elmgreen & Dragsets *Powerless Structures*, Anton Vidokles und Julieta Arandas *Martha Rosler Library* und viele andere Projekte. Wir benutzen dieses Phänomen und entwickeln es weiter in Richtung einer akkumulativen Kunsthalle.

NICOLAUS SCHAFHAUSEN Das scheint ein logischer Schritt in der Post-Bilbao-Ära zu sein: die Architektur wird zur Ausstellung, aber unter den Bedingungen der Kuratoren und der Künstler.

NIKOLAUS HIRSCH Absolut, jedes neue Teil des Gebäudes wird zu einem Teil der Ausstellung. Nicht ad hoc, aber in der typischen Zeitskala von Ausstellungen, z.B. drei Monate. Die Architektur ist kuratiert. Was wir anstreben, ist eine untrennbare Verbindung zwischen dem schweren Gepäck der Architektur und der temporären Struktur der Ausstellung, d.h. ihres zeitlichen Maßstabs, ihrer Finanzierungspolitik und programmatischen Volatilität.

NICOLAUS SCHAFHAUSEN Was hier passiert, ist eine Hybridisierung von Rollenmodellen: der Künstler wird Architekt, die Architektur des Gebäudes wird Ausstellung. Impliziert deine Strategie ein neues Verständnis deiner eigenen Rolle als Architekt?

NIKOLAUS HIRSCH Neu ist dabei die radikale Infragestellung der Autorschaft. In unserer Strategie ist Architektur näher an *Scripting* als an Design. Im Kontext einer zunehmend hysterischen Aufmerksamkeitsökonomie in der internationalen Kunstszene macht es möglicherweise Sinn, meine Rolle nicht durch Design zu definieren. Doch um einem Missverständnis vorzubeugen: es geht immer noch um Planung. Wir definieren einige Spielregeln, wie sich die Evolution der Kunsthalle vollzieht. Wir planen die Logik der Verbindung zwischen den Komponenten, indem auf Typologien musealer Organisationsformen rekurriert wird: lineare und zirkuläre Abfolgen wie im klassischen Parcours, kontinuierliche Verzweigungen oder baulich autonome Einheiten.

NICOLAUS SCHAFHAUSEN Wenn du die Grenzen der Disziplinen und Rollenmodelle in Frage stellst: verstehst du dich dann noch als Architekt im traditionellen Sinn?

NIKOLAUS HIRSCH Es wäre prätentiös zu behaupten, dass ich nicht einem Rollenmodell folge, das traditionell „Architekt" genannt wird. Ob ich will oder nicht: meine Praxis ist Teil einer Kultur des Planens, die bestimmte Instrumente wie Zeichnungen benutzt, um einen zukünftigen physischen Zustand zu beschreiben und zu definieren. Es handelt sich um eine extreme Form der Autorschaft, wenn man sie im Sinn von „Autorität" denkt. Die Konstruktion eines so komplexen und langsamen Phänomens wie eines Gebäudes verlangt eine manchmal perverse Kontrolle über Zeit und Raum. Doch tatsächlich gibt es einen veränderten Begriff von architektonischer Praxis. Sie findet heute in einem *expanded field* statt, in dem das Material und seine kulturellen und politischen Referenzen schneller denn je wechseln. Der Architekt kann sich nicht länger auf sein „langsames" Medium verlassen und wird zu einem hybriden Akteur in einem Feld von Kuratoren, Künstlern und Nutzern. In diesem Sinne wird die Frage der zunehmend umkämpften Autorschaft von Raum immer wichtiger in meiner Arbeit.

NICOLAUS SCHAFHAUSEN Stimmst du überein, dass zeitgenössische Architekten eher in dem Feld zwischen Architektur und anderen Disziplinen arbeiten? Gibt es mehr Bedürfnis nach transdisziplinärer Praxis in der Architektur?

NIKOLAUS HIRSCH Manchmal ist es effizienter, sich von den Rändern der Disziplin zu nähern. Dies bedeutet aber nicht, den harten Kern des Berufs aufzugeben. Tatsächlich glaube ich nicht an die völlige Auflösung der Disziplinen zugunsten eines weichen und freundlichen Cross-Over, sondern eher an eine Kultur der Kollaboration, die ein *friendly fire* zwischen den Disziplinen einschließt. In diesem Sinn geht es weniger um „Architektur & ..." wie Architektur und Tanz, bildende Kunst oder Theater, sondern vielmehr um eine Frage der Konjunktion und Verknüpfung. Mit anderen Worten: es geht um eine Frage von Werkzeugen, die zu einer gemeinsamen Basis werden. Notwendig ist ein physisches Material, das verhandelt werden kann und einen kreativen Konflikt auslöst.

NICOLAUS SCHAFHAUSEN Dieser produktive Konflikt und seine Reflektion im Projekt für die European Kunsthalle muss auch im Kontext deiner vorangegangenen Kollaborationen gesehen werden. Du hast mit dem Choreographen William Forsythe und vor kurzem mit den Künstlern Thomas Bayrle und Raqs Media Collective gearbeitet. Wie funktioniert die Zusammenarbeit zwischen Architekten und Künstlern in der Praxis?

NIKOLAUS HIRSCH Die Zusammenarbeit in der Praxis macht zwei Dinge klarer: das Gemeinsame und das Trennende. Ich war in diesen Kollaborationen mit unterschiedlichen künstlerischen Rollenmodellen und folglich auch verschiedenen räumlichen Strategien konfrontiert. Meine Arbeit mit William Forsythe provozierte ein *friendly fire* zwischen Planung und Improvisation, zwischen einer Disziplin, die Kontrolle durch einen Plan ausübt, und einer anderen, die dies durch den Körper herstellt. Das *Node House* für Raqs Media Collective war eine sehr freie Übersetzung einer durch die Künstler vorgegebenen narrativen Struktur von 18 Monitoren, die eine enorme skulpturale Präsenz hatte. In der Zusammenarbeit mit Thomas Bayrle – dem *Autobahn-Turm* im Frankfurter Museum für Moderne Kunst – haben wir die wesentlichen Parameter von Bayrles 2003 bei der Biennale in Venedig gezeigten *Autobahn* übernommen: ein spezifisches Raster, die Webtechnik, das Material Graupappe. Wir nahmen die Parameter und machten die Autobahn „dreidimensionaler", also zum Gebäude. Der Grad der Erfindung war minimal – als ob mein Stil, meine Signatur und mein Ego in einer zunehmend komplexen Autobahnstruktur verschwunden seien.

NICOLAUS SCHAFHAUSEN Wenn wir von kollaborativen Projekten zur Ausstellungsarchitektur kommen, wechseln wir zu einer Kategorie von Architektur, in der es eher um die Idee von „Service" zu gehen scheint. Tatsächlich wird Ausstellungsarchitektur zunehmend sichtbar in Kunstinstitutionen. Mit ihren temporären Räumen, Grundrissen und Wänden erhält sie häufig eine ähnliche Gewichtung wie Kunstwerke. Siehst du darin eine positive Entwicklung?

NIKOLAUS HIRSCH Es handelt sich auf jeden Fall um eine kritische Entwicklung. Allgemein ausgedrückt: Architektur ist nicht notwendig für das Ausstellen von Kunst. Daher sollte die erste Frage lauten: Wie viel Architektur ist notwendig? Jede architektonische Intervention sollte eine gewisse Notwendigkeit haben – und manchmal ist sie einfach nicht notwendig. Doch das zu realisieren, ist manchmal gar nicht so einfach. So sagte ich den Kuratoren der *Manifesta 4*, dass sie für die Umnutzung ihres alten Gebäudes keinen Architekten brauchen. Ein paradoxer Prozess: sie glaubten mir nicht und so musste ich zum Beweis meiner eigenen Überflüssigkeit Pläne zeichnen.

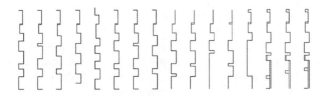

NICOLAUS SCHAFHAUSEN Die fast unsichtbare Position, die du bei der *Manifesta 4* eingenommen hast, ist ein Extrem. Ein anderes ist deine Arbeit für *Frequenzen-Hz* in der Schirn Kunsthalle, die eher dominant auftritt und letztendlich eine eigene Arbeit innerhalb der Ausstellung darstellt.

NIKOLAUS HIRSCH Die Architektur für *Frequenzen-Hz* kann als adaptierbare *superstructure* verstanden werden, die unterschiedliche künstlerische Positionen als räumliche Variablen einer Gruppenausstellung integriert. Doch dies ist nur eine Seite des Phänomens „Ausstellungsarchitektur". Die andere Seite ist, dass nicht wenige Künstler sich in ihrer Arbeit explizit auf Ausstellungsdesign beziehen. Die Idee des Displays wird Teil einer künstlerischen Praxis, wie man in Eran Schaerfs Struktur für *Das achte Feld* im Museum Ludwig oder auch bei Michael Beutlers „Ausstellungsarchitektur" für deinen *Don Quijote* im Witte de With sehen kann. Unabhängig davon, ob eine Struktur von einem Künstler oder einem Architekten konzipiert wird – im besten Fall kann sie eine Selbstreflexivität des Ausstellungsmachens herstellen.

NICOLAUS SCHAFHAUSEN In letzter Konsequenz: würdest du Architektur als eine künstlerische Disziplin bezeichnen?

NIKOLAUS HIRSCH Ich denke, dass Architektur eine Form der Kunst ist, und zwar eine, die tief in Pragmatismus verstrickt ist. Das heißt, das die Autonomie der Architektur ständig bedroht ist. Wie man darauf reagieren kann? Meine Position ist, dass Architektur nicht den Grad an Autonomie einklagen kann, der in der bildenden und darstellenden Kunst herrscht. Im Gegenteil: die Bedrohung durch andere Realitäten ist genau das, was Architektur so spezifisch macht. Du kannst dies entweder als Problem oder als Potential sehen. Ich sehe es als Potential.

DIE EUROPEAN KUNSTHALLE WURDE VON 2005 BIS 2007 VON DEM GRÜNDUNGSDIREKTOR NICOLAUS SCHAFHAUSEN GELEITET. ALS INTEGRALER BESTANDTEIL DER GRÜNDUNGSPHASE HABEN NIKOLAUS HIRSCH, MARKUS MIESSEN, PHILIPP MISSELWITZ UND MATTHIAS GÖRLICH INSTITUTIONELLE MODELLE DER KUNSTHALLE UNTERSUCHT UND DAS PROJEKT *SPACES OF PRODUCTION* ENTWICKELT.

DAS ARCHITEKTUR-DING
THE MAKING OF „MAKING THINGS PUBLIC"

Wenn Politik – wie Bruno Latour und Peter Weibel argumentieren – von Dingen handelt, was ist dann die Politik eines Ausstellungsraumes, in dem Dinge räumlich organisiert werden? Wer organisiert das Territorium? Wie werden Entscheidungen getroffen? Wie wird Raum geteilt, wie wird die Nähe zwischen den Dingen verhandelt?

Nach einem Jahrzehnt intensiver Kritik an Planungsmethoden und deren politischer Territorialisierung ist man versucht zu antworten: jedenfalls nicht, indem die Macht an die Architektur übergeben wird, die klassische Metapher des *state building*. Andererseits: die Verteilung von über 600 Exponaten auf 3.000 Quadratmetern ist kein Fall von Selbstorganisation. Es scheint als gebe es das Verlangen, ein strukturierendes Prinzip – kombiniert mit einer gewissen Autorität – einzuführen. Etwas, das mit dem griechischen Begriff *archè* umschrieben werden kann. Schlussendlich und fast zwangsläufig delegieren die kulturellen Mechanismen das Problem an einen Spezialisten: der *archi-tekt*.

Die Position des Architekten an sich mag schon ambivalent sein, in einer Ausstellung über *Ding-Politik* wird sie vollends fragwürdig. Die Frage ist: wie kann ich als Architekt das problematische Erbe meiner Disziplin vermeiden, d.h. deren Tendenz, einen zukünftigen Endzustand oder *telos* zu prädeterminieren? Wie kann ich dem Primat eines *telos* begegnen, der auf einer Vorgehensweise beruht, die den Platz der einzelnen Teile vorherbestimmt und einem System unterordnet? Eine zeitgenössische Auseinandersetzung mit diesem Problem könnte darin bestehen, die angetragene Autorität zwar anzunehmen, aber – anstatt in die traditionellen Muster der Disziplin zurückzufallen – ein *Ding* zu konstruieren, das mit anderen Disziplinen geteilt werden kann, so dass Autorität zurückgegeben wird.

Die architektonische Strategie für *Making Things Public* untersucht daher ein materiales Element, das zwischen Künstlern, Wissenschaftlern und Kuratoren verhandelt werden kann: die Wand, also das grundlegende Element, durch das Räume definiert werden. Sie ist hier weder klassische weiße Museumswand, noch folgt sie der modernen Ideologie der transparenten Wand. Sie reflektiert ihre eigene Ambivalenz, indem sie verschiedene Aneignungen und wechselnde Environments erlaubt. Eine transluzente Polycarbonat-Haut legt sich auf die sichtbare, nackte Aluminiumstruktur, die üblicherweise hinter der unvermeidlichen weißen Gipsschicht der Museumswände verschwindet. Die weiche Kunststoffoberfläche wird unterschiedlichsten manipulativen Prozessen ausgesetzt: mit Cuttern werden Öffnungen hineingeschnitten, Dispersionsfarbe wird als Projektionsfläche aufgetragen, Kabel durchgeführt, Monitore und Vitrinen integriert, Folien mit Slogans aufkaschiert und, wenn sie nicht passen, wieder abgezogen. Als Instrument zur Verhandlung verschiedener Environments versetzen diese Wände die üblicherweise festen Grenzen in eine ambivalente und kritische Lage. Sie schaffen Übergänge statt rigider Definitionen, Atmosphären statt Zonierungen.

Durch eine einfache Spielregel wird das dominante Industrieraster des ZKM vom Vordergrund zum Hintergrund. Jede vorhandene Stütze muss mit einem neuen Wandelement verknüpft werden, das in jeder beliebigen Geometrie außer im rechten Winkel positioniert werden kann. Das orthogonale Stützenraster verschwindet somit in einem System von 57 transluzenten Wänden, die das geometrische System des Industrieraums in einen komplexen Haufen von Zellen, Agglomerationen und Versammlungen verwandeln. Zu fragen bleibt: sind diese neuen Konfigurationen Resultat einer partizipativen Arbeit? Oder der Selbstorganisation? Weder noch. Diese Begriffe präsentieren Denkmodelle, die dazu neigen, das Moment des Entscheidens zu romantisieren und den antagonistischen Charakter des Politischen in diesem Prozess zu ignorieren. Es handelt sich eher um eine Arbeit, die den Antagonismus in jedem Stück Architektur als eine Voraussetzung für den gemeinschaftlichen Raum verkörpert.

ERSTVERÖFFENTLICHUNG DES ENGLISCHEN ORIGINALTEXTS IN *MAKING THINGS PUBLIC*, HRSG. VON BRUNO LATOUR, PETER WEIBEL, CAMBRIDGE, MA: MIT PRESS, 2005, S. 536-539. DIE VON BRUNO LATOUR UND PETER WEIBEL KURATIERTE AUSSTELLUNG *MAKING THINGS PUBLIC. ATMOSPHÄREN DER DEMOKRATIE* WURDE VOM 20. MÄRZ – 7. AUGUST 2005 IM ZKM KARLSRUHE GEZEIGT. DIE AUSSTELLUNGSARCHITEKTUR WURDE VON NIKOLAUS HIRSCH UND MICHEL MÜLLER ENTWORFEN.

UNITEDNATIONSPLAZA: WISSEN BAUEN
MARKUS MIESSEN IM GESPRÄCH MIT NIKOLAUS HIRSCH

MARKUS MIESSEN Muss ein Architekt immer entwerfen? Es scheint, als propagiere deine Rolle bei unitednationsplaza ein neues Modell von zeitgenössischer Architekturpraxis, das Raumsuche, strategische Raumplanung, das Entwerfen von physischem Material, Wissensproduktion und Lehre verbindet.

NIKOLAUS HIRSCH Ich versuche derzeit, das zu verbinden, was bislang getrennte Teile meiner Arbeit waren. Dies klingt eher simpel, doch tatsächlich löst dieser Ansatz unwillkürlich Konflikte innerhalb des ausdifferenzierten und fragmentierten Berufsbildes „Architektur" aus. unitednationsplaza verlangt mir verschiedene Berufsbilder ab und hinterfragt damit grundsätzlich meine Rolle als Architekt. Ein Ausstellungsgebäude zu entwerfen, das eigentlich keine Ausstellung, sondern eine Schule ist – das impliziert eine Architekturpraxis, die sich nicht nur über das Design definiert. Die Verlagerung von der Ausstellung zur Schule betont vielmehr eine soziale Situation; einen gemeinschaftlichen Zustand, der die Art und Weise, wie Dinge sich physisch manifestieren, zwangsläufig verändert. In mir selbst fand eine permanente Verhandlung zwischen verschiedenen Rollenmodellen statt: dem Planer, dem Handwerker, dem Lehrer, dem Seminarteilnehmer. Einerseits organisiere ich Materie, also träges Material, das die physischen Grenzen eines Instituts bildet. Andererseits bin ich – eingeladen von Anton Vidokle und zusammen mit Boris Groys, Martha Rosler, Walid Raad, Jalal Toufic, Liam Gillick, Natascha Sadr Haghighian und Tirdad Zolghadr – Teil eines akademischen Raumes. In gewisser Weise reflektiert diese Doppelrolle meinen Versuch, Architektur als theoretisches Modell *und* als physischen Raum zu praktizieren. unitednationsplaza ist sowohl ein Modell als auch ein reales Gebäude in Berlin.

MARKUS MIESSEN In welchem Zusammenhang steht dies zur zunehmenden Institutionalisierung zukünftiger Produktion – oder anders gesagt: zu der Tendenz von Kunstinstitutionen zu Orten der

Wissensproduktion zu werden und damit auch langfristig zu Initiatoren von Aktualitäten und Objekten. Wie würdest du das Verhältnis zwischen Akademien und „ausstellenden" Kunstinstitutionen wie Museen und Kunsthallen beschreiben?

NIKOLAUS HIRSCH Ohne Zweifel: es ist eine neue Dynamik zwischen Museen und Akademien zu beobachten. Dies hängt einerseits mit der Kritik von Wissensproduktion zusammen, und andererseits, in einem größeren Zusammenhang, mit der Suche der Kunst nach politischsozialer Relevanz. Wenn man sich die Ausstellungsgeschichte der vergangenen 15 Jahre in Erinnerung ruft, wird deutlich, dass sich einige der wichtigsten Ausstellungen als Initiatoren von sozialen Projekten definierten. Ziel war es, die Ausstellung neu zu positionieren als ein Projekt, das etwas im sozialen Maßstab aktiv verändert – etwas, das übrigens die Architektur ohnehin (manchmal auch unabsichtlich) immer tut. Doch nach der Erfahrung der vergangenen Jahre wird es immer offensichtlicher, dass Ausstellungen mit den Problemen fast ausschließlich auf der Ebene der Repräsentation umgehen und damit vielleicht einfach nicht das richtige Format sind, um die hochgesteckten Ziele zu erreichen. Diese Einschränkung erklärt für mich zum Großteil das aktuelle Interesse von musealen Kunstinstitutionen an akademischen Strukturen. Museen versuchen, sich zu legitimieren und neu zu erfinden. Sie erweitern ihr Programm und rekurrieren damit – auch auf die Gefahr der politischen Instrumentalisierung hin – explizit auf ihre aufklärerische Mission. In gewisser Weise fängt unitednationsplaza von der anderen Seite her an: vom Modell der Schule.

MARKUS MIESSEN Die genealogische Spur von unitednationsplaza kann zur gescheiterten Manifesta School in Nikosia zurückverfolgt werden. Kannst du den Weg von Nikosia nach Berlin beschreiben?

NIKOLAUS HIRSCH Die Kuratoren Anton Vidokle, Mai ElDahab und Florian Waldvogel beauftragten mich mit der Entwicklung einer Raumstrategie für die Manifesta School in Nikosia, genauer gesagt: mit der Planung einer kohärenten Struktur für die drei konzeptionell verschiedenen, über die geteilte Stadt verteilten „Departments". Ein Jahr später wurde das Projekt auf Grund der Querelen zwischen der griechischen und türkischen Seite abgesagt. Nach dem Scheitern des Projekts erhielten wir Angebote von einigen europäischen Kunstinstitutionen, die sich anboten, die Gastgeberrolle zu übernehmen. Am Ende jedoch entschieden wir gegen diese „freundlichen Übernahmen" und für die Gründung eines autonomen Instituts in Berlin.

MARKUS MIESSEN Wie würdest du deine Erfahrungen in Bezug auf den räumlichen Kontext in Zypern zusammenfassen?

NIKOLAUS HIRSCH Der kritische Faktor war die Reibung zwischen der theoretischen und der physischen Seite des Modells. Das Konzept einer „Schule als Ausstellung" in Nikosia war ungewöhnlich, da es im Gegensatz zu fast allen anderen eingereichten kuratorischen Vorschlägen nicht mit den allzu offensichtlichen geopolitischen Klischees des zypriotischen Kontexts operierte, sondern mit einem eher abstrakten Format: der Schule. Der Ansatz war nicht ortsspezifisch. Aus diesem Grund wollte ich auf der räumlichen Ebene mit einer eher neutralen Infrastruktur operieren. Die klassischen räumlichen Typologien der Schule wie Auditorium, Seminarraum, Büros, Küche, Cafeteria und Dormitorium wurden als logistische Komponenten geplant, geliefert von „neutralen" Organisationen wie den *peacekeeping forces* der Vereinten Nationen oder weniger neutralen, privaten Dienstleistern – ein Ansatz, den Liam Gillick und ich als unser *Halliburton-Modell* bezeichneten. Doch letztendlich hatte die Geopolitik das letzte Wort: der Versuch, Anton Vidokles Department in einem leer stehenden Hotel auf der türkischen Seite zu implementieren, führte zur Absage der gesamten Manifesta School durch die griechisch-zypriotischen Behörden. Es war buchstäblich nicht möglich, die Dinge auf den Boden der Tatsachen zu bringen, sie physisch zu implementieren.

MARKUS MIESSEN Wie sieht die Zusammenarbeit des Architekten mit den teilnehmenden Künstlern, insbesondere mit Anton Vidokle aus? Wie hat dieses Verhältnis die Raumstrategie in Berlin beeinflusst?

NIKOLAUS HIRSCH Mein Verhältnis zu Anton Vidokle, dem Gründer von unitednationsplaza, war nie eine Architekt-Bauherr-Beziehung, sondern eine offene Kollaboration. Folglich ist das gebaute Resultat auch nicht die Antwort auf einen bestimmten Auftrag oder ein spezifisches Raumprogramm, sondern vielmehr das Produkt einer experimentellen Konstellation. Was die Zusammenarbeit fast „natürlich" machte, ist etwas, das man als den architektonischen Aspekt in Vidokles Arbeit bezeichnen könnte: sein Interesse an Infrastrukturen wie e-flux, die *Martha Rosler Library*, die Agency for Unrealized Monuments oder e-flux Video Rental. Tatsächlich war der Ausgangspunkt für das Projekt einer „Schule als Ausstellung" in Berlin keine Frage des Designs. Es ging um das Finden eines strategischen Orts. Wir waren auf der Suche nach einem Paradox: einem *objet trouvé*, das als Infrastruktur funktioniert.

MARKUS MIESSEN Wichtig erscheint es mir, an dieser Stelle mit einem Missverständnis aufzuräumen: sobald Projekte in der Welt der Architektur eine alternative räumliche Strategie verfolgen, entstehen missverständliche Analogien zu Methoden des Situationismus. Wie verhält sich eure Strategie dazu?

NIKOLAUS HIRSCH Unser Arbeitsprozess basiert weder auf situationistischer *dérive* noch auf den Techniken eines Flaneurs, der sich in der Stadt verlieren will. Wir versuchen die – immer sorgfältig versteckten – romantischen Motivationen dieser Ansätze zu vermeiden. Im Gegenteil: während unseres 3-Tage-Marschs durch Berlin ging es Anton Vidokle und mir darum, Kriterien für einen Raum zu entwickeln. Gehen und Sehen waren Mittel, um Optionen zu reduzieren; fast stochastisch. Durch eine Art räumlicher Wahrscheinlichkeitsrechnung haben wir versucht, die Möglichkeiten in einer Stadt zu reduzieren, in der es fast zu einfach ist, freien Raum zu finden – in Berlin stehen mehr als 100 000 Wohnungen und eine ähnliche Zahl von Gewerberäumen leer. Nach zwei Tagen Wanderung erfasste uns ein zunehmendes Unwohlsein, das in erster Linie auf den hohen Grad an räumlicher „Freiheit" zurückzuführen war. Uns wurde bewusst, dass *Ökonomie*, hier das Verhältnis zwischen Miete und Quadratmetern, und *Zentralität*, also die Nähe zu den kulturellen Hubs von Berlin-Mitte, keine ausreichenden Kriterien für unsere Raumsuche waren. Wir brauchten noch einen anderen Parameter.

MARKUS MIESSEN Welchen Parameter meinst du?

NIKOLAUS HIRSCH Wir reflektierten nochmals den Begriff der Autonomie in unserem Konzept. Im Gegensatz zur klassischen Typologie der Galerie, die als ladenähnliche Situation meist nur ein Teil eines größeren Gebäudevolumens ist, bietet das autonome Gebäude, dessen 470 Quadratmeter ausschließlich von unitednationsplaza genutzt werden, ganz spezifische Vorteile: es ist freistehend, sichtbar, zugänglich. Die trockene Typologie eines Instituts. Dieser dritte Parameter reduzierte die Optionen von mehreren hundert Räumen auf drei autonome Gebäude in Berlin-Mitte. Ganz abgesehen von der großartigen Adresse *Platz der Vereinten Nationen* (als unitednationsplaza schließlich Namensgeber des Projekts) und deren willkommenen Referenzen an den vorangegangenen zypriotischen Kontext, hat das schließlich ausgesuchte Gebäude für uns die Qualität, dass es auf die berüchtigte *site specificity* verzichtet. Der dreistöckige Quader verfängt sich weder in der Rhetorik der nahen Karl-Marx-Allee, noch in der romantischen Patina der Boheme von Berlin-Mitte. Es geht eher um etwas Generisches, um etwas Allgemeines, dessen Alter –

obwohl offensichtlich modern – schwer zu schätzen ist. Diese banale architektonische Qualität lässt die Besucher an ein Gebäude der 70er Jahre denken, tatsächlich ist es aber erst 1993 erbaut worden. Für mich war der Findungsprozess eine andere Art des Architekturentwurfs.

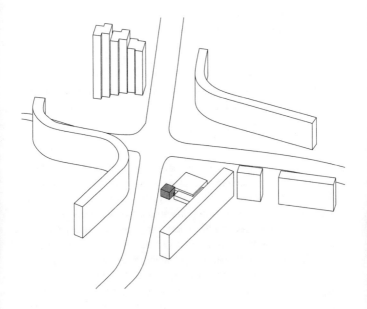

MARKUS MIESSEN Wie weit ging im nächsten Schritt die Intervention in die bauliche Struktur?

NIKOLAUS HIRSCH Die Intervention war weniger ein Addieren als ein Subtrahieren innerhalb der Gebäudestruktur. Wir entfernten einige Wände, entnahmen eine Bodenlage, vereinfachten das Beleuchtungssystem und entwickelten für Liam Gillicks unitednationsplaza-Zeichen eine vierseitige Fassadenlogik.

MARKUS MIESSEN Du hast den Umbau des Gebäudes und dessen öffentlichen Raum geplant, eine Art Auditorium. Mit welchen Typologien institutioneller Praxis und Kritik hast du dich dabei auseinandergesetzt?

NIKOLAUS HIRSCH Das Raumkonzept von unitednationsplaza bezieht sich auf den ambivalenten Charakter zeitgenössischer Kunstinstitutionen. Die Frage ist heute: geht es um einen Ausstellungsraum, ein Theater, ein Kino oder ein Auditorium? Für diesen hybriden Zustand haben wir ein leichtes modulares System – das Material ist ein verdichteter weißer und verblichener Schaum – entwickelt, das in verschiedenen künstlerischen Formaten konfiguriert werden kann: von der Ausstellung zum Seminar, vom Videoscreening zur Performance, vom Vortrag zu unvorhersehbaren Arrangements. unitednationsplaza ist ein Raum, in dem institutionelle Modelle als Display ihrer selbst gezeigt werden.

MARKUS MIESSEN Wie lässt sich die Rolle von Display in solch einem Institutionsmodell beschreiben? Mit anderen Worten: wie viel Display ist noch notwendig?

NIKOLAUS HIRSCH Ein Modell funktioniert immer auch als Display seiner selbst. So gesehen ist Display unvermeidbar. Du kannst versuchen, es durch geschickt maskierte Strategien zu verstecken. Du kannst einen *Non-Plan* oder so etwas wie die Selbstorganisation des Publikums behaupten – doch selbst das ist eine spezifische Entscheidung und eine Form von Display, oder anders gesagt: eine räumliche Konfiguration, die ich hinsichtlich quantitativer Logik und geometrischer Muster präzise beschreiben kann.

MARKUS MIESSEN Wie hängt das Problem des Ausstellens von sozialen Prozessen mit der Arbeit zusammen, die du für Bruno Latour und seine Ausstellung *Making Things Public* am ZKM in Karlsruhe gemacht hast?

NIKOLAUS HIRSCH unitednationsplaza könnte als ein *reality check* dessen gesehen werden, was Bruno Latour als *Ding* bezeichnet und in einer Weiterentwicklung des Begriffs der Realpolitik in den Neologismus *Dingpolitik* umdeutet. Es geht um das Potential eines physischen Dings, zu teilen und zu versammeln. Um etwas, das eine öffentliche Sache im Sinne einer *res publica* wird. Eine Architektur, die verschiedene, häufig widersprüchliche Formen des Zusammenseins auf sich zieht.

MARKUS MIESSEN Wie versammeln die Seminare von unitednationsplaza ein Publikum?

NIKOLAUS HIRSCH Die Seminare sind als Seminar- und Residencyprogramm angelegt, das trotz des eher kleinen Gebäudes eine relativ große Zahl von Künstlern und Theoretikern involviert. In der Tradition der *Free Universities* sind die Veranstaltungen offen für alle, die interessiert sind. Die Seminare von Boris Groys, Martha Rosler, Walid Raad, Jalal Toufic, Liam Gillick, Natascha Sadr Haghighian, Tirdad Zolghadr und mir implizieren sehr unterschiedliche Konfigurationen und Versammlungsformen. Das entscheidende Problem ist die Frage des Formats: was ist ein Seminar? Was ist ein Vortrag? Wie interagiert der Sprecher mit den anderen Anwesenden? Für Liam Gillick und die ihn kommentierende Maria Lind ging es mir um eine Architektur, die das Formale eines Seminars verstärkt: ein rigides Raster von Bänken und Stühlen mit einer frontalen Position zwischen Sprecher und Publikum, das die Autonomie von Liam Gillicks Vortrag exponiert. Am folgenden Tag der Eröffnungskonferenz „Histories of Productive Failures: from the French Revolution to Manifesta 6" wurde der Raum für Diedrich Diederichsen und sein auf direkte Einbeziehung der Teilnehmer abzielendes Seminar völlig verändert: die Raumelemente funktionierten in einer zufälligeren, zerstreuten, nur vage zu einem Halbkreis tendierenden Geometrie. In Martha Roslers Seminar „Art & Social Life: the Case of Video Art" mit seinem Schwerpunkt auf Projektionsformate wiederum mutierte der Raum in einen Hybrid aus Seminarraum und Galerie. In Tirdad Zolghadrs Seminar verwandelte sich die vertikale, zuvor für Projektionen genutzte Wand in eine horizontale Bühne.

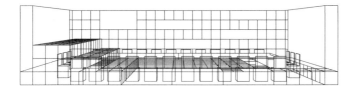

MARKUS MIESSEN Welchen Raum würdest du als deinen Ort der Wissensproduktion bezeichnen? Deine Lehrtätigkeit umfasst Institutionen wie die Architectural Association in London, die Universität Gießen, HfG Karlsruhe und die University of Pennsylvania in Philadelphia. Derzeit, so scheint mir, entwickelst du einen neuen Ansatz, der akademische Forschung und physische Praxis zusammenbringt. Aus dieser Perspektive kann unitednationsplaza als Teil einer Trilogie in deiner Arbeit gesehen werden – zusammen mit dem Projekt für das Institut für Theaterwissenschaften in Gießen und dem *Mohalla Lab*, das du derzeit mit dem Think Tank *Sarai* in Delhi baust.

NIKOLAUS HIRSCH Ja, ich versuche, die Lehrformate, die ich von Institutionen wie der Architectural Association kenne, zu erweitern. Ich bin interessiert an einer Konstellation, in der Lehren zum Bauen wird, und umgekehrt Bauen zur Lehre. Ich versuche Wissensproduktion mit der Produktion eines realen Gebäudes im Maßstab eins zu eins zu koppeln.

MARKUS MIESSEN Wie lässt sich das auf das Projekt übertragen, das du mit dem Komponisten und Theatermacher Heiner Goebbels für das Institut für Theaterwissenschaften an der Universität Gießen planst?

NIKOLAUS HIRSCH Unser Ziel ist eine Situation, in der baulicher Lernkontext und Wissensproduktion in wechselseitiger Abhängigkeit stehen. Architektur wird dabei zum selbstreflexiven Instrument der Institution. Wir haben eine Struktur entwickelt, die verschiedene performative Typologien erlaubt: von der Black Box zum Seminarraum, vom künstlichen zum natürlichen Licht, von hermetischen Räumen zu offenen Konfigurationen, die den Blick nach Außen als Bühnenbild integrieren. Dieser Ansatz wird noch weiter getrieben beim *Mohalla Lab* (hindi für „Nachbarschaft") in Delhi, einem Projekt, das wir derzeit mit dem Think Tank *Sarai*, dem NGO *Ankur – Alternatives in Education* und einer Gruppe von jungen Medienpraktikern entwickeln. Dabei ist der Begriff der Kulturproduktion essentiell. Die Produktion, das Ausstellen und das Archivieren von Bilderbibliotheken, Texten, Weblogs und akustischem Material wird nicht von der Struktur des Gebäudes getrennt. Das Gebäude ist Display.

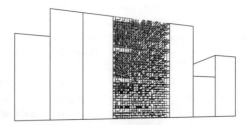

MARKUS MIESSEN Wie schätzt du dabei deine Rolle als Architekt ein?

NIKOLAUS HIRSCH Die Frage ist: bin ich Dienstleister oder Autor? Wohl immer beides: ich werde als Autor eingeladen und biete gleichzeitig einen Service. Die daraus entstehende Architektur hat dann verschiedene Autoren. Mich und andere. Das ist etwas wie Co-Autorenschaft.

MARKUS MIESSEN Stimmst du mit mir überein, dass der Begriff der Kollaboration einerseits eine kritische Dimension zu einem Projekt beisteuert, andererseits aber bedeutet, dass Verantwortung abgegeben wird? Gab es einen Moment bei unitednationsplaza, in dem du eine Art konfliktuelle Partizipation, also einen produktiven Konflikt zwischen widerstreitenden Stimmen, gespürt hast, die dann neue Wissensformen produziert hat?

NIKOLAUS HIRSCH Die Arbeit für unitednationsplaza legt das Gegenteil von Verantwortungs-Outsourcing nahe: eher eine Zunahme von Verantwortung, eine Verbindlichkeit auf persönlicher Ebene, zwischen Autoren. Diese Partizipation schafft keine Welt des faulen Kompromisses oder der versteckten Agenda, ja nicht einmal die so beliebte Konfliktrhetorik. Die gemeinschaftliche Situation ist Teil der Forschung und kein Selbstzweck.

UNITEDNATIONSPLAZA WIRD ORGANISIERT VON ANTON VIDOKLE IN KOLLABORATION MIT LIAM GILLICK, BORIS GROYS, MARTHA ROSLER, NIKOLAUS HIRSCH, WALID RAAD, JALAL TOUFIC, NATASCHA SADR HAGHIGHIAN UND TIRDAD ZOLGHADR. DAS ARCHITEKTONISCHE KONZEPT WURDE VON NIKOLAUS HIRSCH UND MICHEL MÜLLER ENTWICKELT UND REALISIERT.

ERSATZSTADT: REPRÄSENTATIONEN DES URBANEN

Was ist „Stadt" und weshalb sollte diese Frage im Theater verhandelt werden? Vielleicht weil das Theater aufs Engste mit der Entwicklung von Stadt und der Entstehung einer städtischen Öffentlichkeit verknüpft ist. Wie jedoch die Stadt von heute als öffentliche Sache, als *res publica*, verstanden werden kann, ist unklarer denn je. Im Zuge der zunehmenden Mobilisierung von Arbeit und Kapital im globalen Maßstab hat sich eine Krise der Repräsentation breit gemacht: die gute, alte *res publica* der Stadt scheint zu verschwinden, da sie kaum noch als politisch-ästhetischer Gegenstand zu erkennen ist. Sie ist unanschaulich geworden.

Was gerade im europäischen Kontext seit der Entwicklung der athenischen Demokratie einen ablesbaren Zusammenhang zwischen räumlichen Parametern und gesellschaftlichen Organisationsformen aufgewiesen hatte, ist einem ubiquitären und diffusen Zustand des Städtischen gewichen. Stadt ist überall und nirgends. Deregulierung und Globalisierung haben Kartographien umgeschrieben und neue räumliche Bedingungen etabliert, welche die Art und Weise, wie sich Gesellschaft formiert und repräsentiert, radikal geändert hat. In der vielbeschworenen homogenen „europäischen Stadt" sind Parallelgesellschaften, Ersatzmodelle, Gegenkulturen und Schattenökonomien entstanden. Diese stellen das sozialdemokratisch-konsensuale, in unendlichen Kompromissen verhandelte Stadtmodell der repräsentativen Demokratie in Frage, könnten aber auch als potentielle Gegenmodelle gesellschaftlich-räumlicher Organisation fungieren.

Die Stadt, wie sie einmal existierte und in Bezugnahme auf eine imaginierte „europäische Stadt" als Scheinexistenz weiterlebt, gibt es nicht mehr. Das traditionelle Bürgertum als Träger der Stadtgesellschaft löst sich im globalisierten Raum auf. Doch die klassischen Kunst-Orte der städtischen Selbstvergewisserung sind geblieben: das Theater, das Museum. Sie bestehen fort und wirken doch zunehmend anachronistisch. Kein Wunder also, dass zunehmend neue Topoi und Formate in die alten Gehäuse eindringen: das Lager, der verstörend schöne Slum in de Rijke/de Rooijs *Bantar Gebang*, der Flohmarkt, informelle Stadtentwicklungen, Anarchitekturen (im Rückgriff auf einen später von Gordon Matta-Clark übernommenen Begriff von Robin Evans), die Utopia Station, der Ausnahmezustand, die Ersatzstadt. Doch was passiert eigentlich, wenn urbanistische und geopolitische Diskurse ins Theater kommen? Werden Soja, Davis und Lefebvre hysterisch herausgeschrieen wie im Monolog von René Pollesch, der Textfragmente aus seinem Stück *Stadt als Beute* aktualisiert und auf die aktuelle Stadtdebatte in Berlin bezieht?

KRITIK ODER HEUCHELEI
Umgekehrt proportional zum Rückzug kommunaler und staatlicher Strukturen ist eine zunehmende Verbreitung von urbanistischen Diskursen in der Kunst zu verzeichnen. Wie lässt sich das inflationäre Interesse an städtischen Interventionen erklären, mit denen Theater und Museen nach draußen gehen oder das Draußen nach innen holen? Eine These wäre, die Orte der Kunst als Räume der Kritik oder gar des Widerstands zu interpretieren, wie dies auf die strategische Position zutrifft, die durch die Volksbühne im wiedervereinten Berlin eingenommen wurde. Bei dem Versuch, den Motiven und Potentialen des Stadtdiskurses in Theater, bildender Kunst, Musik und Architektur auf die Spur zu kommen, stößt man aber auch auf Widersprüche. Im Vordergrund steht dabei die Ambivalenz zwischen urbaner Intervention und den eingesetzten künstlerischen Mitteln. Mit Brian Holmes' *Reverse Imagineering* lässt sich fragen: Mit Hilfe welcher Strategien kann vermieden werden, dass die Kunst nicht genau das tut, was das zeitgenössische Stadtmarketing von ihr erwartet? Denn so unschuldig ist die Kunst nicht in ihrer urbanistischen Praxis. Ob in Berlin-Mitte, dem New Yorker Chelsea oder dem Londoner Shoreditch: Künstler sind immer auch – ob sie wollen oder nicht – Agenten der Gentrifizierung. Wenn die Avantgarde tatsächlich auch die Speerspitze des *Real*

Estate ist, so würden die kapitalistischen Deregulierungsprozesse im städtischen Raum genau durch jene befördert, die sie am heftigsten kritisieren. Der Grat zwischen Kritik und Heuchelei kann schmal sein.

DAS FESTE HAUS

Analog dem White Cube der bildenden Kunst ist die Black Box der darstellenden Künste ein architektonisches Paradigma, das auf totale Kontrolle angelegt ist: autonomer, neutraler, stabiler Raum mit gleichbleibenden Licht- und Klimazuständen. Anders als die Museen moderner Kunst ist das klassische Stadttheater ein „festes Haus" mit einer weitgehend stabilen Soziostruktur, die meist ein fest gebundenes Schauspielensemble und organisierte Bühnentechniker umfasst.

Das „feste Haus" und die Statik seiner Strukturen rücken damit fast zwangsläufig ins Zentrum zeitgenössischer Kulturdebatten: Ist das „feste Haus" ein Modell, das in Zeiten der ökonomischen und sozialen Deregulierung einen geschützten Raum bietet und damit ein notwendiges Gegenmodell darstellt? Oder müsste das Theater seine starren Strukturen auflösen und die Entwicklung flexibler Modelle vorantreiben, die letztlich auch den veränderten künstlerischen Strategien und Produktionen entsprechen? Die strategische Öffnung des Theaters betrifft den unmittelbaren physischen Raum, aber auch die Akteure selbst. Schon dort, wo das Licht, der Ton und der Raum eines Theaters produziert werden, ist eine Tendenz unübersehbar: Die bislang streng gewerkschaftlich organisierten Techniker lösen sich zunehmend in flexible freiberufliche Produktionseinheiten auf. Auf der künstlerischen Seite stehen der Struktur des festen Ensembles nicht nur befristete Engagements gegenüber, sondern auch zunehmend Strategien, die Laiendarsteller oder Fachleute anderer Disziplinen integrieren und wie *Rimini Protokoll* zum integralen Bestandteil ihrer Werke machen. Die Außenbeziehungen des festen Hauses werden neu verhandelt. Es finden Grenzverschiebungen statt. Ob die

Erweiterung der Grenzen jedoch unter den Prämissen des Theaters oder der Stadt geschieht, bleibt umstritten.

HEISSE LUFT
Wenn von Grenzen die Rede ist, so sind diese auch unmittelbar physisch zu verstehen. Jedes Gebäude, und das Theater insbesondere, schafft konkrete Grenzen. Wand, Boden und Decke agieren dabei als materiale Grenzen zwischen dem internen System „Theater" und seiner Umwelt. Sie sind zuständig für Umweltkontrolle, d.h. sie dämmen, schützen, speichern. Das Material konkretisiert unterschiedliche Wahrnehmungen und verhandelt die Instabilität externer Environments: Gradationen von visueller Protektion und Exposition, akustische Zustände zwischen Lärm und Stille, klimatische Bedingungen zwischen konstanter, jahreszeitunabhängiger Temperierung und saisonaler Temperaturschwankung.

Das Gebäude selbst und seine Umweltbedingungen werden performativ. So wird der physische Gegensatz zwischen interner Stabilität und externer Instabilität vom britischen Künstlerduo Lonetwin in heiße Luft umgesetzt. Der geschützte Binnenraum des Theaters wird explizit mit den Bedingungen der Außenwelt in Beziehungen gesetzt. Dabei wird der Körper des Performers zum Medium dieser Beziehung. Er ist nicht nur Speicher von Narrationen, sondern auch von Temperatur. Er bringt etwas von außen nach innen und wieder zurück. Warm gekleidet und schwer bepackt von ihren Stadtwanderungen drehen Gregg Whelan und Gary Winters ihre Runden auf der Bühne des geschützten, klimatisierten Binnenraums. Sie erzählen Geschichten, Witze und Anekdoten aus der Stadt. Am Ende – heißgelaufen und wieder auf der kalten Straße – produzieren ihre Körper eine riesige Wolke aus Kondensat.

WIE GEFÄHRLICH IST DIE STRASSE?
Ganz im Gegensatz zum festen Haus des Theatergebäudes mit

seinen abgesicherten Formaten, scheint die Straße – so zumindest das landläufige Gerücht – das Potential des Anderen zu bieten: Ort von unvorhersehbaren Konflikten, von Interaktion, Situationismus und *dérive*. Es ist der Raum des Poeschen „Man in the Crowd" und des Benjaminschen Flaneurs. Der Akteur kann anonym werden und sich verlieren in der Masse. Verschluckt von der Stadt wie der legendäre Jazzmusiker und Bassist Henry Grimes, der sein Instrument verpfändete und erst drei Jahrzehnte später wiederauftauchte.

Vom geschützten Haus auf die Straße. Das Gefährliche der Straße existiert heute in dem, was Eyal Weizman als *Urban Conflict as Spatial Practise* bezeichnet. Die Beschreibung von Stadt als homogenem gesellschaftlich-räumlichem Körper weicht Analysen und Theorien, die den Verlust an Kohärenz in den Vordergrund stellen. Es geht um Desintegration, Überlagerung und das Entstehen neuer räumlicher Strukturen. Die urbanen Akteure werden, so Weizman, zu *Builders and Warriors*.

Wo der politische Konflikt weniger offensichtlich als in der Westbank ist und sich stattdessen die Langeweile sozialdemokratischer Wohlfahrtsstaaten breitmacht, muss die Gefahr der Straße inszeniert werden. Sie wird ins System reintegriert und am Ende doch wieder zur Unterhaltung. Wer aus der Langeweile ausbrechen will, kann die Gefahr allenfalls noch bei den illegalen Highspeedfahrten suchen, die Matias Faldbakkens *Getaway* auf den Stadtautobahnen skandinavischer Musterländer dokumentiert.

EINE LIZENZ ZUR ÖKONOMIE

Das einstige situationistische Spektakel ist Teil einer neoliberalen Eventökonomie geworden. Alles wird zum Produkt. Jede kleine Geste, jeder noch so unscheinbare Gegenstand. Die *commodification* schreitet unaufhaltsam voran. Außerhalb dieser Logik zu operieren, wird zunehmend schwierig.

Widerstand, inzwischen selbst ein Paradigma der Kulturindustrie geworden, scheint zwecklos. Relevanter könnte es daher sein, in die Produktwelt einzutauchen und nach der Genealogie eines Produkts zu fragen. Woher kommt es? Wie wird es vermarktet? Wer hat es gemacht? Wem gehört es?

Die dänische Künstlergruppe Superflex, die sich seit Mitte der 90er Jahre mit der Entwicklung von alternativen Produktionsmodellen von Radiostationen, Energieproduktion und Raubkopien auseinandersetzt, entwickelt für die dreitägige *ErsatzStadt* eine spezifische Infrastuktur in der Volksbühne: den *Free Beergarden*. Er fungiert nicht nur als räumliche Intervention, sondern in erster Linie als ökonomisches Modell, das auf der Produktion eines eigenen Biers beruht. *Free Beer* ist ein Open-Source-Projekt und lässt sich als Gegenmodell zur Praxis multinationaler Konzerne lesen. Die Rezeptur ist allgemein zugänglich. Es kann in *Creative Commons*-Lizenz von jedem verwendet sowie modifiziert werden und unter Veröffentlichung des ursprünglichen Produkts und der spezifischen Zusammensetzung kommerziell genutzt werden. Dieser Ansatz gibt sich nicht dem sozialromantischen Glauben an Subversivität oder illegale Ökonomien hin, sondern dreht an den Parametern des ökonomischen Systems. Lizenzen, intellektuelles Eigentum und Autorenschaft werden zu Parametern der künstlerischen Praxis.

STADTMUSIK ODER LAUTMALEREI
Wenn Diedrich Diederichsen, Björn Gottstein, Christian von Borries und Ekkehard Ehlers in ihrem *ErsatzStadt*-Workshop *Der letzte Metro* fragen, wie Beton zum Gitarrenriff werde oder was das Quietschen der Straßenbahn in den hohen Streichern eines Orchesters verloren habe, so geht es um mehr als Übersetzungsprobleme. Es geht um die Frage, inwieweit Musik selbst einen aktiven Part in der Herstellung von Stadt übernimmt, ja letzendlich, ob Musik das Urbane produziert oder nur reflektiert.

Wie Christoph Gurk zu Diedrich Diederichsens Vortrag *Keine Sorge wegen der Regierung* schreibt, steht die Stadt in der populären Musik bis 1950 zwar als Chiffre für Verheißung, Abenteuer und Jammertal, wird dabei jedoch weitgehend passiv als Natur beschrieben. „Erst in der Popmusik tauchen Formeln zu der Frage auf, wie man sich die Stadt aneignen könnte – vom Straßenkampf bis zum *Dancing in the Streets*. Hier brennt die Stadt häufiger als alles andere: *London's Burning, Motor City is Burning* …" Im Laufe der Zeit hat es jedoch den Anschein, als gehe es in der Popmusik seit den achtziger Jahren eher um Selbstreflexion. Die Protagonisten der reflexiv gewordenen Popmusik scheinen die Städte eher lesen zu wollen, als sie zu besetzen oder zu besitzen. Die Zeit des Kampfs um die Stadt scheint erst einmal vorbei zu sein.

STADT ALS ERSATZ
Zu fragen ist, ob es bei *ErsatzStadt* um eine theatrale Strategie geht, die das politische Vakuum nutzt und in der Schnittmenge zwischen politischen und künstlerischen Diskursen selbst zum urbanen Ersatz-Akteur werden will oder ob es sich um eine Legitimationsstrategie, vielleicht gar um einen Kontextualisierungstrick, handelt.

Das Gefährliche der Straße ist inzwischen Unterhaltung geworden. Das situationistische Spektakel mit seinen einstmals politischen Implikationen ist als Eventkultur zu einem Segment neoliberaler Raumstrategien geworden. Die Konflikte und Straßenschlachten, die noch in den frühen 80er Jahren in dem Hörstück *Q-Damm 12.4.81* von Heiner Goebbels bearbeitet wurden, sind zu *Surrogate Cities*, so das 1998 uraufgeführte Stück von Goebbels, geworden. Was meint nun *ErsatzStadt*? Einen Ersatz als politischen Gegenort oder Ersatz als manipuliertes Surrogat?

Das was man „Stadt" nannte, hat sich aufgelöst in unzählige Verwaltungsebenen und hoheitliche Vorgänge. Ein permanenter Maßstabssprung zwischen Mikro und Makro, vom Bürgerbüro bis zum supranationalen Gebilde. Unanschaulich und langweilig. Wo ist hier das Politische? Eine exzessive Veranschaulichung von Stadtpolitik zeigt Anri Sala in seiner Videoarbeit *Dammi i Colori*, in dem er ein urbanistisches Projekt seiner Heimatstadt Tirana dokumentiert. Ein Farbkonzept im urbanen Maßstab macht die Wiederaneignung der Stadt zum Thema. Die Arbeit entstand während einer Autofahrt mit dem Initiator des Projekts, dem ehemaligen Künstler und jetzigen Bürgermeister Edi Rama, und hinterfragt die aktive Rolle von Künstlern und Politikern im zeitgenössischen Urbanismus. Ein seltener Fall, der einen alten Traum (oder Alptraum?) verwirklicht: der Künstler und Politiker in Personalunion.

In Berlin funktioniert dies arbeitsteiliger. Doch auch hier wird die Problematik einer Kulturpolitik deutlich, die angesichts schwindender Kohäsionskräfte des Staates zur Kompensation zu werden droht und die „Stadt" mitsamt ihrer Bauwerke als Ersatz in der Krise der Repräsentation benutzt. Zur Diskussion steht damit ein Begriff des Urbanen, der in einer immer unübersichtlicher werdenden Situation noch einen letzten Rest von Anschaulichkeit verspricht und eine mimetische Sehnsucht nach Konkretisierung von Politik und Gesellschaft bedient.

Gemeint ist dabei nicht nur die traditionelle apologetische Repräsentationspolitik eines im Verschwinden begriffenen Bürgertums, sondern eine Repräsentationskritik, die noch in der Kritik weiterhin in Kategorien des Werks denkt und damit die Einheit von Werk und Gemeinschaft aufrechterhält. Die Stadt wird, den Theorien von Henri Lefebvre folgend, zum kollektiven, lebendigen Kunstwerk. Diese Interpretation der Stadt und ihrer Bewohner schafft dem Künstler eine willkommene Legitimation. Doch nach einem Jahrzehnt intensiver Stadtdebatte melden sich zunehmend Zweifel: Gibt es hier ein stillschweigendes Einverständnis zwischen Politikern und Künstlern? Handelt es sich um eine gegenseitige Instrumentalisierung, in der urbane Konflikte zum Vorwand verkommen? Ein Repräsentations- und Übersetzungsproblem: die Stadt nicht als Werk denken.

DER TEXT BASIERT AUF NIKOLAUS HIRSCHS EINFÜHRUNGSVORTRAG ZU *ERSATZSTADT: REPRÄSENTATIONEN DES URBANEN* AN DER VOLKSBÜHNE AM ROSA-LUXEMBURG-PLATZ IN BERLIN (20. – 22. MAI 2005). KURATOR DES PROJEKTS WAR NIKOLAUS HIRSCH, UNTERSTÜTZT VON EINEM BERATERTEAM BESTEHEND AUS DIEDRICH DIEDERICHSEN, EKKEHARD EHLERS UND NICOLAUS SCHAFHAUSEN SOWIE CHRISTOPH GURK (DRAMATURGIE) UND CELINA NICOLAY (PRODUKTIONSLEITUNG). DIE *ERSATZSTADT* UMFASSTE VORTRÄGE, PERFORMANCES, DISKUSSIONEN, INSTALLATIONEN, WORKSHOPS, KONZERTE UND FILMVORFÜHRUNGEN VON FATMA AKINÇI, MARYANNE AMACHER, JAKOB BOESKOV, CHRISTIAN VON BORRIES, ALICE CREISCHER, FRIEDRICH DIECKMANN, DIEDRICH DIEDERICHSEN, DE RIJKE/DE ROOIJ, EKKEHARD EHLERS, HEINZ EMIGHOLZ, MATIAS FALDBAKKEN, HARUN FAROCKI, GANG GANG DANCE, GOB SQUAD, HEINER GOEBBELS, HENRY GRIMES, BJÖRN GOTTSTEIN, CARL HEGEMANN, BRIAN HOLMES, HANS-THIES LEHMANN, LONE TWIN, BART LOOTSMA, OLAF METZEL, ASTRID MEYERFELDT, MARKUS MÜLLER, BERT NEUMANN, PHILIPP OSWALT, RENÉ POLLESCH, JULIANE REBENTISCH, RECHENZENTRUM, ANRI SALA, SABINE SANIO, WERNER SEWING, ANDREAS SIECKMANN, SUPERFLEX, ALBRECHT WELLMER, EYAL WEIZMAN.

DER ARCHITEKT UND SEINE GRENZEN
DAVID ADJAYE IM GESPRÄCH MIT NIKOLAUS HIRSCH

DAVID ADJAYE Als ich dein Erstlingswerk besichtigte, war ich beeindruckt vom Maßstab und dem Anspruch eines architektonischen Anfangs. Das 1996 realisierte Projekt für die Jüdische Gedenkstätte in Frankfurt eröffnet einen umfassenden Diskurs über die Natur des Berufs: die Rolle des Architekten und ganz allgemein, die gesellschaftliche Relevanz von Architektur.

NIKOLAUS HIRSCH Im Gegensatz zur traditionellen Annahme, dass ein Architekt erst einmal im kleinen Maßstab (z.B. mit einem Haus) „üben" sollte, bevor er sich an Größeres heranwagen darf, war unser erstes Projekt ein öffentliches Monument im großen urbanen Maßstab. Dabei sind beide Aspekte ungewöhnlich: sowohl der städtebauliche Maßstab, als auch der Begriff des Monuments als solcher. Das Projekt war extrem instruktiv in Bezug auf die Rolle des Architekten und seiner Grenzen in der zeitgenössischen Gesellschaft. Uns wurde die Möglichkeit gegeben, in einem *expanded field* zu arbeiten – aber mit den Grenzen, die diese Disziplin so spezifisch machen. Wir mussten dabei zwei Aspekte verbinden: ein komplexes Feld von miteinander verstrickten Disziplinen wie Kunst, Design, Politik und Geschichtswissenschaft, die letztendlich die Frage nach der kulturellen Relevanz von Architektur aufwarfen; andererseits die architektonische Tradition der Planung, d.h. eine Kultur der Kontrolle, die einen physischen Gegenstand zeichnet und für die Zukunft prädeterminiert. Ich denke, dass beide Aspekte bestimmend in unserer Arbeit sind: auf der einen Seite die Freiheit eines größeren gesellschaftlichen Kontexts, auf der anderen Seite die penible Präzision des Ingenieurs. Das Resultat in Frankfurt verbindet beide Pole: kein autonomes, isoliertes Objekt, sondern eine dreihundert Meter lange Wand, die auf einem kleinmaßstäblichen Element basiert und dennoch ein Stück Urbanismus herstellt.

DAVID ADJAYE Was mich fasziniert, ist die repräsentative Qualität des Projekts. Seine „Monumentalität" operiert im Rahmen von zeitgenössischer Kunst und Architektur, zugleich aber innerhalb einer Idee der kritischen Konstruktion von Geschichte. Wie hast du als Architekt diese Bedingungen miteinander vereinbart?

NIKOLAUS HIRSCH Ich sehe diese Bedingungen nicht separat. Sie sind beide Teil desselben Problems: wie definiere ich meine Rolle an einem bestimmten Ort? Ich bin zwar vorsichtig gegenüber dem allzu Narrativen, doch interessiert an dem Potential, das im Material der kleinen und großen Geschichten liegt. Es bietet Widersprüche und Probleme. Tatsächlich ging es in Frankfurt um die Fähigkeit, ein Problem zu finden. Wir haben das Wettbewerbsprogramm in Frage gestellt und das Grundstück erweitert bzw. verlassen, haben es mit dem alten Friedhof verknüpft und so den physischen Widerstand geschaffen, der nötig war für solch ein Projekt.

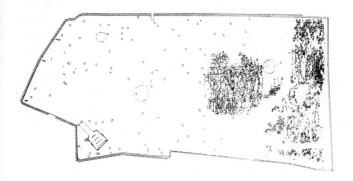

DAVID ADJAYE Traditionell wird vom Architekten erwartet, dass er eine Lösung zu einem Problem findet, das der Bauherr gestellt hat. Die Idee eines Architekten, der das Problem findet, scheint wie eine Umkehrung dieser Rolle. Ein neues Paradigma: nicht nur der Bauherr definiert, was notwendig ist, sondern auch der Architekt kann das latente Potential des Programms formulieren. Ich mag die Art wie du das sagst. Es hat eine gewisse Poesie. Das Problem wird von dir als Architekt formuliert, und dann wird die Lösung gewissermaßen, was sie werden muss. Das hat eine bestechende Eleganz, was die Idee der Autorschaft betrifft. Du scheinst ein neues Modell des Architekten als Autor zu suchen.

NIKOLAUS HIRSCH Zumindest sehe ich die Frage der Autorschaft als eines der zentralen Probleme von Architektur.

DAVID ADJAYE Durch deine Arbeiten zieht sich eine kohärente Idee des Infragestellens von Wahrnehmung und Bedeutung. Wie siehst du die Rolle des Materials in diesem Prozess? Wenn man deine Gebäude betrachtet, beispielsweise die Synagoge in Dresden, unterstreicht die Materialstrategie ganz wesentlich die Bedeutung.

NIKOLAUS HIRSCH Die Arbeit beginnt für uns mit einer Suche nach dem Material. Der Materialzustand von Dresden ist durch zwei traumatische Zerstörungen geprägt: jene von Gottfried Sempers Synagoge in der Kristallnacht 1938 durch die Deutschen, und jene der kompletten Altstadt durch alliierte Bomber 1945. Die Zerstörungen sind zwar historisch miteinander verknüpft, doch die architektonischen Konsequenzen könnten nicht unterschiedlicher ausfallen. Zum einen rekonstruiert Dresden seine historischen Monumente und stellt damit eine problematische Behauptung von architektonischer Stabilität her. Im anderen Fall, der Synagoge, versuchen wir den Konflikt zwischen Stabilität und Fragilität zum Thema zu machen, die Spannung zwischen dem Dauerhaften und dem Provisorischen, oder – auf die historischen Typologien bezogen – zwischen dem Tempel und dem Zelt. Dieser Konflikt wurde zum Ausgangspunkt für unsere Materialstrategie. Die Implikationen von Stabilität und Fragilität untersuchend, ist das Material der Synagoge durch einen Dualismus geprägt: eine monolithische äußere Struktur von vorgefertigten Betonwerksteinen und eine innere Struktur aus einem weichen Messingtextil.

DAVID ADJAYE Wie habt ihr die Materialstrategie in eine volumetrische Logik übersetzt?

NIKOLAUS HIRSCH Die Frage war: Wie können wir ein spezifisches Gebäude bauen, und nicht nur eine generische Wiederholung von existierenden Typologien und Mustern? Im Gegensatz zum Wettbewerbsprogramm haben wir zwei unterschiedliche, voneinander getrennte Volumina entworfen: einen eher introvertierten religiösen Raum und einen Baukörper, der alle sozialen Funktionen aufnimmt. Auf der Grundlage des orthogonalen Grundstücks verdreht sich das Volumen der Synagoge um wenige Grad nach Osten. Was uns an dieser Rotation von Mauerwerkslagen interessiert hat, war eine komplexe, zweifach gekrümmte Geometrie, die auf einem einfachen Prinzip beruht: ein Stein und eine Schalung für das ganze Gebäude. Interessant ist dabei, dass die Wahrnehmung des gebauten Volumens von einer Perspektive zur anderen dramatisch wechselt. Am Ende geht der Prozess der Wahrnehmung weit über die operative Planungslogik hinaus.

DAVID ADJAYE Traditionell denkt man Materialität im Sinne von elementaren Baumaterialien. Beeindruckend bei dem Dresdener Projekt ist, dass man es zunächst als Steingebäude wahrnimmt, es sich tatsächlich aber um ein Betongebäude handelt. Es gibt hier einen Bedeutungswechsel, der nicht romantisch ist, sondern der Realität Substanz gibt.

NIKOLAUS HIRSCH Der Materialdiskurs, den du ansprichst, hat verschiedene Aspekte: Tragwerk, Wahrnehmung und Urbanismus. Das Projekt befindet sich in einer städtebaulichen Position zwischen dem sandstein-süchtigen historischen Zentrum der Stadt und den Plattenbauten der sozialistischen Moderne. So gesehen, ist die Materialstrategie auch eine kritische Auseinandersetzung mit der Frage: Was ist dieser Ort? Wir haben zwei gleichermaßen problematische

Tendenzen verhandelt: den kontextuellen oder regionalistischen Ansatz des Sandsteins und die industrielle, globalisierte Logik des Betonfertigteils. Das Resultat dieser Materialverhandlung ist ein spezifisch für dieses Projekt entwickelter künstlicher Stein, eine Fusion von vorfabriziertem Beton und natürlichen lokalen Zuschlagstoffen.

DAVID ADJAYE Die Intensität der Materialforschung in diesem und anderen Projekten ist erstaunlich. Die Entwicklung des künstlichen Steins und des Messingtextils sind da nur Beispiele in deiner Arbeit. Wie würdest du die Rolle des Materials in deiner Praxis beschreiben?

NIKOLAUS HIRSCH Unser Arbeitsprozess ist nicht linear, sondern produziert ständig iterative Rückkopplungen zwischen kleinem und großem Maßstab. Im Gegensatz zur üblichen Linearität von Entwurfsphasen, die sich nur Schritt für Schritt dem Detail nähern, beginnen wir von Anfang an mit dem Maßstab 1:1. Als tektonisches Detail wird das Material zum konzeptuellen Träger der Architektur.

DAVID ADJAYE Ein anderes Phänomen zeigt sich in der Dresdner Synagoge und schafft eine Verknüpfung mit dem Projekt für das Dokumentationshaus Hinzert. Ich sehe hier eine Verbindung zwischen einer Materialstrategie und einer Umwelt-Agenda, die sich in deiner Arbeit zu entwickeln beginnt.

NIKOLAUS HIRSCH In unseren Bauten versuchen wir einen erweiterten Umweltbegriff zu untersuchen, der unterschiedliche perzeptive Kriterien umfasst: visuelle, akustische, klimatische. Wir entwickeln spezifische Umweltsysteme für jedes Projekt. Mit anderen Worten: wir versuchen die Besonderheiten und Widersprüche des Programms als konzeptuellen Vorteil zu nutzen. Für die Synagoge in Dresden entwickelten wir ein System, das sich die Trägheit des monolithischen Gebäudes zu Nutze machte. In unserem neuen Projekt, dem Dokumentationshaus Hinzert, ist die Situation völlig anders, weil das Museum in einer abgelegenen Landschaft liegt, vier Kilometer entfernt vom nächsten Dorf und dessen technischer Infrastruktur. Aus diesem Grund operieren wir bei diesem Projekt mit Geothermie und anderen autonomen Umwelttechniken.

DAVID ADJAYE Kannst du das Gebäude aus der perspektivischen Verschiebung deines Arbeitsgebiets von der Stadt zur Landschaft beschreiben? In Frankfurt und in Dresden hast du unter urbanen Bedingungen gearbeitet, nun agierst du plötzlich in einer extremen Landschaft.

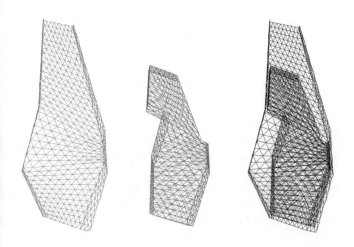

NIKOLAUS HIRSCH Im Gegensatz zu den präzisen räumlichen Limitierungen in urbanen Kontexten hat das Dokumentationshaus keine besondere spezifische Begrenzung in der Landschaft. Wir konnten uns ausdehnen, und zwar im wörtlichen Sinn. Wir haben nicht von Grundstücksgrenzen nach innen entworfen, sondern von Innen nach Außen. Wir haben das ständig veränderte Raumprogramm kontinuierlich angepasst, indem wir die Geometrie der Außenhülle immer weiter manipulierten und nach außen in die Landschaft gedrückt haben. Um den zentralen Ausstellungsraum herum haben wir eine Reihe von *Pockets* wie kleine Bibliotheken, Archive, Research Studios und dreidimensionale Exponate angelagert, die immer wieder die Konturen der äußeren Hülle verändern und eine komplexe Geometrie aus unregelmäßigen dreieckigen Flächen bilden.

DAVID ADJAYE Eine andere Seite deiner Arbeit sind die kollaborativen Arbeiten mit Künstlern aus so unterschiedlichen Bereichen wie Theater, Musik, Bildende Kunst und Ballett. Einige dieser Arbeiten sind temporäre Projekte; Bauten, die für einen Moment „stattfinden" und wieder verschwinden. Wie lässt sich die Rolle dieser Projekte als Teil einer meist sehr langsamen Architekturpraxis verstehen?

NIKOLAUS HIRSCH Du hast Recht. Das Verhältnis zwischen Planung und zeitlichen Rhythmen und Maßstäben hat eine enorme, häufig unterschätzte Auswirkung auf die architektonische Praxis. Um ehrlich zu sein: ich brauche diese unterschiedlichen Rhythmen in meiner Arbeit. Bauten wie die Dresdner Synagoge setzen sich mit Kriterien der Dauer auseinander, während die temporären Projekte nach einer kurzen, aber intensiven Nutzung wieder verschwinden. Wichtig ist, dass die Idee der Zeit ein wesentlicher Parameter des Planungsprozesses *und* des gebauten Resultats ist.

DAVID ADJAYE Wie manifestiert sich die Idee der Zeit in der kollaborativen Arbeit? Wie verhandelst du Zeit?

NIKOLAUS HIRSCH Ich begegne immer wieder der klischeehaften Annahme, dass Kollaborationen zur Auflösung der Disziplinen führen. Meine romantische Seite unterstützt diese Idee, doch andererseits sind die produktivsten Resultate nicht das Ergebnis von weichen Grenzen, sondern von Differenz oder sogar Konflikt zwischen den

Disziplinen. Eine kritische Differenz bleibt der Rhythmus der Produktion. In der Zusammenarbeit mit William Forsythe für das Bockenheimer Depot Theater kollidierten zwei fundamental unterschiedliche Rhythmen: die Tendenz des Architekten, einen zukünftigen Endstatus über einen langen Zeitraum zu fixieren und Forsythes Tanzstrategie, die auf Improvisation in Realzeit basiert.

DAVID ADJAYE Zurück zur Rolle des Physischen: all diese temporären Projekte haben eine starke Materialstrategie. Wie verbindest du diesen Fokus auf das Material mit der Idee der Grenze als einem deiner räumlichen Schlüsselbegriffe?

NIKOLAUS HIRSCH Ich denke, wir brauchen das physische Material, um eine Art Widerstand herzustellen, der geteilt und verhandelt werden kann. Eine starke Materialstrategie kann zur gemeinsamen Basis einer Zusammenarbeit werden, vergleichbar mit unserer Schaumstruktur für *Frequenzen-Hz* in der Schirn Kunsthalle oder dem Musikpavillon im Park des Museu Serralves in Porto. Der Begriff der Grenze kann in zweierlei Art operieren. Einerseits beschreibt er die zunehmend komplexe Zusammenarbeit mit Experten aus anderen Disziplinen. Andererseits benutze ich den Begriff der Grenze im wörtlichen Sinn: als Wand, Decke und Boden. Als materiales Element, das einen Übergang zwischen einem architektonischen System und seiner Umwelt herstellt. Als eine tektonische Grenze, die Öffnung und Schließung verhandelt.

DAVID ADJAYES INTERVIEW MIT NIKOLAUS HIRSCH FAND IN DER BERLINER VOLKSBÜHNE AM
ROSA-LUXEMBURG-PLATZ STATT UND WURDE ERSTMALS IN *BUILDING DESIGN* (AUSGABE VOM
15. JULI 2005) VERÖFFENTLICHT.

GEOPOLITISCHE TEKTONIK
TIFLIS ODER WIE MAN EINEN KONTEXT FÜR SEINE ARCHITEKTUR FINDET

Auf der Suche nach dem Lokalen. Einem Kontext für meine Arbeit. Oder ist es ein Prä-Text, ein Vorwand? Die räumlichen Fakten sind eindeutig: Entwurf eines 35 000-Quadratmeter-Gebäudes in Tiflis, Integration eines komplexen Raumprogramms mit Büros, Geschäften, Konferenzbereich und Apartments, Fertigstellung bis 2008. Weniger eindeutig ist der politische Raum. Georgien ist ein Land, das irgendwo dazwischen liegt: nicht mehr im Kommunismus und schon fast angekommen im westlichen Parlamentarismus, ein Pipelineland zwischen Öl fördernden und kaufenden Staaten, zwischen den imperialen Ambitionen der Vereinigten Staaten und Russland. Doch wirkt sich Geopolitik auf Architektur aus? Sicherlich tut sie es im großen territorialen Maßstab. Aber was geschieht im Maßstab eines einzelnen Gebäudes? Kann aus der territorialen Logik heraus eine Materialstrategie entwickelt werden? Wie wird das Material von A nach B gebracht, wie wird es zusammengefügt? Können wir eine geopolitische Tektonik erfinden?

Die Disziplin „Architektur" bietet uns diverse Instrumente der Kontextualisierung (oder sind es Techniken der List?), um das Lokale zu finden und anzueignen: Typologien, Gebäudehöhen, Dachformen und Materialstrategien mit lokalen Referenzen. Nach all den ignoranten Zerstörungen der Moderne bevorzugen wir verständlicherweise eine Architektur des Respekts. Doch ist das möglich: höfliche Architektur? Ein Tag mit unserem georgischen Bauherrn beweist, dass Kontextualisierung zwar gut gemeint sein mag, doch letztlich im besten Fall romantisch, im schlimmsten Fall bevormundend ist. Neugierig auf dieses neue Land auf meiner architektonischen Landkarte stellte ich Fragen. Viele Fragen – nennen wir es „research". Doch nach einem langen Verhör über lokale Materialien, Muster, Steine, Hölzer und Teppiche realisierte mein Bauherr, wonach ich suchte, und sagte: „Bevormunde uns nicht. Du musst uns nicht die georgische Kultur erklären – du bist hier, weil wir eine international kompatible Architektur wollen". Hier sind sie: die Grenzen der Kontextualisierung. Und ich befinde mich in der Sackgasse einer Kultur des guten Willens.

Zurückgeworfen auf meinen Status als „internationaler Architekt" muss ich nach etwas suchen, das jenseits von Alt-Tiflis und seiner hölzernen Balkone liegt. Die Frage ist: kann die immer weiter expandierende Welt der Konstruktion reterritorialisiert werden? Was ist denn überhaupt lokal? Fürs erste bin ich versucht zu antworten: vor allem Regeln und Standards. Jenseits aller pittoresken Diskurse über den Kontext, ist es das Gesetz, das definiert, was spezifisch lokal ist. Ein Schriftstück, dessen Paragraphen nicht Stile, sondern Daten festlegen: maximale Dichte, Volumen, Höhe und minimale Isolierung, Brandschutz und Sicherheitsauflagen. In einer Welt, in der sich Standards immer weiter angleichen, sind es die kleinen Unterschiede in einem langweiligen Text, die das Lokale ausmachen. So haben unspektakuläre, kleine Paragrafen zur natürlichen Belichtung von Arbeitsplätzen spektakuläre Auswirkungen auf die Form eines Gebäudes. Die Distanz von einem Fenster zu einem Arbeitsplatz wird zu einem bestimmenden Parameter lokaler Differenz. Während die von natürlicher Belichtung besessenen deutschen Baugesetzbücher einen maximalen Abstand von 4,50 Meter erlauben (und deshalb landauf, landab eine endlose Wiederholung von schmalen Hochhäusern produzieren), eröffnen die georgischen Auflagen spezifisch neue Möglichkeiten: tiefe Gebäude. Folglich testet unser Gebäude die Grenzen dessen, was das Gesetz erlaubt: eine Tiefe von 48 Metern auf Grundlage eines porösen Systems von tiefen Lichtlöchern und modulierten Fassadenelementen. Die Frage lautet: ist dies eine neue Version der *site specificity*?

Die alte Frage nach dem Ortsspezifischen könnte zu einer Frage der Logistik werden: wie kommt das Material zum Grundstück und wo kommt es her? Diese banale Frage wird zu einer architektonischen

Frage, zu einer Entwurfsentscheidung. Eine Territorialisierung von Material und Tektonik entwickelt sich. Details, Verbindungen, Oberflächen – jedes Teil des Gebäudes wird gegen die Ungewissheiten eines instabilen, durch das russische Embargo noch prekärer gewordenen geopolitischen Kontext geprüft und entsprechend einer geo-ökonomischen Logik evaluiert. Plötzlich kann das Gebäude als Genealogie der Konstruktion verstanden werden. Es kann als eine geopolitische und geo-ökonomische Materialisierung beschrieben werden, die ein bislang unbekanntes Potential für architektonische Manipulation bietet. Wir können etwas zeichnen, das wir so nicht kannten: ein Diagramm des Gebäudes als Weltatlas; eine Zeichnung, welche die Herkunft jedes Gebäudeelements darstellt. Die Welt im Gebäude.

Mit den neuen Werkzeugen der geopolitischen Tektonik zu spielen, heißt dann: was im Untergrund ist, der Dreck der Erdarbeiten und die grobe Substruktur aus Beton, wird zu einer lokalen Sache, wogegen die Materialentscheidung für die *superstructure* einer Strategie des forcierten Imports folgt. Beunruhigt durch die Ungenauigkeiten des lokalen Betons, wählen wir die auf Millimeter präzise und auf Minuten pünktliche Stahlvariante, die – auf Grund der völligen Abwesenheit von georgischem Stahl – zwangsläufig von weiter westlich (Türkei) importiert werden muss. Mit der Fassade, dem sensibelsten und eigens entwickelten Gebäudeteil, weitet sich das geo-materiale System noch weiter in den Westen aus. Das Fassadenmuster im Maßstab 1:1 steht weit entfernt in einem kleinen oberschwäbischen Dorf und definiert die Qualität der Ausführung. In ihrer perversen Logik scheint die Kohärenz der Arbeit von dem Grad der Autonomie vom Lokalen abzuhängen. Mit anderen Worten: die Kohärenz meiner Arbeit steigt mit der Entfernung vom Lokalen. Willkommen in der unheimlichen Welt der Planung. Einer Welt, in der Kontrolle alles ist und der Verlust von Kontrolle zum letzten Tabu der Architektur wird.

WIE DIE TÜRME STEHEN

„Im Bauwerk soll sich der Stolz, der Sieg über die Schwere, der Wille zur Macht versichtbaren: Architektur ist eine Art Macht-Beredsamkeit in Formen, bald überredend, selbst schmeichelnd, bald bloss befehlend. Das höchste Gefühl von Macht und Sicherheit kommt in dem zum Ausdruck, was grossen Stil hat. Die macht, die keinen Beweis mehr nöthig hat; die es verschmäht, zu gefallen; die schwer antwortet; die keinen Zeugen um sich fühlt; die ohne Bewusstsein davon lebt, dass es Widerspruch gegen sie giebt; die in sich ruht, fatalistisch, ein Gesetz unter Gesetzen."[01]

Es scheint, als seien die Zeiten des „autistischen" Bauwerks vorbei. Die „Zeugen", von denen Nietzsche spricht, haben sich zurückgemeldet und vor allem gegen jene Gebäude Einspruch erhoben, die sich weiter als andere hervorwagten. So muss insbesondere das Hochhaus Rücksichten nehmen. Es soll „stadtverträglich" und „umweltfreundlich" sein.

Der Paradigmenwechsel zum Kontextualismus rührt buchstäblich an der Basis des Hochhausbaus. Denn es wird weniger das Spezifische des Hochhauses – seine Höhe – in Frage gestellt als vielmehr sein unmittelbares „Stehen" auf dem Boden der Stadt. Diese Boden-Ständigkeit meint jenen Ort, wo globale Phänomene wie die weltweite Konzentration von Dienstleistungen auf lokale Traditionen stossen, wo ein auf Fernwirkung und Skylinebildung angelegtes Objekt auf die Perspektive der Straße trifft. Vor diesem Hintergrund erscheint die Basis als wunder Punkt des Hochhauses.

SCHLIESSUNG
Im Frankfurt der sechziger und siebziger Jahre war das auf sich selbst bezogene „autistische" Hochhaus die Regel. Unter den

---

[01] FRIEDRICH NIETZSCHE, „GÖTTERDÄMMERUNG", IN FRIEDRICH NIETZSCHE, *KRITISCHE STUDIENAUSGABE*, MÜNCHEN/BERLIN 1988, S. 118–119.

Bauten, die der Stadt den – damals – wenig schmeichelhaften Namen „Mainhattan" einbrachten, stellt das Hochhaus der Dresdner Bank, erbaut von ABB Architekten in den Jahren 1971 bis 1980, ein aufschlussreiches Beispiel dar. Neben der Logik des Entwurfs und seiner Umsetzung betrifft dies vor allem die Dramaturgie des Ortes. Die zwischen außen liegenden Kernen gegeneinander versetzten Baukörper erheben sich inmitten des gründerzeitlichen Bahnhofsviertels. Vermittlung zum Kontext im Sinne heutiger „Stadtverträglichkeit" sucht man hier vergeblich. Wer sich vom Bahnhof aus dem Hochhaus nähert, bemerkt schon von weitem an der Ecke des Grundstücks einen hell reflektierenden Versorgungskern, der sich hart gegen die kleinmaßstäbliche, steinerne Blockstruktur absetzt. Unvermittelt, ohne überflüssige Differenzierung führen geschosshohe Aluminiumpaneele vom Boden bis in eine Höhe von 166 Metern.

Die Wahl der flächig gefügten Materialien Aluminium und Glas für die Kerne wie auch für die Bürogeschosse mit ihren vorfabrizierten Fassadenelementen widerspricht jeder Art von Tiefe. Weder ist die Fassade durch Vor- und Rücksprünge gegliedert, noch kann ein Alterungsprozess eine zusätzliche Bedeutung, gleichsam als semantischen Mehrwert, hinzufügen. So strahlt das Gebäude noch heute jenes Verhältnis zwischen Material und Zeit aus, das Robert Smithson, einer der Protagonisten der Minimal Art, in seinem Aufsatz „Entropy and the New Monuments" als charakteristisch für die Kunst und Architektur der sechziger Jahre bezeichnet: „Anstatt aus natürlichen Materialien wie Marmor, Granit oder anderen Arten von Gestein sind die neuen Skulpturen und Monumente aus künstlichen Materialien gefertigt: aus Kunststoff, Chrom und elektrischem Licht. Sie sind nicht für die Zeit, sondern eher gegen die Zeit gebaut."[02]

[02] ROBERT SMITHSON, „ENTROPY AND THE NEW MONUMENTS", IN: *ARTFORUM* (JUNI 1966).

Die Schnittstelle zwischen der „selbstbezogenen Zeit" des Dresdner-Bank-Hochhauses und der „prozesshaften Zeit" der Umgebung bildet der Eingangsbereich. Allein hier wird die Geschlossenheit des aluminiumbekleideten Baukörpers aufgebrochen. Weit hinter die Bürogeschosse zurückspringend, zieht sich das Gebäude auf seine Erschließungsfunktion zurück und beansprucht nur noch ein Drittel der Grundstücksfläche. Rund 2000 Beschäftigte nähern sich jeden Morgen dem in braungetöntem Glas gefassten Eingangsbereich und passieren einzeln – jeweils registriert von einer Überwachungskamera – eine der fünf Drehtüren. Nachdem die erste Außen-Innen-Barriere überwunden ist, durchqueren sie mit wenigen Schritten das Foyer und kommen vor den Aufzügen zur Sicherheitsschleuse, wo die persönlichen Codekarten gelesen werden. Die Drehkreuze markieren den inneren Bereich, der nicht einmal zur Mittagspause verlassen werden muss, da sich im zweiten Obergeschoß eine Großkantine befindet. Angemeldeten Besuchern werden Magnetkarten am Empfang ausgehändigt. Mit ihrem runden Glasschutz nimmt die Theke das Motiv der allgegenwärtigen abgerundeten Ecken auf, das auch im Luftraum des Foyers mit auskragenden, braun eloxierten Raumkapseln wiederkehrt. Durch eine weitere Sicherheitsstufe geschützt, befindet sich hier die Leitzentrale, das Gehirn des Gebäudes.

Bis ins Detail zeigt sich das Hochhaus der Dresdner Bank als geschlossenes System, das allein eigenen Gesetzen gehorcht. In Anlehnung an Niklas Luhmanns Theorie selbstbezüglicher Systeme ließe sich sagen: Die Abkopplung von der städtischen Umwelt wird ermöglicht durch funktionale und formale Schließung und stellt die Bedingung des Funktionierens dar. So ist es auch nur konsequent, wenn nach Büroschluss das Gebäude tatsächlich schließt. Zwischen den frei stehenden, aluminiumverkleideten Stützen werden Rollgitter herabgefahren. Der Eingangsbereich verschwindet. Die Vorfläche der Bank – tagsüber der transitorische Raum der Geldhändler – gehört nachts dem Rotlichtmilieu des Bahnhofsviertels.

SPIEGEL

Als Heinrich Klotz 1984 im neu eröffneten Frankfurter Architekturmuseum die „Revision der Moderne" verkündete, wurde auf der anderen Mainseite das Hochhaus der Deutschen Bank fertiggestellt. Bis in die neunziger Jahre hinein beherrschten die 155 Meter hohen, spiegelverglasten Doppeltürme das Panorama der Stadt, doch stand die bauliche Präsenz in einem eigentümlichen Kontrast zur Aufmerksamkeit einer Architekturdiskussion, die sich zu jener Zeit vornehmlich mit Museen und „Stadthäusern" auseinandersetzte. Ein Grund für die Missachtung könnte darin zu finden sein, dass sich das Gebäude bewusst der Lesbarkeit entzieht. Die polygonalen Türme sind so zueinander gestellt, dass sie sich keiner eindeutigen Form zuordnen lassen. Zudem verleiht die spiegelverglaste Hülle dem massiven, im Tube-in-Tube-System errichteten Stahlbetongebäude ein – je nach Wetter – ständig wechselndes Aussehen. Der Blick, der nach Gliederungen und Übergängen sucht, findet keinen Halt, ja, im Gegenteil: das Spiegelglas wirft ihn zurück. Fast scheint es, als beobachte nicht die Stadt das Gebäude, sondern umgekehrt das Gebäude die Stadt.

Die Logik von sichtbarem, öffentlichem Raum auf der einen und unsichtbarem, privatem Raum auf der anderen Seite kippt an der Basis des Gebäudes, einem viergeschossigen Breitfuß, der zwar vage an einen städtischen Block erinnert, aber in erster Linie der formalen und mit – Ausnahme eines Steakhouses – monofunktionalen Logik des Hochhauses folgt. Bei zunehmender Nähe lässt die Wirkung des Spiegels nach. Der Blick beginnt einzudringen. Um unerwünschte Einblicke in die auch im Erdgeschoß liegenden Büroräume zu verhindern, ist hinter der Fassade eine zweite Schicht aus Stofflamellen installiert. Das Schließen des Vorhangs bleibt als letzter Rückzug.

Obwohl ursprünglich eingesetzt, um den Gebäudekomplex zu vereinheitlichen, kann das Spiegelglas nicht verhindern, dass ein Ganzes in seine Einzelteile zerfällt. Die Dinge werden sichtbar: So können die erst nach Ende der Arbeitszeit sich schließenden spiegelverglasten Tore nicht den dunklen Schlund der Tiefgaragen verdecken. Und auch die schräg über dem Haupteingang verlaufende Spiegelglasschürze ist nichts anderes als ein Vordach. Allem Reden von der „Hochhausskulptur" zum Trotz gibt es einen unauflösbaren Unterschied zwischen dem als Großplastik intendierten Hochhaus und einer künstlerischen Skulptur. Diese braucht sich nicht um das Problem des Eingangs zu kümmern.

ÖFFNUNG
In den neunziger Jahren wird das Hochhaus zunehmend weniger als Solitär in einem gleichgültigen Raumkontinuum denn als integraler Bestandteil eines Stadtensembles gesehen. Damit ist das Verhältnis von privatem zu öffentlichem Raum zu einem entscheidenden Kriterium für die Akzeptanz von Hochhäusern geworden. So genannte „Unternehmenskulturen" öffen sich der Stadt. Im firmeneigenen Prospekt zur DG-Bank in der Westendstraße ist zu lesen: „Der Gebäudekomplex gehört zu einer neuen Generation von Hochhäusern, mit denen visionäre Konzepte, wie zum Beispiel die Integration von Arbeiten, Wohnen und Leben, umgesetzt werden. Seine kontextuelle, d. h. auf die Umgebung bezogene Gestaltung berücksichtigt die unterschiedlichen Bedürfnisse der Menschen." Dieses „menschenfreundliche", 1993 fertiggestellte, wie ein Abziehbild des Kontextualismus funktionierende Hochhaus der Architekten Kohn Pedersen Fox nimmt vielerlei Rücksichten und hat eine dementsprechend komplexe Gestalt: Eine zwanzig Meter hohe Randbebauung vermittelt zum gründerzeitlichen Wohnviertel Westend, ein fünfzig Meter hoher Flügelbau bezieht sich auf die Maße der Geschäftshäuser aus den sechziger Jahren, ein quadratischer Turm von 150 Metern nimmt die vertraute Höhe der vorangegangenen Hochhausgeneration (Dresdner Bank und Deutsche Bank) auf, und schließlich ragt ein halbseitig gerundeter Körper in eine Höhe von über zweihundert Metern. Wesentlich bei der Integration des Hochhauses in den Kontext erscheint

die Ausbildung des Sockels. Nach Christian Norberg-Schulz geht es hierbei um nichts Geringeres als um die Versöhnung von (architektonischer) Unabhängigkeit und (städtebaulicher) Abhängigkeit.[03]

Die „Versöhnung" zwischen dem Neubau der DG-Bank und der Stadt Frankfurt beginnt bereits mit der Art und Weise, wie das Hochhaus „steht". Während sich fünfzehn Jahre zuvor artifizielles Material in bewusster Indifferenz über die gesamte Fassade zog, werden nun historische Typologien der Gliederung reaktiviert, die den Bezug zur umgebenden Bebauung herstellen sollen. Das kalte, artifizielle Material hat „natürlichem" Material Platz gemacht. Dunkelgrauer Granit formuliert den Übergang vom Bodenbelag der Stadt zum hellen Granit der Fassade. Dass Differenzierung allerdings nicht heißt, unterschiedlichen Nutzungen auch eine unterschiedliche Materiallogik zu verleihen, sondern primär ein Bild der Differenzierung meint, zeigt die Südseite des Blocks. Hier trifft die Maßstäblichkeit der kontextuell begründeten Gliederung auf die gewaltige Infrastruktur des Hochhauses. Notausgänge, Technikräume und Tiefgarageneinfahrten zwängen sich in den vorgegebenen steinernen Rahmen.

Die Hoffnung auf Belebung der Sockelzone hat sich nicht erfüllt. Eine wesentlicher Grund hierfür könnte die Orientierung des Komplexes auf seine Mitte sein, den „Wintergarten". Erschlossen durch zwei Passagen und ein tempelartiges Portal, das den daneben liegenden Eingang des Investors fast bescheiden aussehen lässt, ist die 27 Meter hohe, von Palmen flankierte Halle als „Bindeglied zwischen Geschäftsviertel und Wohnquartier" konzipiert. Holzbänke im Kolonialstil sollen zum Verweilen einladen. Die Geräusche der Klimaanlage werden sanft übertönt vom herabfließenden Wasser einer in die Steinfas-

---

[03] CHRISTIAN NORBERG-SCHULZ, „THE HIGH-RISE-CITY", IN WARREN A. JAMES (HRSG.), *KOHN PEDERSEN FOX. ARCHITECTURE AND URBANISM. 1986-1992*, NEW YORK 1992, S. 9.

sade integrierten Wasserwand. Ein China-Restaurant, eine Parfümerie, ein Blumengeschäft, ein Frisör und eine Cocktail-Bar sollen einem Raum Leben einhauchen, der alle Anzeichen einer privatisierten Öffentlichkeit trägt. Das Publikum der Bankangestellten und -kunden bleibt unter sich. Wie der Ort für „Veranstaltungen vom Konzert bis zur Modenschau" zu verstehen ist, zeigt ein Blick in den „Wintergarten" zur Zeit der Internationalen Automobilausstellung. Ein neues Modell wird vorgestellt. Der „Wintergarten" wird zur Bühne für ein chromglänzendes Auto, das in das gleißende Licht der Theaterbeleuchtung gestellt ist. Dazwischen diskret verteilte Verkaufstische.

INDIFFERENZ

Für Leon Battista Alberti war das Haus eine kleine Stadt und die Stadt ein großes Haus. In Zeiten zunehmender Segregation scheint man sich dieses Diktums zu erinnern. Kann, so möchte man fragen, das Hochhaus ein Stück Stadt im Kleinen sein? Ist es offen für Prozesse, die nicht von vornherein determiniert sind? Die bisherige Erfahrung legt die Vermutung nahe, dass die wirtschaftliche Logik das Gebäude weitgehend determiniert. Öffentlichkeit wird zur Public Relation. Vor diesem Hintergrund erscheint das kontextuelle Hochhaus nur als Ausdifferenzierung des autistischen Hochhauses, das nach Büroschluss die Gitter herunterfährt. Da Differenzierung sich immer auf eine Grenze bezieht, ist die Einbeziehung von Mischnutzungen nicht zuletzt auch eine Erweiterung der Innen-Außen-Grenze. Das Gebäude wäre in diesem Sinn zwar offen für Einflüsse der Umwelt, doch handelte es sich bei diesen Einflüssen gewissermaßen nur um äußere Reize, die inneren Selektionskriterien unterworfen blieben. Der geheime Plan ist der Bau des eigenen Kontextes.

ERSTVERÖFFENTLICHUNG IN *BAUWELT* **46 (1995), S. 2645–2647.**

WALDSTADT
EIN DIALOG ZWISCHEN MICHAEL HIRSCH UND NIKOLAUS HIRSCH

MICHAEL HIRSCH Föhrenwald. Fängt man beim Namen an, denkt man an Buchenwald …

NIKOLAUS HIRSCH … oder, weniger große Geschichte als die eigene kleine Geschichte: Waldstadt, das suburbane bundesrepublikanische Idyll bei Karlsruhe, in dem wir beide aufgewachsen sind. Hier wie dort ist es unheimlich.

MICHAEL HIRSCH Ja, der Ort ist unheimlich, irgendwie gespenstisch. Zugleich sehe ich die Ähnlichkeit mit anderen suburbanen Reihenhaussiedlungen und Gartenstädten; und dann gibt es die verschiedenen Bedeutungsschichten. Wir haben es mit einer tiefgreifenden Transformation von politisch-historischen Kontexten und Bevölkerungsstrukturen zu tun. Zunächst eine Planung für einen sehr konkreten Zweck: die Errichtung von Wohnungen für die Arbeiter einer Rüstungsfabrik tief in der oberbayerischen Landschaft in einem Föhrenwald an der Isar. Zuerst als nationalsozialistische Mustersiedlung geplant, dann zum Lager für Zwangsarbeiter umfunktioniert, dann bis 1957 Lager für jüdische *displaced persons* („Regierungslager für Heimatlose Ausländer"), dann – nach dem Kauf durch die Katholische Kirche – eine Siedlung für sozial schwache, kinderreiche Familien von Heimatvertriebenen. Und heute deren Nachkommen.

NIKOLAUS HIRSCH Was mich dabei interessiert, ist die ständige Überformung des Gebauten durch neue Nutzer. Das Charakteristische an der Geschichte von Föhrenwald bzw. dem heutigen Waldram ist eben auch die Trägheit von Architektur. Sie scheint sich physisch kaum zu verändern. Sie läßt alles zu.

MICHAEL HIRSCH Eigentlich sieht man aber nur, was man schon weiß. Dieser Gedanke macht die Tür auf zur Kontingenz aller Bewertungen und Bedeutungen. Und Kontingenz heißt: Abhängigkeit vom jeweiligen Beobachterstandpunkt, der immer auch anders möglich wäre.

NIKOLAUS HIRSCH Ich denke, wir stehen hier vor einem Problem der Anschaulichkeit. Und zwar im doppelten Sinne. Zunächst, was den konkreten Gegenstand unserer Beobachtung betrifft. Dann aber auch – und dies ist möglicherweise das Hauptmotiv dieses Dialogs – das Verhältnis zwischen Architektur und politischer Philosophie als einem Problem der Gestalt oder Mimesis betreffend. Bei dem Problem des Lesbarmachens handelt es sich um eine Schwierigkeit, die bereits die Väter der derzeitigen Urbanismusdebatten, nämlich Lefebvre, de Certeau und Soja, beunruhigt hatte: ein prekäres Verhältnis zwischen physischem und mentalem Raum. Während Lefebvre auf den komplexen Beziehungen zwischen diesen beiden Sphären auf Basis alltäglicher sozialer Praxis insistiert, beunruhigte ihn gleichwohl die „Dominanz des Lesbaren und Sichtbaren" in der Interpretation des Raumes. Interpretation, so Lefebvre, kommt später, gleichsam ein Hintergedanke der Produktion von sozialem Raum. Das „Lesen" folgt der Produktion in allen Fällen – außer dort, wo der Raum produziert wird, damit er gelesen werde (was im Fall von Föhrenwald zutrifft). Die Frage ist also: macht Architektur Politik sichtbar? Bekommt Politik durch Architektur eine Gestalt? Der aktuellen Faszination von Urbanismus und Architektur in der Kunst liegt auch eine gewisse Überforderung des Gebauten zugrunde. Als seien Bauten eine letzte Möglichkeit, Politik anschaulich werden zu lassen. Nicht verstellt durch die weitgehend abstrakten und unanschaulichen Prozesse, die Politikwahrnehmung üblicherweise prägt, sondern unmittelbarer Ausdruck von Gesellschaft.

MICHAEL HIRSCH Das ist ein Gedanke, der für die politische Theorie wichtig ist. Gerade im avancierten französischen Theoriekontext gibt es einen Begriff des Politischen, der sozusagen autotelisch ist, das heißt keinen Gegenstand außer sich selbst hat. Das Politische als ontologisches

Urphänomen. Obwohl die meisten Autoren hier eher aus dem linken Theoriespektrum kommen, wie zum Beispiel Jacques Rancière, Chantal Mouffe und Ernesto Laclau, Alain Badiou, Giorgio Agamben, Claude Lefort, übernehmen sie ein zentrales konservatives Theorem: das Politische als Form der Konstituierung und Darstellung von Gemeinschaft; als die Form ihrer Identifikation. Während in rechten Modellen eines solchen Begriffs des Politischen eine Mythologie der Einheit gepflegt wird, eine Mythologie des harmonischen Volkskörpers sozusagen, der sich gegen Fremde und Feinde richtet, gibt es bei den linken Modellen eine Art Mythologie des Konflikts. Das ist eine Art Ästhetizismus, eine Ästhetisierung der Politik von links. Dieses Modell des Politischen ist agonal oder antagonistisch, nicht an Einheit, sondern an Differenz, am Streit orientiert. Hier steht die Idee der Auseinandersetzung verschiedener Positionen im öffentlichen Raum im Mittelpunkt. Das ist eine Metaphysik der leeren Stelle der Macht; eine Ästhetik der Repräsentation von Konflikten. Die Einheit oder Gestalt der Gemeinschaft wird nicht verkörpert, sondern bleibt leer, in Bewegung. Nicht umsonst übernimmt heute die Kultur, vor allem zeitgenössische Kunst und Urbanismus, die Aufgabe, eine solche widersprüchliche Gesellschaft „dokumentarisch" anschaulich zu machen.

NIKOLAUS HIRSCH Aber ist das Links-Rechts-Schema tatsächlich so scharf zu trennen?

MICHAEL HIRSCH Die scheinbar klare Differenz von links und rechts verschwimmt sogleich, sobald wir Hannah Arendt betrachten, welche dieses „ästhetizistische" Paradigma des Politischen vielleicht am deutlichsten ausgearbeitet hat. Sie hat definiert, dass Politik keinen Gegenstand hat außer ihrem eigenen Erscheinen oder Erscheinungsraum. Ihr Thema ist nicht *Gesellschaft*, die Verteilung sozialer und ökonomischer Machtpositionen und Rechte. Dieser Bereich ist bei ihr ganz konservativ aus dem politischen Diskurs ausgeschlossen. Arendts Thema ist vielmehr *Gemeinschaft*, die rituelle Artikulation der

Gestalt des Gemeinwesens, der Kampf um Anerkennung im öffentlichen Raum. Es ist kein Zufall, dass heute angesichts der politischen Resignation in Bezug auf eine progressive, egalitäre Veränderung der Gesellschaft, solche strukturkonservativen ontologischen Modelle des Politischen eine immer größere Rolle spielen. Wenn schon keine politische Veränderung der Gesellschaftsstruktur, dann wenigstens eine kritische Artikulation der Widersprüche der Gesellschaft. Die *Stadt* und das *Urbane* werden zu Metaphern dieser neuen politischen Kultur des Konflikts. Im Unterschied zu den faschistischen Formen führt diese Streit-Kultur nicht zu einer einheitlichen Gestalt des Volkes, nicht zu einem einheitlichen Bild der Gemeinschaft. Es handelt sich eher um eine Ästhetik des Diskurses als des Bildes. In gewisser Weise entstehen in dieser neuen politischen Kultur „Monumente" nicht einer organisch gedachten Gemeinschaft, sondern einer kritischen Öffentlichkeit. Diskursive Monumente der Zivilgesellschaft.

NIKOLAUS HIRSCH *Diskurs* zu bauen ist nicht ganz einfach, möglicherweise gar ein Widerspruch, den ein Architekt nicht lösen kann. Das Eigentümliche des Architektonischen liegt – ob man will oder nicht – im Organisieren von Ordnung, mehr noch: im Vorhersehen und Prädeterminieren eines künftigen Endzustandes.

MICHAEL HIRSCH Eines *telos*. Ein Sichüberkreuzen von Architektur und Politik. Jede Seite holt sich dabei von der jeweils anderen Seite ihren Gegenstand.

NIKOLAUS HIRSCH Kein Wunder also, dass der Architekt von jeher im Verdacht steht, auf der Seite der Autorität zu stehen, auf der Seite eines Systems, das die Gesellschaft organisiert und ihr Gestalt gibt. Er ist eben, wenn man der Etymologie folgt, ein „Architekt". Diese Wortzusammensetzung legt nahe, dass es um mehr geht als das reine Herstellen eines Gebäudes, um mehr als die pragmatische Tätigkeit eines *tektonikos*, der die Bedürfnisse von Nutzern befriedigt und anschließend wieder unsichtbar wird. *Archè* impliziert eine koordinierende Autorität und ein Prinzip, welches das Ende vorherbestimmt. Ein Ansatz, dieses Dilemma zu überwinden, ist das *Organische*. Der Begriff des Organischen taucht denn auch in vielfältiger und widersprüchlicher Form immer wieder im Laufe der Moderne auf, immer mit dem Ziel, die dem Architektonischen inhärente Tendenz zur Entfremdung zu überwinden. Er geht aus von Louis Sullivans als organisch – nicht funktionalistisch – verstandenem *form follows function*, entwickelt sich weiter über die Gartenstadtbewegung, den Jugendstil, Hugo Härings von Mies van der Rohe abgegrenzter organischer Architektur und in gewisser Weise bis hin zu den komplexen, auf natürlichen Wachstumstheorien basierenden Geometrien der Diagrammarchitektur der neunziger Jahre. Die Genealogie des Begriffs umfasst aber auch parallele Entwicklungsstränge, die uns über ambivalente Figuren wie Heinrich Tessenow direkt zum Architekten von Föhrenwald führen. Die Planung dieser Siedlung war in den späten 1930er Jahren der Versuch, ein künstliches Dorf zu bauen, oder, um es mit den Worten des Architekten zu sagen, der Versuch, ein „organisch gewachsenes Ortsbild" entstehen zu lassen.

MICHAEL HIRSCH Eine künstliche Heimat sozusagen. Wenn Heidegger sagt: „die Heimatlosigkeit wird ein Weltschicksal", stelle ich ihn mir automatisch vor seiner Hütte in Todtnauberg vor. Der, der noch wirklich wohnt im emphatischen Sinne, sagt uns, dass wir nicht mehr wohnen. Auf das Problem der Architektur und ihres Begriffs angewendet heißt das, dass die *archè*, der Grund oder das Prinzip der Architektur verschwindet, und nur noch das *Tektonische*, die nutzbare Wohnfläche und Bauhülle übrigbleibt.

NIKOLAUS HIRSCH Die Häuser werden zu leeren Behältern, Containern. Das ist die gängige Kritik der Moderne im 20. Jahrhundert. Schachtelförmige Reihenhaussiedlungen wurden immer wieder, auch in der Bildenden Kunst, zu Symbolen einer allgemeinen Kulturkritik der Moderne. So auch in der Arbeit *Homes for America* von Dan Graham. Die dort, auch in einer ironischen Kritik an den Parametern der Minimal Art gezeigten Häuser sind bezeichnenderweise ebenfalls für Arbeiter einer Rüstungsfabrik gebaut worden. Sie sind Zeichen für die Austauschbarkeit des Wohnens, für den Verlust an Heimat und für die fehlende Einbindung in die Landschaft. Die Siedlung Föhrenwald – paradoxerweise an einem der Herstellung von Menschen-, Landschafts- und Häuserzerstörungsmitteln geweihten Ort – scheint gerade das Umgekehrte anzuzeigen: den Willen zur bildnerischen Verklärung und Gestaltung, zur artifiziellen Herstellung von Heimat.

MICHAEL HIRSCH Hier zeigt sich eine grundsätzliche Paradoxie des Nationalsozialismus, in gewisser Hinsicht des modernen Konservatismus überhaupt. Moeller van den Bruck, ein Wortführer der Konservativen Revolution und prägend für die Heimatschutzbewegung, sagte: „Konservativ sein heißt Dinge zu schaffen, die zu bewahren sich lohnt". Für diesen modernen Konservatismus ist Architektur ein Versuch, Orte der Heimat und Gemeinschaft zu bauen; ein Versuch, das Organische und Gewachsene künstlich herzustellen. Man wollte gediegene Dinge und Häuser machen, die so aussehen, als ob sie schon immer dagewesen wären. Betonte die klassische Moderne das Konstruktive und Abstrakte, das Durchsichtige und damit die Kontingenz der Konstruktion, geht es bei der faschistischen Moderne darum, ein Erbe zu fingieren und damit etwas zu erschaffen, worauf man sich in Zukunft wird beziehen können. Alle konservativen und gegenaufklärerischen Begriffe der Moderne sind nach dem paradoxen Modell einer konservativen Revolution gebaut. Eine künstliche Heimat schaffen, Werte, an die sich glauben lässt, Formen und Gebilde, die so aussehen, als seien sie schon immer da gewesen. Der Inbegriff dieser Grundparadoxie ist der moderne Begriff der Nation. Er verweist auf das Natürliche, das aus sich heraus Entstandene. Aber in der Moderne muss das Natürliche und Organische eben künstlich hergestellt werden; es muss fingiert werden. Es ist mit anderen Worten ein Mythos.

NIKOLAUS HIRSCH Deshalb bezeichnen sich Politiker oder Gesetzgeber häufig als Architekten. Architektur als klassische Metapher der Politik. Und Architekturen als Denkgebäude: der Turm zu Babel, die Pyramide, das Labyrinth, das Netz.

MICHAEL HIRSCH Ja. Philippe Lacoue-Labarthe nannte den Nationalsozialismus in diesem Sinne *Nationalästhetismus*. Das Programm des politisch und intellektuell relevanten Konservatismus ist im Kern immer auch ein ästhetisches. Seine Protagonisten sind immer auch Architekten des Volkes, dem eine Identität und eine Gestalt gegeben werden soll. Wie Goebbels es ausdrückt: Politik ist die Bildende Kunst des Volkes. *Organisch* ist an dieser ganzen Ideenwelt immer nur die Vision des Volkes als Gestalt oder Körper. Die Vision von Volk und Gemeinschaft als Werk und gemeinsame politische Aufgabe. Das Volk als Gesamtkunstwerk.

NIKOLAUS HIRSCH Interessant ist dabei, dass die Tendenz, das Volk oder eine Gemeinschaft räumlich zu repräsentieren, ideologisch und ikonologisch weit weniger eindeutig zuzuordnen ist als zunächst zu vermuten. Das Etikett „Naziarchitektur" ist da problematisch und entspringt eher einem Freund-Feind-Schema, das eher der Legitimation anderer Positionen dient. Die Versuche dem entfremdeten Dasein in der Moderne zu entkommen, gehen zurück zur Gartenstadt, darüber hinaus zu den Gemeinschaftsarchitekturen des Frühsozialismus. Das Prinzip des Organischen ist eng verknüpft mit dem Prinzip *Gemeinschaft.* Auffällig in Föhrenwald ist das hohe Maß an Gemeinschaftsbauten. Eine merkwürdige Proportion zwischen Gemeinschaftsbauten und Wohnhäusern. Ein Übermaß an Gemeinschaft. In der Typologie den Wohnhäusern mit ihren steil aufragenden Dächern verwandt, doch skaliert, ins Großmaßstäbliche vergröbert. Den Wohnhäusern werden wesentliche Funktionen entzogen, die üblicherweise ein Haus und das Leben seiner Bewohner definieren. Die Küche wird zur Gemeinschaftsküche.

MICHAEL HIRSCH Das gemeinschaftliche Leben war nicht in Haushalten organisiert, im „Privaten" der bürgerlichen Kleinfamilie, sondern ausgelagert in eine öffentliche Struktur der Ernährung und der kulturellen und politischen Freizeitorganisation. Es gab keine Haushalte im eigentlichen Sinne des Wortes *oikos*. Denn es gab keine Küche, das heißt der „heimische Herd", die eigentliche Mitte jeden Hauses fehlte. Die heile, heimische Welt im Kleinen, Grundideologie des Nationalsozialismus, konnte sich nicht entfalten, weil die andere Seite dieser Ideologie, die "totale Mobilmachung" (Ernst Jünger), die Grundlage der bürgerlichen Gesellschaft, nämlich Haushalt und Familie, zerstörte. Die Dominanz der Gemeinschaftsbauten in der Siedlung zeigt den streng kollektivistischen Ansatz dieser Mustersiedlung: kollektive Organisation des Arbeitens, der Verpflegung und der Freizeit. Ideologische Beeinflussung und räumliche Überwachung sind in dieser Struktur fast total. Eine radikale Form der Zwangsvergemeinschaftung.

NIKOLAUS HIRSCH Das macht es so deprimierend. Unheimlich. Und merkwürdig, dass mir einzig die Welt der Baumärkte, die sich langsam über die alten Fassaden legt, etwas Hoffnung macht. Die falsche, gekaufte Individualität der Hauseingänge, der Carports, der Dachgauben und Gartenzäune. Aber immerhin. Hauptsache dem Übermaß an Gemeinschaftsarchitektur etwas entgegensetzen.

MICHAEL HIRSCH Die Lässigkeit der heutigen Bewohner mit dem historischen Erbe der Siedlung hat vor allem etwas mit den konkreten Bedürfnissen der Leute zu tun. Sie suchen bezahlbaren Wohnraum in einer einigermaßen ruhigen Umgebung. Sie sind die ersten, die hier jetzt freiwillig wohnen. Sie bewohnen gewissermaßen ein Monument, vermutlich in größter Indifferenz gegenüber der Bedeutung dieses Monuments.

NIKOLAUS HIRSCH Die Spuren der Praxis – oder auch wie de Certeau sagen würde: die List der Nutzer im Umgang mit dem Monument –

könnte man als etwas Positives interpretieren. Als etwas Subversives, das die Planung und den daraus resultierenden Ort umdreht. All die kleinen Details scheinen wie ein – wenn auch vielleicht unbeabsichtigter – ironischer Kommentar zur Geschichte des Ortes. Das *An-Archische* wäre die positive Lesart. Die andere ist: es handelt sich nicht um kleinmaßstäbliche, individuelle List, sondern um eine neue homogene Schicht, die eingebettet ist in die Landschaft eines sich natürlich gebenden Kapitalismus und seines Warenfetischismus. Das Gemeinschaftliche bleibt dann diskreditiert zurück.

MICHAEL HIRSCH Wenn man die riesigen, den ganzen Ort dominierenden Gemeinschaftsbauten (Kantine, Versammlungsräume, Kino usw.) betrachtet, stellt man fest, dass sie heute verwaist sind in Bezug auf ihre ursprüngliche Funktion. Sie beherbergen nun kirchliche Schuleinrichtungen. Die Gemeinschaftsbauten sind einfach stehengeblieben mitten in der Siedlung, als eine von den Bewohnern der Siedlung vernachlässigte Mitte. Der Ort in seiner besonderen Geschichte und politischen Bedeutung wird durch die heutige Nutzung partiell ausgelöscht oder zumindest von ihr überlagert. Die kleinbürgerliche Idylle der Reihenhaussiedlung ist ja ein fester Topos in der politischen Ikonographie der progressiven Gesellschaftskritik des 20. Jahrhunderts.

NIKOLAUS HIRSCH Aber die Verhältnisse haben sich verkompliziert.

MICHAEL HIRSCH Richtig, solche Siedlungen symbolisieren nicht mehr nur einfach die kleinbürgerliche Ideologie von Eigentum und heiler Welt unter Seinesgleichen, die Ideologie einer gewissen soziokulturellen Homogenität, die an die Stelle der totalitären Homogenitätsideale getreten ist. Das eigene Heim am Stadtrand oder auf dem Land ist inzwischen längst auch zu einer Ikone des Pragmatismus im aktuellen Kapitalismus geworden. Gerade in Städten mit teuren Mieten wie München oder Frankfurt hat der Erwerb von Wohneigentum vor den Toren der Stadt als Lebensform sich weit in linke

Milieus hinein ausgebreitet. Da der gesellschaftliche Kontext inzwischen von sozialer Verunsicherung und Prekarisierung der Existenzen geprägt ist, wird plötzlich so etwas wie *Sicherheit* und *Immobilität* des Wohnens zu einer auch für erklärte Nichtspießer plausiblen Option.

NIKOLAUS HIRSCH Und hier wird die Sache – der historische Vergleich – interessant. Spätestens seit Götz Alys Buch *Hitlers Volksstaat* weiß man, wie sehr der Nationalsozialismus auch ein Sozialstaat war, der die sozial schwächere Bevölkerung mit allen möglichen sozialen Leistungen bestochen hat. Das steuerbegünstigte Eigenheim ist ja nicht nur eine Ideologie, sondern auch eine konkret von unserem politischen System massiv wirtschaftlich, steuerlich begünstigte Lebensform. Es ist eine Lebensform, die ihrerseits Lebensformen generiert, konkrete Stile und Abhängigkeiten, Flächenversiegelung, Landschaftszerstörung, automobile Verkehrsströme …

MICHAEL HIRSCH Es handelt sich um eine praktische Ideologie mit einem offensichtlich realen Gebrauchswert. Wie alle anderen Ideologien hat die Ideologie des Wohnens eine reale Funktion in unserem Leben, solange andere Lebens- und Wohnformen nicht gefunden werden. Und ich würde sagen, dass heute – nach einem deklariert anti-bürgerlichen Intermezzo – politisch die Suche nach anderen urbanen Lebensformen weitgehend aufgegeben wurde. Mangels realer Alternativen werden dann auch wieder die scheinbar obsoleten bürgerlichen Formen als Option plausibel. Die sogenannte Ideologie der Familie, die sich in solchen Reihenhaussiedlungen und in den in sie eingeschriebenen Lebensmodellen und Vorstellungen geschlechtsspezifischer und professioneller Arbeitsteilung verkörpert, wurde ja immer nur kulturell-ideologisch angegriffen, nie in bezug auf ihre reale gesellschaftsstrukturelle Funktion (die Gewährleistung von Sicherheit, Inklusion, Anerkennung für alle Beteiligten). Deswegen kann sie heute – nach dem sich abzeichnenden Scheitern aller egalitären

Utopien der klassischen Moderne – so problemlos restauriert werden. Wir leben heute, wie Alain Badiou kürzlich in *Le siècle* schrieb, in einem Zeitalter der Restauration. Die Familie steht darin ja nicht allein: auch alle anderen „autoritären" Institutionen der bürgerlichen Gesellschaft erleben heute wieder eine triumphale Wiederauferstehung: der Staat, die Justiz, die Eliten, die Experten, das Unternehmen, die „feste Stelle" usw.

NIKOLAUS HIRSCH „Regierungslager für Heimatlose Ausländer". So stand es seit 1952 auf einem Schild an der äußeren Grenze des Lagers für *displaced persons*. Dieses Schild und überhaupt die Abgrenzung nach außen sind wichtig. Es handelt sich um einen exterritorialen Ort. Nicht nur ist es ein künstliches Dorf für jüdische Flüchtlinge mit einer komplett autarken Infrastruktur (Polizei, Gerichtsbarkeit, Lebensmittelhandel, Synagogen, Schulen, Bibliothek, Kino, Versammlungsräume, Badehaus usw.). In diesem Lager haben sich die jüdischen sogenannten heimatlosen Ausländer eine provisorische, aber dann eben doch sehr lange andauernde künstliche Heimat errichtet. Später wohnen hier sogenannte Heimatvertriebene und Spätaussiedler. Zuvor wurde der Bezug zu den eroberten Territorien des nationalsozialistischen Deutschlands hergestellt. Im Text des Architekten heißt es: „Die Straßen und Plätze sind im Hinblick auf das Zeitgeschehen nach wiedergewonnenen Gebieten benannt." Auch hier wird der Wille deutlich, in der Architektur die jeweilige historische und politische Lage anschaulich werden zu lassen.

MICHAEL HIRSCH So wird Föhrenwald zu einem Ort der mehrfach überlagerten historischen Bezüge. Die heutigen Bewohner eignen sich diesen Ort nach ihren eigenen Bedürfnissen an. Anbauten an den Eingängen, individuell gestaltete Gartenzäune usw. Sie verwischen immer mehr die Spuren der ursprünglichen architektonischen Gestalt. Mit anderen Worten: sie verwandeln die Siedlung immer mehr von einem historischen Monument in eine „normale" Reihenhaussiedlung. Deren architektonische Form ist per se in den Augen der Bewohner/Benutzer sekundär. Sie sind Pragmatiker, deren Horizont quer steht zum Horizont der Beobachter/Theoretiker. Sie neutralisieren den ganzen historisch-politisch-ästhetischen Bedeutungskontext. Der ganze Ort lebt von dieser Neutralisierung und Verdrängung der historischen Bedeutungsschicht – von einem Vergessen im Dienste des Lebens. Aber das Vergessene bleibt anwesend. Das ganze semantische Feld von Wohnen, Gewöhnung und Gewöhnlichkeit, von Heimat, heimelig, heimlich und unheimlich ist hier von Bedeutung. Das Gewöhnliche überlagert das Ungeheuerliche und umgekehrt.

NIKOLAUS HIRSCH „Gewöhnung", ein Begriff, den Walter Benjamin in Bezug auf die Rezeption von Architektur benutzt, zeigt das ganze Dilemma. Die Rezeption von Architektur geschieht in einem Prozess der Gewöhnung, in einer eher zerstreuten Wahrnehmung, und nicht in der konzentrierten Aufmerksamkeit, die durch ein Gegenüber geprägt ist wie in der Rezeption eines Kunstgegenstands. Das Problem ist allerdings: als Architekt oder Philosoph befindet man sich dann doch eher in der Kunstsituation. Eine Schwierigkeit – wenn nicht Unmöglichkeit, sich außerhalb systemischer Ordnungen zu stellen. Es fällt beiden schwer, das zu tun, was die Bewohner machen: die Architektur unscharf werden zu lassen, die harten Linien weich werden zu lassen.

DER DIALOG ZWISCHEN MICHAEL HIRSCH UND NIKOLAUS HIRSCH FAND ANLÄSSLICH DER AUSSTELLUNG *FÖHRENWALD* VON MICHAELA MELIÁN STATT UND WURDE VERÖFFENTLICHT IN *FÖHRENWALD*, HRSG. VON HEIKE ANDER, MICHAELA MELIÁN, FRANKFURT AM MAIN 2005, S. 129–144.

PERMANENZ UND SUKZESSION
MONUMENTALE FRAGEN ZUM GLEIS 17 /
BAHNHOF BERLIN-GRUNEWALD

Nach tiefgreifenden historischen Einschnitten wurde einst Vergessen verordnet. Nichts weniger als „ewige Vergessenheit und Amnestie" – oder *perpetua oblivio et amnestia*[01] wie es im Westfälischen Frieden von 1648 heißt – sollte gelten. Als Grundlage eines dauerhaften Friedens wurden sämtliche Schuldzuschreibungen und Strafmaßnahmen ausgeschlossen. Mit den Ereignissen des 20. Jahrhunderts änderte sich diese Praxis jedoch grundlegend. „Verbrechen gegen die Menschlichkeit", vor allem der Genozid, sind seit den Nürnberger Kriegsverbrecherprozessen von Amnestie ausgeklammert. Aus dem verordneten Vergessen wird auf kultureller Ebene eine Verpflichtung zur Erinnerung. Diese Umkehrung ist gut gemeint, eröffnet aber einige Fragen: Lässt sich Erinnerung festschreiben? Lässt sie sich über die fortschreitende Zeit hinweg aufrechterhalten? Und in welcher Form geschieht dies?

Erinnerung ist angewiesen auf Gedächtnisstützen: Das gesprochene oder geschriebene Wort, Rituale, Monumente. Die Schwierigkeit liegt nun jedoch darin, dass in den Mnemotechniken, die Erinnerung gewährleisten, zugleich das Potential des Vergessens angelegt ist. Die Stützen der Erinnerung sind unzuverlässig. Sie können erstarrte, inhaltsleere Formen annehmen. Sie werden beliebig und austauschbar. Aufschlussreich ist in diesem Zusammenhang eine alltägliche Mnemotechnik, die Heidegger in *Sein und Zeit*[02] beschreibt: Der Knoten im Taschentuch. Der Knoten ist geknüpft an ein Ereignis, das man zu vergessen fürchtet. Als reines Zeichen kann er für eine unendliche Menge von Erinnerungsaufgaben stehen. Doch welche ist jeweils die bezeichnete Aufgabe? Verwirrung ist unter solchen Umständen immer möglich. So kommt es nicht nur vor, dass der Knoten nur für Eingeweihte lesbar ist, sondern auch, dass zum Verständnis

---

[01] VGL. HARALD WEINRICH, *LETHE. KUNST UND KRITIK DES VERGESSENS*, MÜNCHEN 1997, S. 217.

[02] VGL. MARTIN HEIDEGGER, *SEIN UND ZEIT*, TÜBINGEN 1986, S. 81

des Zeichens weitere Zeichen notwendig werden. Dem Knoten muss also unter Umständen ein weiterer Knoten hinzugefügt werden. Damit verliert das als Zeichen unverwendbare *monumentum* zwar nicht seinen Zeichencharakter, erhält aber die Aufdringlichkeit eines disponiblen Objekts.

BEILÄUFIGES BEMERKEN
Einen Ansatz gegen die Tendenz zur Verselbständigung von Monumenten bietet der Bezug auf den Ort. Gewiss, *site specificity* als solche ist auch eine Konstruktion. Eine Konstruktion, die Kontext herstellt. Doch im Gegensatz zur *tabula rasa* des leeren Grundstücks bietet der vorhandene Ort die Möglichkeit, das Problem der Erinnerung nicht räumlich zu isolieren, sondern mit anderen Parametern zu konfrontieren und darüber hinaus über die eigene Rolle als Konstrukteur von Erinnerung zu reflektieren. Vorsichtig gesagt: das genaue Hinschauen hat zumindest den Vorteil, dass Dinge vor Ort gefunden und auch belassen werden können wie sie sind. Es geht dabei weniger um die Überformung eines Ortes als um ein Hinzufügen und Einfügen. Während autonome Grundstücke wie der historisch unpräzise Ort des zentralen Berliner Holocaust-Mahnmals die Zusammenhanglosigkeit zwischen Zeichen und Bezeichnetem eher verstärken (und dies in der Logik des Eisenmanschen Formalismus noch als besondere Qualität interpretiert wird), bieten Tat-Orte die Möglichkeit einer Verknüpfung struktureller Art.

Der Bahnhof Berlin-Grunewald ist ein Tatort und dennoch ein ganz gewöhnlicher Ort. Kaum etwas verweist darauf, dass von hier aus im Oktober 1941 die Deportation der Berliner Juden begann. Heute wie damals ist das Gleis 17 eingebettet in einen Kontext von alltäglichen, parallel ablaufenden Nutzungen. Pendler aus dem Villenvorort fahren mit der S-Bahn zur Arbeit. Spaziergänger suchen Erholung. Hochgeschwindigkeitszüge rauschen vorbei. Am Gleis 16 steht ein Wohnzug für Bahnarbeiter. Gardinen an den Fenstern, Parabolantennen auf dem Dach, im Sommer einige Stühle und ein Grill vor den Waggons. An der Rampe warten diesmal Urlauber auf die Verladung in Autoreisezüge.

Das Gleis 17, ein seit Kriegsende weitgehend ungenutztes und infolgedessen überwuchertes Gleis, ist kein abgesondertes Grundstück. Es handelt sich nicht um eine vom Alltag ausgegrenzte, autonome Situation, sondern um ein lineares Element unter anderen, um einen gewöhnlichen Ort innerhalb eines Kontextes von parallelen, transitorischen Phänomenen. Die Gewöhnlichkeit des Ortes verweist auf einen Wahrnehmungsmodus, den Walter Benjamin als charakteristisch für die Architektur bezeichnete: „… sie findet von Hause aus viel weniger in einem angespannten Aufmerken als in einem beiläufigen Bemerken statt. Diese an der Architektur gebildete Rezeption hat aber unter gewissen Umständen kanonischen Wert. Denn: Die Aufgaben, welche in geschichtlichen Wendezeiten dem menschlichen Wahrnehmungsapparat gestellt werden, sind auf dem Wege der bloßen Optik, also der Kontemplation, gar nicht zu lösen. Sie werden allmählich nach Anleitung der taktischen Rezeption, durch Gewöhnung bewältigt".[03] Gerade an transitorischen Orten wie Bahnhöfen vollzöge sich Wahrnehmung damit eher in einer gewissen Flüchtigkeit. Auf die Frage des Monuments bezogen, ginge es damit weniger um objekthafte Dinge, die einem Betrachter gegenüberstehen und damit eher statisch wahrgenommen werden, als vielmehr um „beiläufige" Dinge; wörtlich verstanden also um Dinge, die im unmittelbaren Zusammenhang mit Fortbewegung und Gehen erfahren werden.

AUF DAUER
Wie lässt sich die Ambivalenz zwischen dauerhaftem Erinnern und Vergessen als Materialfrage verstehen? Lässt sich Ambivalenz

---

[03] WALTER BENJAMIN, „DAS KUNSTWERK IM ZEITALTER SEINER TECHNISCHEN REPRODUZIERBARKEIT", IN DERS., *GESAMMELTE SCHRIFTEN*, BD. I.2, FRANKFURT AM MAIN 1980, S. 466.

bauen? Kann „Flüchtigkeit" oder gar „Zweifel" in ein Monument eingebaut werden? Nichts wäre einfacher als sich vom *monere* des Mahnmals, also von allzu gut gemeinter Ermahnung und Didaktik zu distanzieren und sich gänzlich auf die Seite des Flüchtigen und Prozessualen zu schlagen. Die zunehmend verdächtig wirkende, auf Dauer zielende Erinnerung würde damit einer Erinnerung weichen, die Sache der Alltagspraxis ist; immer in Bewegung, sich ständig verändernd durch individuelle Interaktion. Dieser Ansatz, wie er zum Beispiel von Jochen Gerz in seinem Harburger „Mahnmal gegen Faschismus" mit Tausenden von eingeritzten Privatkommentaren realisiert wurde, ist sicherlich der einfachste Weg, die Frage des Monumentalen von staatspolitischer Erinnerungskultur zu entkoppeln und ganz nebenbei noch zu dokumentieren, dass man auf „der richtigen Seite steht".

Weniger bequem, aber möglicherweise umso relevanter ist es hingegen, die Problematik des Monuments inklusive der fragwürdigen, auf Dauer angelegten Erwartungen der staatlichen Erinnerungspolitik anzunehmen und sie gleichzeitig in ein Spannungsverhältnis zu kontingenten und weitgehend unkontrollierbaren Prozessen zu setzen. Es geht darum, die Parameter der Permanenz den alltäglichen Veränderungen auszusetzen. Das Flüchtige mit dem Dauerhaften in Beziehung zu setzen. Sich nicht entscheiden. Vielleicht ist das Zweifel.

Was bedeutet nun Permanenz als Materialstrategie? Zunächst, dass der Ort „Gleis 17" nicht erst erfunden oder rekonstruiert werden muss. Er existiert bereits. Die Intervention beschränkt sich daher auf das Definieren einer horizontalen Struktur, die den Ort sichtbar und begehbar macht. Diese Struktur versiegelt nicht, sondern legt sich mit ihrem offenen Raster auf das bestehende Gelände, folgt dessen leicht gekrümmten Verlauf und einer eigentümlich verzogenen Topographie. Die Anzahl und Abfolge der horizontalen Elemente ist durch die numerische Logik der Transporte bestimmt. Horizontale jeweils

1,42 x 3,12 Meter große Elemente bilden zwei Bahnsteige auf einer Länge von je 132 Metern und ermöglichen so einen Rundgang um das Gleis 17. Beiläufig, also im Gehen, ergibt sich die Chronologie eines Fahrplans, dessen Koordinaten in einer Kopfzeile zum Bahnsteig hin aufgeführt sind: Datum des Transports, Anzahl der Deportierten, Bestimmungsort.

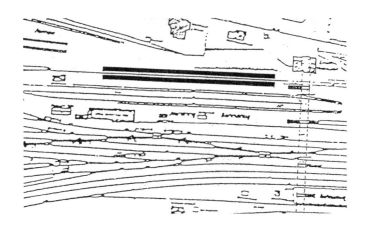

Wenn Dauer ein wesentlicher Parameter eines Monuments ist, kommt dem Material eine besondere Bedeutung zu. Es muss so beschaffen sein, dass die Daten dem Ort möglichst dauerhaft eingeschrieben werden. Mit der unbarmherzigen Präzision des Ingenieurs können die zeitlichen Faktoren bauphysikalisch untersucht und weiterentwickelt werden. Auch kann die Materialstrategie kontextuell begründet sein – schließlich ist die Geschichte der Bahnhöfe aufs Engste verknüpft mit der Entwicklung von Gusseisen. Das Material wird zum Verweis auf

Reisen und Warenzirkulation. Doch wie transitorisch bzw. dauerhaft ist das Material? Inwieweit ist man verantwortlich für die Implikationen, die ein Material mit sich bringt? Und in welchem Maß sind diese Diskurse zeitlich gebunden? Auch das scheinbar transitorische Material Eisen unterliegt einem Diskurswandel, den bereits Walter Benjamin bemerkte: „Die ersten Eisenbauten dienten transitorischen Zwecken: Markthallen, Bahnhöfe, Ausstellungen. Das Eisen verbindet sich also sofort mit funktionalen Momenten im Wirtschaftsleben. Aber was damals funktional und transitorisch war, beginnt heute in verändertem Tempo formal und stabil zu wirken."[04] Das Material Gusseisen kann sogar noch stabiler werden. Auf die Intervention am Gleis 17 angepasst, kann seine Dauerhaftigkeit durch das Hinzufügen von Lamellengraphit verlängert werden. Doch letztlich handelt es sich bei der Beantwortung der Materialfrage um eine kontingente Entscheidung. Sie ist keine Entsprechung, keine Übersetzung, keine Nachempfindung oder gar gebautes Mitleid in Bezug auf das zu erinnernde Ereignis. Am Ende ist es eine Entscheidung für korrosionsbeständigen Grauguss GG 30.

STABILITÄT UND INSTABILITÄT

Die Frage wie sich Materialzustände mit historisch-politischen Diskursen verknüpfen lassen, ist geprägt durch „stabile" und „instabile" Strategien. Zwei konkurrierende, um 1900 von Alois Riegl und Georg Dehio entwickelte Denkmalbegriffe stehen zur Debatte. Die Frage lautet: geschehen lassen oder statisch werden? Einig waren sich die Erfinder der modernen Denkmalpflege in der Forderung, Relikte der Vergangenheit zu erhalten und sie rechtlich zu schützen. Fundamental werden die Unterschiede jedoch beim Umgang mit dem konkreten Material und seinen zeitlichen Parametern.

---

[04] WALTER BENJAMIN, *DAS PASSAGEN-WERK*, BD. 1, HRSG. VON ROLF TIEDEMANN, FRANKFURT AM MAIN 1983, S. 216.

Dehio fordert nichts weniger als die Unterbrechung des Materialprozesses.[05] Die Zeit soll angehalten werden. Ein vergangener Materialzustand wird eingefroren. Doch um das Material auch nur annähernd zu stabilisieren, muss Denkmalpflege zu einer aktiven Handlung werden: Reparaturen, Ausbesserungen, im äußersten Fall gar Wiederherstellungen.

Für Alois Riegl und seinen „modernen Denkmalkultus"[06] hingegen ist ein „Alterswert" entscheidend, der sich nicht durch die Vergangenheit, sondern einzig und allein durch die Gegenwart legitimiert. In der Konsequenz geht es nicht um die aktive Konservierung eines vergangenen Materialzustands, sondern um Verfall. Dieses Denkmalkonzept verweist explizit auf den natürlichen Verfallsprozess einer Ruine. Das Ziel ist nicht das Festhalten von Zeit, sondern das Geschehenlassen.

Welche Strategie ist nun die richtige: geschehenlassen oder festhalten? Möglicherweise geht es ja gar nicht um eine Entscheidung für das eine oder andere, sondern um die Kritik einer Dichotomie, die schon immer mehr mit ideologischen Positionskämpfen als mit realen Materialbedingungen zu tun hatte. Die Arbeit am Gleis 17 ist so gesehen ein Ansatz, der sich irgendwo in der Konfliktzone zwischen den Begründern des modernen Denkmalbegriffs zu orientieren sucht, also zwischen Alois Riegls Ästhetik des natürlichen Verschwindens einerseits und Georg Dehios materialer Stabilisierung andererseits.

[05] VGL. GEORG DEHIO, „DENKMALSCHUTZ UND DENKMALPFLEGE IM 19. JAHRHUNDERT. FESTREDE AN DER KAISER-WILHELM-UNIVERSITÄT ZU STRASSBURG, DEN 27. JANUAR 1905", IN GEORG DEHIO, ALOIS RIEGL, *KONSERVIEREN, NICHT RESTAURIEREN. STREITSCHRIFTEN ZUR DENKMALPFLEGE UM 1900*, BRAUNSCHWEIG/WIESBADEN 1988, S. 88-103.

[06] VGL. ALOIS RIEGL, „DER MODERNE DENKMALKULTUS, SEIN WESEN UND SEINE ENTSTEHUNG", IN GEORG DEHIO, ALOIS RIEGL, A.A.O., 1988, S. 43-87.

ERINNERN UND VERGESSEN

Der Ort *Gleis 17* ist geprägt durch ein historisches Ereignis, das festgeschrieben und damit statisch werden soll. Andere Dinge sind einfach geschehen. So unterscheidet ein Phänomen das Gleis 17 von allen anderen Gleisen des Bahnhofs: Sukzession. Dies ist – allem Anschein zum Trotz – kein geschichtsphilosophisches Theorem, sondern ein Begriff der Ökologie, der Vegetation in Beziehung zu zeitlichen Parameter setzt. Zwischen den Schienen des Gleises 17 ist in den vergangenen sechzig Jahren ein Wald gewachsen. Die lineare Baumstruktur entstand spontan in einem, etwa die Hälfte der Gleislänge messenden Bereich, der seit Kriegsende nicht mehr genutzt wurde. Dort liefen Sukzessionen von verschiedenen Vegetationen ab, die Zeitabstände, ja ganz allgemein Veränderung markieren.
In einer Initialphase siedelten sich Pionierpflanzen wie kleinwüchsige Kräuter und Gräser an. Anschließend entwickelte sich auf den kargen Schotterböden zwischen Schiene und Schwelle ein dichter Birkenwald. Diese Vegetationsphase war so lange stabil bis sich genügend Humus gebildet hatte und der heutige Bestand von Buchen und Eichen entstand.

Der selbstorganisierte Prozess der Sukzession wird weitergehen. Er wird möglicherweise übergreifen auf die Bahnsteige und sich innerhalb des Rahmens der 186 Elemente entwickeln. Hierbei fungieren die Perforationen der einzelnen Gusselemente als offenes Raster für Veränderungen. Über die Bahnsteige könnte sich in Zukunft eine Schicht legen, die in Abhängigkeit von Benutzung entsteht. Das Begehen durch den Besucher wird damit zu einem Parameter, der reguliert, ob und wieviel Gras über die Sache zu wachsen vermag.

Vielleicht ist dies ein Versuch, das Monument und seine auf Dauer abzielenden Parameter ernst zu nehmen, dabei jedoch eine Art Zweifel einzubauen. Ein Versuch, einen strukturellen Zusammenhang zwischen Erinnerung und Vergessen zu entwickeln. Der ungewisse

Status der Erinnerung würde damit ins Zentrum der Intervention am Gleis 17 rücken: Auf der einen Seite die Determiniertheit der Daten, auf der anderen Seite die Indetermininiertheit der Zeit; zum einen die dauerhafte räumliche Definition des Ortes durch einen sich im Gehen erschließenden Rahmen, zum anderen die sukzessive Veränderung durch Vegetation. Die Strukturen unternehmen den vergeblichen Versuch, die Zeit festzuhalten. Die Prozesse gehen darüber hinweg und markieren die Unumkehrbarkeit von Zeit.

DAS GLEIS 17 AM BAHNHOF BERLIN-GRUNEWALD WURDE 1998 VON DEN ARCHITEKTEN NIKOLAUS HIRSCH, WOLFGANG LORCH UND ANDREA WANDEL GEBAUT.

ARCHITEKTURWERKE,
ZUR VEREINIGUNG DER VÖLKER ERBAUT

Die Rekonstruktion des Berliner Stadtschlosses, so der Regierungschef des wiedervereinigten Deutschland, soll dem Volk etwas für die Seele geben. Dieses Projekt überrascht zu Beginn des 21. Jahrhunderts. Wenn ein Volk in einem Bauwerk zu sich selbst kommen soll, wiederholt sich unvermutet eine architektonische Denkfigur, die Hegel in seinen Vorlesungen über die Ästhetik entwickelte: „Architekturwerke, zur Vereinigung der Völker erbaut". Im Hegelschen System steht am Anfang aller Kunst die symbolische Architektur. Sie ist eine „selbständige Architektur", die im Gegensatz zu Haus und Tempel, also zu Behausungen für Menschen und Götter, keinen äußeren Zweck voraussetzt. Es handelt sich um Bauwerke, durch die sich die Gesellschaft in einem mimetischen Prozess gleichsam selbst konstruiert. Architektur ist hier ganz bei sich selbst: ein politisch-ontologisches Projekt.

Konsequent zu Ende gedacht, müsste die „Selbständigkeit" des Bauwerks strukturelle Folgen für das Berliner Schloss haben. Angenommen die Anhänger der Schlossrekonstruktion hätten recht, und die Frage der inneren Funktionen sei tatsächlich irrelevant – was läge da näher, als dem strukturellen Konstruktionsprinzip des Turms zu Babel und anderer von Hegel angeführter Beispiele zu folgen und ohne schlechtes Gewissen zu sagen: Das Schloss muss massiv sein. Und daher unzugänglich.

MONUMENTALE FUNKTIONALISIERUNG

Wenn Funktionslosigkeit die Voraussetzung für die Selbständigkeit des Schlosses ist, so ist umgekehrt eine monumentale Funktionalisierung wesentlich für die Interpretation des Palasts der Republik als „Fun Palace". Diesem Ansatz geht es, so scheint es zunächst, nicht mehr um einen mimetischen Kurzschluss zwischen Gesellschaft und Werk, sondern um eine strukturelle Offenheit des Bauwerks für äußere Zwecke und Funktionen. Unvorhersehbare Prozesse führen zu immer neuen Überformungen, Kolonisierungen und Anpassungen. Architektur wäre eher Hintergrund als Vordergrund. In Analogie zu Cedric Prices „Fun Palace" wird eine Strategie der Instabilität verfolgt: ein Gebäude als Rahmen für unterschiedlichste Formen der Aneignung, ein prozessorientiertes Gebilde, eine Kultur des *Non-Plan*.

Das Neue an diesem Ansatz wäre ein Denkmalbegriff, der sich wesentlich von dem bereinigten, geradezu ahistorischen Zustand unterscheidet, in den viele Monumente im ausgehenden 19. Jahrhundert und vor allem im Laufe des 20. Jahrhundert versetzt wurden. Vorgeblich ästhetische Verunreinigungen wurden beseitigt, banale Funktionen wie Wohnen und Arbeiten wurden entkernt, Monumente wie die Kathedrale von Paris durch großflächige Abrisse der unmittelbar angrenzenden Bebauung freigestellt. Vielleicht ist es heute möglich, diese Logik umzukehren. Prozesse wie jene, die das Colosseum mit seinen jahrhundertelangen funktionalen Überformungen bis zur architekturpolitischen Säuberung unter Mussolini durchlief, würden nun umgekehrt ablaufen. Das Ziel wäre die ständige Veränderung – bis zur Unkenntlichkeit des originalen Monuments.

NON-PLAN HEUTE: KRITIK ODER AFFIRMATION DER VERHÄLTNISSE?

Der Ansatz eines organischen *Non-Plans* hat jedoch zwei problematische Aspekte zu berücksichtigen: zum einen müsste kritisch hinterfragt werden, ob es dabei letztlich nicht doch um die Sehnsucht nach Verkörperung von Gesellschaft geht und damit letztlich nicht auch – analog zum Schloss, aber aus einer anderen Perspektive – um ein politisch-ontologisches Projekt. Unbehagen bereitet auch die inzwischen unübersehbare Nähe zwischen situationistischen und neoliberalen Strategien. Die in den späten 50er und 60er Jahren entwickelten, vor allem auf zeitlichen Parametern basierenden situationistischen Aktionen sind inzwischen durch neoliberale Marktstrategien adaptiert und perfektioniert worden. *Non-Plan* ist somit kein Wert an sich. Es drängt sich sogar der Verdacht auf, dass dieser Begriff inzwischen weniger die Kritik als vielmehr die Affirmation der herrschenden Verhältnisse ausdrückt. Der „Fun" des Fun Palace ist eine Industrie geworden, perfekt integriert in die Mechanismen des deregulierten Marktes. Insofern läuft eine Strategie, die sich vor allem auf die vermeintliche Gegen-Ökonomie temporärer Veranstaltungen verlässt, zunehmend Gefahr, Teil der allgemeinen Eventkultur zu werden und dabei die Tendenz zu verstärken, „feste Häuser" wie die Berliner Theater zu flexibilisieren oder gar aufzulösen. Als perpetuierte Eventmaschine würde, so steht zu vermuten, der Palast der Republik das absurde Schicksal des Tacheles teilen: Sub- und Gegenkultur unter Denkmalschutz.

ZURÜCK ZUR PLANUNG

Es ist merkwürdig, dass sich der Architekturdiskurs in den vergangenen zehn Jahren zwar intensiv mit den Begriffen „Zeit" und „Prozess" auseinandergesetzt hat, zugleich aber ignorant gegenüber historischer Zeit und dem Phänomen des Denkmals geblieben ist. Woher rührt diese Ignoranz? Einerseits ist sie zurückzuführen auf einen kaum gebrochenen Glauben an die Allmacht von „Design" und seiner Fähigkeit, inkommensurable Prozesse in Form von Diagrammen zu integrieren. Andererseits scheint das theoretische Rüstzeug zu fehlen, um die Frage „Palast oder Schloss" als eine Frage zeitgenössischer Architektur diskutieren zu können. Was benötigt wird, ist eine Strategie, die geschichtspolitische Fragestellungen und aktuellen Architekturdiskurs zu koppeln vermag. Vielleicht hilft hier ein Rekurs auf Alois Riegl, den Begründer des „Modernen Denkmalkultus". Die Ambivalenz seiner Theorie des Monuments, die sich einerseits auf einen Erinnerungswert als historisch-dokumentarischen Wert und andererseits auf einen Gegenwartswert als Gebrauchswert stützt, kommt der aktuellen Problematik schon recht nahe. Um allerdings in der zeitgenössischen Debatte anzukommen und daraus eine kreative Entwurfsoption zu entwickeln, müsste sie ihren Aufgabenbereich radikal erweitern: nicht nur der Umgang mit bereits existierenden, also aus der Vergangenheit stammenden authentischen Objekten sollte auf der Agenda stehen, sondern ebenso neue und virtuelle Materialien. Denkmalpflege als neue paradoxe Avantgarde, die nach vorne und hinten schauen kann.

SCHLOSS *UND* PALAST
Ausgehend von einem Denkmalbegriff, der ausschließlich auf authentischem Material basiert, wäre dem Palast der Republik der Vorzug vor dem Schloss zu geben; ganz einfach, weil er physisch existiert. Der Palast der Republik, ein historisches Dokument der DDR und des Umbruchs von 1989, muss als Teil eines städtebaulichen Ensembles begriffen werden, das sich vom Palast über den Fernsehturm bis hin zum Alexanderplatz erstreckt, und neu zu programmieren ist. Aber, gibt es überhaupt genügend Programm, um das Riesengelände sinnvoll zu füllen? Käme es zu mehr als harmlosem Retrodesign der sozialistischen Moderne oder bestenfalls zu einer nostalgischen Wiederholung der Appropriationstechniken der neunziger Jahre?

Möglicherweise ist die zugespitzte Alternative „Palast oder Schloss" ja zu einfach gestrickt, verfangen in einem Lagerdenken, das sich weitgehend mit der Identifizierung des Gegners begnügt und damit jedes zeitgenössische Risiko vermeidet. Die wirkliche Herausforderung in Berlins Mitte könnte daher in einem Ansatz liegen, der Palast und Schloss endlich als untrennbare, aufeinander bezogene „Gegenbauten" zusammendenkt und zu einer architektonischen Zwangsehe verurteilt. Dabei ginge es nicht mehr um ein „entweder ... oder ...", welches das bestens eingespielte und so bequeme Freund-Feind-Schema perpetuiert, sondern um eine Strategie, welche die physische Ruine des Palasts mit der virtuellen Ruine des Schlosses verschmelzt: Erhaltung *und* Rekonstruktion, Volkskammer *und* Schlüterhof. Es entstände ein hybrides Gebilde, das aus widersprüchlichen Komponenten neu zusammengesetzt ist. Der ost-westlich ausgerichtete Baukörper des Palasts der Republik würde überlagert von der Nord-Süd-Orientierung des in Kubatur und Proportion annähernd identischen Stadtschlosses. Ein architektonischer Mutant, der Palast und Schloss in etwas Neues verwandelt.

ERSTVERÖFFENTLICHUNG IN *FUN PALACE 200X. DER BERLINER SCHLOSSPLATZ*, HRSG. VON PHILIPP MISSELWITZ, HANS ULRICH OBRIST, PHILIPP OSWALT, BERLIN 2005, S. 166-169.

MATERIALZEIT
NOTIZEN ZUR SYNAGOGE DRESDEN

Der Entwurf einer Synagoge scheint vor allem Fragen nach dem Verhältnis zwischen architektonischem Material und zeitlichen Parametern aufzuwerfen. Wie verhält sich Architektur gegenüber einer Kultur, die zwar über Jahrtausende hinweg eine kohärente schriftliche Tradition aufzuweisen hat, deren architektonische Tradition jedoch eher inkohärent ist und weitgehend von instabilen Raumkonstellationen geprägt ist? Wie reagiert ein zeitgenössisches Gebäude auf einen städtebaulichen Kontext, dessen Leitbild durch die Rekonstruktion eines „Dresden wie es einmal war" bestimmt ist? Und wie schließlich sehen die Rückwirkungen zeitlicher Faktoren auf das architektonische Material und seine Tektonik aus?

STABILE UND INSTABILE ZUSTÄNDE
Schon der Versuch, den Entwurf einer zeitgenössischen Synagoge aus einer historisch tradierten Typologie herzuleiten, endet fast zwangsläufig in einer Sackgasse, oder anders gesagt: mit der Erkenntnis, dass ein spezifischer Bautypus „Synagoge" gar nicht existiert. Die Baugeschichte der Synagoge ist zu einem hohen Grad abhängig von wechselhaften, häufig prekären lokalen Umständen. Mal schlüpft die Synagoge in das Gewand eines Wohnhauses, mal kommt sie als Pseudokirche daher. Einen prägnanteren Ausgangspunkt für eine Materialstrategie bieten dagegen die Zustandsbeschreibungen dessen, was man die architektonischen Grunderfahrungen des Judentums nennen könnte: der Tempel und das Stiftszelt. Bereits in den zwanziger Jahren hatte der Wiener Kunsthistoriker Max Eisler anlässlich des Wettbewerbs für eine Synagoge in Wien-Hietzing das „Zelt" als angemessene Bauform „für ein Volk auf Wanderschaft"[01]

---

[01] MAX EISLER, „DER WETTBEWERB UM EINE WIENER SYNAGOGE", IN: *ÖSTERREICHISCHE BAU- UND WERKKUNST*, 2. JG. (1925/26), S. 1-7. ZIT. NACH RUTH HANISCH, OTTO KAPFINGER, „DER WETTBEWERB UM EINE SYNAGOGE IN WIEN-HIETZING", IN MATTHIAS BOECKL (HRSG.), *VISIONÄRE & VERTRIEBENE. ÖSTERREICHISCHE SPUREN IN DER MODERNEN AMERIKANISCHEN ARCHITEKTUR*, BERLIN 1995, S. 249FF.

bezeichnet; zuletzt wies Salomon Korn[02] auf die Bedeutung des Gegensatzpaares „Tempel" und „Zelt" hin. Der Vorteil dieses Ansatzes: Das Gegensatzpaar verknüpft Materialzustände mit dem gesellschaftlichen Kontext und stellt damit ein konkretes, zugleich aber immer auch prekäres Verhältnis zum Ort her.

TEMPEL UND ZELT

Das erste Gotteshaus der Juden war ein Provisorium: Das Stiftszelt, jederzeit zum Abbau und Umzug bereit, bildete eine ephemere Hülle für die tragbare Bundeslade. Im Gegensatz zu diesem mobilen Heiligtum war das zweite jüdische Gotteshaus ein festes Haus: der Salomonische Tempel. Fest mit dem Heiligen Land und der Topografie des Bergs Zion verbunden, von gewaltigen Substruktionsbauwerken unterstützt, formulierte der Tempel einen massiven Anspruch auf Dauerhaftigkeit. Ganz allgemein ließe sich sagen, dass die Synagoge sowohl Elemente des Tempels als auch solche des Stiftszeltes mit jeweils unterschiedlichem Akzent aufweisen kann. Abhängig von internen Verhältnissen und externen Kontexten ist die Architektur der Synagoge mehr oder weniger dauerhaft – respektive temporär. So waren bis Anfang des 19. Jahrhunderts die äußeren Bedingungen in Deutschland derart prekär, dass die in gesellschaftlichen und räumlichen Peripherien gebauten Synagogen sich eher am provisorischen Charakter des Stiftszelts orientierten. Mit der einsetzenden Emanzipation im 19. Jahrhundert zeichnete sich auch ein architektonischer Paradigmenwechsel ab: Nicht mehr das portative Gotteshaus, sondern der dauerhafte Tempel mit seinen Versprechungen auf Heimat war nun das bestimmende Motiv. Die politische Emanzipation zieht eine Verfestigung durch Architektur nach sich. Emanzipation und Assi-

---

02 SALOMON KORN, „SYNAGOGENARCHITEKTUR IN DEUTSCHLAND NACH 1945", IN HANS-PETER SCHWARZ, DEUTSCHES ARCHITEKTURMUSEUM, JÜDISCHES MUSEUM (HRSG.), *DIE ARCHITEKTUR DER SYNAGOGE*, STUTTGART 1988, S. 287 FF. AKTUALISIERTE FASSUNG IN SALOMON KORN, *GETEILTE ERINNERUNG*, BERLIN 1999, S. 35 FF.

milation werden manifest. Christlichen Typologien des Sakralbaus werden übernommen. Die Semper-Synagoge, im Innenraum mit orientalisierenden Motiven auf eine „fremde" Herkunft anspielend, ist nach Außen hin ganz Neoromanik. So wurde der „deutsch-romanische Styl"[03] im öffentlichen Raum zum Zeichen eines patriotischen Bekenntnisses – ein architektonisches Bekenntnis, das die Synagogen in Deutschland jedoch nicht vor ihrer Zerstörung bewahrt hat.

MATERIALSUCHE
Was heißt es überhaupt, etwas Neues zu bauen? Bevor wir neues Material erfinden, suchen wir nach dem alten, häufig zerstörten und endgültig verschwundenen Material. „Dresden" ist eine Chiffre für „Zerstörung". Weniger verankert im öffentlichen Bewusstsein ist, dass in Dresden eine doppelte Zerstörung stattgefunden hat: jene der Dresdner Altstadt durch alliierte Bomber am 13. und 14. Februar 1945, die auf immer und ewig die Stadt auf eine Opferrolle festgelegt zu haben scheint, und jene, eher verdrängte Zerstörung der Semper-Synagoge am 9. November 1938. Die Zerstörungen sind zwar räumlich und historisch miteinander verknüpft, doch die Reaktion auf das Verschwinden der Bauten könnte kaum unterschiedlicher sein. Mit der Rekonstruktion von Frauenkirche und anderer, tief im kollektiven Gedächtnis verwurzelten Bauten wird nach über fünfzig Jahren der Versuch unternommen, den architektonischen Phantomschmerz zu heilen und die Kontinuität zwischen Vergangenheit und Gegenwart wiederherzustellen. Die räumlichen Zäsuren der Zerstörungen, die Geschichte sichtbar machen, verschwinden allmählich. Im Zeitalter der Rekonstruktion entsteht ein neuer Städtebau, der keinen Plan braucht. Der inoffizielle Masterplan des heutigen Dresdens ist ein Luftbild aus den späten 1930er Jahren. Tausendfach in der Stadt plakatiert, zeigt es die heile Welt des alten Dresden – oder

[03] EDWIN OPPLER, „GUTACHTEN VOM 05.08.1863 ÜBER DIE SYNAGOGE IN HANNOVER", IN
DIE ARCHITEKTUR DER SYNAGOGE, STUTTGART 1988, S. 221

wie es im Titel heißt: „Dresden wie es einmal war". Mein Blick wandert nach rechts oben, an den östlichen Rand der Altstadt, dorthin, wo die Semper-Synagoge zu sehen sein müsste. Sie ist nicht da. Verschwunden. Getilgt aus dem „Dresden wie es einmal war", das schon damals nicht mehr ganz so heil war wie es heute behauptet. Das Sehnsuchtsbild, der inoffizielle Masterplan für die Rekonstruktion von heute, ist nach der Zerstörung des 9. November 1938 aufgenommen und schließt daher die Synagoge nicht ein.

RECYCLING
Die Geschichte der Rekonstruktion ist komplexer als es einem Architekten recht sein kann, der sich in einem zeitgenössischen, ständig nach dem „Neuen" suchenden Architekturdiskurs wähnt. In Dresden beginnt diese Geschichte mit der Rekonstruktion des Zwingers, die weniger ein restaurativer Akt, als vielmehr ein Akt des Widerstands gegen die Abriss- und Modernisierungspolitik der Sozialistischen Einheitspartei war. Sie geht weiter mit einer – aufgrund neuer Brandschutzanforderungen – nicht ganz genauen Kopie der Semperoper und führt schließlich zur Frauenkirche, deren Ruine bis 1989 als antifaschistisches Antikriegsdenkmal diente und danach rekonstruiert wurde. Was dort schon ambivalent ist, ist als Behauptung ungebrochener Kontinuität im Fall der Synagoge mehr als fragwürdig. Die Synagoge ist – so gibt auch das Wunschbild des vermeintlich intakten Dresden zu verstehen – nicht Teil der Rekonstruktionsgeschichte. Im Gegensatz zur Frauenkirche sind nicht einmal Ruinen übriggeblieben. Ein noch Ende 1938 gedrehter Lehrfilm des Technischen Hilfswerks dokumentiert am Beispiel der Dresdner Synagoge den fachgerechten Abbau von Ruinen. Es ist wie ein obszöner Fall von angewandtem Ökofaschismus: die Ruine der ausgebrannten Synagoge wird nach der Reichskristallnacht abgetragen, ihr Material geschreddert und als Straßenbaumaterial recycelt.

VOM GRUNDSTÜCK ZUR BÖSCHUNG UND WIEDER ZURÜCK
Das Material war weg. Das Grundstück lag da, verfügbar für die
Ambitionen der Nachkriegsmoderne. In der Annahme, dass hier nie
wieder eine Synagoge stehen werde, konnte das Gelände mit den
Infrastrukturen der neuen Gesellschaft beplant werden. Wasser, Gas-
und Stromleitungen wurden verlegt. Eine neue überdimensionierte
Brücke mit anschließender sechsspuriger Verkehrsmagistrale wurde
gebaut und veränderte radikal Geometrie und Topographie des
Grundstücks. An der Schnittstelle zwischen der Dresdner Altstadt
und den östlich angrenzenden Plattenbauten der sozialistischen
Nachkriegsmoderne entstand ein Restgrundstück – kaum mehr als
eine lang gestreckte Böschung. Was kann man – Jahrzehnte später
– damit machen? Lässt sich hier bauen? Die „Erfindung" einer neu-
en Konfiguration operiert jenseits von Bezügen auf historische Bau-
linien und basiert eher auf dem, was wir finden: dem vagen, eher zufällig entstandenen Grundstück, seiner Vermessungsdaten, einer
komplexen Topographie von gegenläufigen Gefällen, in das sich die
neue Synagoge hineinzuzwängen hat. In einer Serie von Schicht-
modellen verschleifen wir die unterschiedlichen Höhen und Neigun-
gen zu einem Sockel, der sich mit der zur Elbe abfallenden Topographie verbindet und damit unterschiedliche Zugangssituationen zu
einem neuen öffentlichen Raum zwischen Synagoge und Gemein-
dehaus schafft. Ein Ort, der sowohl exponiert als auch geschützt ist.
Doch was heißt hier überhaupt Öffentlichkeit? Wie öffentlich kann –
andere würden sagen: darf – eine Synagoge sein?

SICHTBARKEIT
Öffentlichkeit und Sichtbarkeit waren einst aufeinander bezogene
Begriffe der städtischen Raumpolitik. Was öffentlich war, war auch
sichtbar und umgekehrt. Das hat sich radikal geändert. Nicht nur
durch Fernsehen und Internet. Der physisch sichtbaren Stadt miss-
trauen wir – Öffentlichkeit scheint immer woanders zu sein.

Architektur als Medium der Sichtbarmachung öffentlicher Belange –
das Thema scheint erledigt. Doch was passiert eigentlich, wenn eine
soziale oder religiöse Gruppe öffentlich sichtbar wird, wenn sie eine
taktile *res publica* wird? Nach Jahrzehnten in einer verborgenen und
peripheren Position in der Dresdner Neustadt kehrt die schnell wachsende, nun mehrheitlich aus Migranten der ehemaligen Sowjetunion
bestehende Gemeinde an den historischen Ort der Semperschen
Synagoge, also in die Mitte der Stadt, zurück. Die Kritik lässt nicht
auf sich warten: zu groß, zu zentral, nichts als räumliche Wieder-
gutmachung[04]. Doch was ist die Alternative: eine fragmentierte Gemeinschaft, deren Räume in Hinterhöfen über die Stadt verteilt
werden? Doch nicht nur die anhaltenden Diskussionen um den Bau
von Moscheen in deutschen Vorstädten zeigen, dass die Strategien
des Fragmentarischen, Unsichtbaren und Peripheren widersprüch-
lich sind. Am Ende sind sie vielleicht nicht mehr als neue, subtile Formen der Ausgrenzung unter veränderten, mitunter sogar gut ge-
meinten politischen Vorzeichen.

Warum nicht in die Mitte gehen? Dorthin, wo es weh tut. Es mit
den hegemonialen Kräften aufnehmen und das architektonische Problem der Sichtbarkeit annehmen. Zu sehen ist die Rückkehr einer
Gemeinschaft in die Mitte der Stadt, in den direkten Kontext der monumentalen Bauwerke und Identitätspunkte der Stadt, aufgereiht
im Elbpanorama neben Albertinum, Frauenkirche, Kunstakademie,
Schloss, Hofkirche und Semperoper. Sichtbar wird der kritische
Moment, in dem eine Gemeinschaft durch Architektur manifest wird
und zu konkretem, festem Material wird. Das Material wird zum
öffentlichen Träger politisch-kultureller Diskurse – und gehorcht doch
dem Gesetz der eigenen Trägheit.

---

04 VGL. MARK JARZOMBEK, „DISGUISED VISIBILITIES: DRESDEN/'DRESDEN'", IN: *LOG* (HERBST 2005),
S. 73-82.

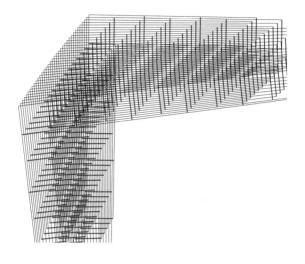

EINDEUTIGE GEOMETRIE UND UNEINDEUTIGE WAHRNEHMUNG
Geometrische und perzeptive Prozesse stehen beim Entwurf der Dresdner Synagoge in einem bewusst mehrdeutigen Verhältnis zueinander. Was in der geometrischen Konstruktion eindeutig ist, erscheint in seiner räumlichen Wahrnehmung uneindeutig. Aus der beengten, orthogonalen Geometrie des Grundstücks heraus verdreht sich der massive Baukörper der Synagoge kontinuierlich nach Osten. Die komplexe Form der zweifach gekrümmten Wandflächen basiert hierbei auf der einfachen geometrischen Operation einer sukzessiven Rotation orthogonaler Schichten, die wiederum aus 120 x 60 x 60 cm großen, monolithischen Betonwerksteinen bestehen. Trotz der einfachen geometrischen Operation entstehen zweifach gekrümmte Flächen, deren Wahrnehmung sich je nach Perspektive ändert und damit einer eindeutigen geometrischen Rekonstruktion durch das Auge entzieht. Ein Indiz für das Auge

bieten die Konstruktion und ihr Schattenwurf. Aufgrund der Rotation der einzelnen Mauerwerkschichten um den Mittelpunkt des Gebäudes entstehen an den Gebäudeecken maximale Auskragungen von 55 mm, deren Schatten die geometrische Operation sichtbar machen. Von den Gebäudeecken ausgehend entsteht ein Schattenverlauf bis zum Nulldurchgang des rotierten Baukörpers. Jenseits der Wandmitte kehrt sich die Logik des Schattens um.

MASSIVE PROBLEME ODER: WAS IST EIN STEIN?
Im Kontext einer Baukultur, die „Stein" als bloßes Oberflächenphänomen versteht und folgerichtig in zunehmenden Maße Steintapeten produziert, ein massives Gebäude zu planen, heißt auch, sich einiger vertrauter Vorurteile zu entledigen. In erster Linie jenes, wonach ein Stein natürlich zu sein hat. „Unser" Stein *soll* – aus Gründen persönlicher Vorliebe – und *muss* – aus konstruktiven Gründen – künstlich sein. Der Begriff „Kunststein" umschreibt, worum es geht: ein Material, das den Bereich zwischen der lebendigen Mineralität des natürlichen Steins und der industriell standardisierten Neutralität des Betonfertigteils auslotet; ein Material, das eine kritische Position zwischen der Sandsteinseeligkeit des rekonstruierten Alt-Dresden und den technokratischen Fantasien der sozialistischen Plattenbauten einnimmt und damit auch die Lage der Synagoge an der Schnittstelle zwischen Alt- und Neu-Dresden reflektiert.

GEWAND
Architektur und Kleidung gelten üblicherweise als gegensätzliche Pole: Hart vs. weich, kalt vs. warm, dauerhaft vs. ephemer. Umso ungewöhnlicher erscheint in diesem Kontext die von Gottfried Semper in seiner 1860 veröffentlichten Abhandlung "Der Stil" entwickelte Theorie der Bekleidung, die den Ursprung der Architektur auf das Textil bezieht. Demzufolge ist die Wand als wesentliches Element des räumlichen Eingrenzens auf gefilzte Gewänder, geflochtene und verwobene Materialien zurückzuführen. Die Geschichte

der Architektur wäre damit als eine Geschichte der zunehmenden Verfestigung des "Gewandes" zu lesen.

Während Gottfried Semper, unser Vorgänger als Architekt der Dresdner Synagoge, der massiven Wand die Anmutung einer Bekleidung gab, nimmt unser Ansatz die Elemente wieder auseinander. Das Textile sollte nicht in einer mimetischen Logik als Abbild eingesetzt werden, sondern wieder weich werden und in seiner visuellen und taktilen Eigenheit zur Geltung kommen: umhüllend, fließend, die Farben changierend, Licht reflektierend. Vom Deckenrost abgehängt, umhüllt ein Messingtextil den rituellen Raum im Inneren der Synagoge. Scheinbar ein Widerspruch: Bekleidung bauen.

RAUMKONFLIKTE

Nach Bruno Latour sind es *Dinge*[05], um die sich Menschen versammeln. Sie sind keine bloßen Objekte, sondern Dinge, die selbst aktiv sind und das politische, soziale und religiöse Verhalten der Versammelten prägen. Die räumliche Disposition der Synagoge ist dabei ungewöhnlich: die Dinge agieren gegeneinander. In den textilen Raum sind hölzerne Möbel von unterschiedlicher Größe eingestellt: Empore, Bänke, die Bima als zentrales Vorlesepult und der Thoraschrein. Die Anordnung der wesentlichen rituellen Elemente verdeutlicht dabei einen „synagogalen Raumkonflikt"[06]: einerseits tendiert die Ausrichtung auf den am östlichen Ende des Raums stehenden Thoraschrein zu einem Longitudinalraum, andererseits fokussiert die mittige Anordnung der Bima auf einen Zentralraum. Die Richtung des Gebets wird ambivalent. Die Bewegungen im Raum laufen durcheinander.

---

[05] VGL. BRUNO LATOUR, *DAS PARLAMENT DER DINGE. FÜR EINE POLITISCHE ÖKOLOGIE*, FRANKFURT AM MAIN 2001.

[06] SALOMON KORN, OP.CIT., S. 292.

Durch die mittige Anordnung des Vorlesepults geht die räumliche Disposition gewissermaßen hinter Reformsynagogen wie die Semper-Synagoge in Dresden zurück, die im Zuge der Assimilierung des 19. Jahrhunderts altarähnliche Anordnungen im Chor einführten. Während mit diesen architektonischen Anpassungsarbeiten an das Modell der christlichen Kirchen neue räumliche und rituelle Hierarchien geschaffen wurden, entsteht mit der mittigen Positionierung der Bima eine unhierarchische Bewegung im Raum, die zwischen zentralen und longitudinalen Richtungen schwankt. Es findet eine Verlagerung von einer architektonisch eindeutig definierten Situation zu einer räumlichen Indeterminiertheit statt.

ZWISCHEN TAUTOLOGIE UND NARRATION
Beim Versuch, materiale Zustände mit politischen, sozialen und historischen Zeiträumen zu verbinden und dies zum Ausgangspunkt einer Entwurfsstrategie zu machen, betreten wir eine Grauzone. Die Parameter des Entwerfens werden uneindeutig. Es ist heikel, diese Zone zwischen parametrischem Entwerfen und etwas, das mit Narration umschrieben werden könnte, zu betreten. Wir verlassen den sicheren Grund der Übersetzungstechnik, der Verräumlichung von Raumprogrammen und der Antworten auf technische Probleme. Keine Frage, es geht uns um eine konsistente Organisation von Material, aber nicht mit dem Ziel der Tautologie oder einer simplen Gleichung. So sehr sich Architekten auch darum bemühen, ihre Arbeit als parametrisch entwickelte Produkte zu erklären und sich durch diesen scheinbar willenlosen „no style" als Autoren zu entlasten – es entsteht so etwas wie Mehrwert. Ein Überschuss, der zwar problematisch, aber auch unabdingbar für jede Form von Architektur ist. In den 1990er Jahren konzentrierten sich die avanciertesten Formen der Architekturpraxis auf eine Architektur der Emergenz und des „parametrischen Designs". Doch nach einem Jahrzehnt der Emergenz und der damit einhergehenden Verweigerung von Narrationen tut sich eine tiefe Kluft auf zwischen den scheinbar unendlichen Variationen

von formalen, materialen und organisatorischen Möglichkeiten und deren konkreter Umsetzung in politische, soziale und ökonomische Zusammenhänge. Notwendig könnte nun ein architektonischer Praxisbegriff werden, der gerade erst im Konflikt zwischen den internen physischen Möglichkeiten der autonomen Disziplin und den externen politisch-kulturellen Narrationen spezifisch wird. Das Material der Architektur wäre dann beides: Handwerk und Politik.

DER TEXT BASIERT AUF DEM GLEICHNAMIGEN MANUSKRIPT FÜR EINEN VORTRAG, DER 2001 IN DER FRAUENKIRCHE GEHALTEN WURDE. DIE 2001 GEBAUTE SYNAGOGE DRESDEN WURDE VON NIKOLAUS HIRSCH, WOLFGANG LORCH UND ANDREA WANDEL ENTWORFEN.

BIOGRAPHY / BIOGRAFIE

born/geboren 1964 in Karlsruhe, Germany/Deutschland
lives and works/lebt und arbeitet in Frankfurt am Main

PROJECTS (SELECTION) / PROJEKTE (AUSWAHL)
Mohalla, Cultural Center/Kulturzentrum, Dehli, 2007–2008
European Kunsthalle, Cologne/Köln, 2005–2007
Hybrid Highrise, Tbilisi/Tiflis, 2006–2008
unitednationsplaza, Berlin, 2006–2007
Node House, Space for Raqs Media Collective, Museum für Kommunikation, Frankfurt am Main, 2006, Kunstmuseum Bern, 2007
Autobahn Tower (with/mit Thomas Bayrle), Museum für Moderne Kunst, Frankfurt, 2006
Manifesta School, Nicosia/Nikosia, cancelled/abgesagt 2006
Visitors Center/Besucherzentrum, Ravensbrück, 2004–2007
Making Things Public, exhibition architecture/Ausstellungsarchitektur, ZKM Karlsruhe, 2005
Hinzert Document Center/Dokumentationshaus Hinzert, 2004–2006
Music Pavilion, Museu Serralves, Porto, 2003
Theater, Institute of Applied Theatre Studies/Institut für Theaterwissenschaften, Universität Gießen, 2004–2008
Conversion of/Umbau des Bockenheimer Depot Theater (with/mit William Forsythe), Frankfurt am Main, 2002–2003
Exhibition system/Ausstellungssystem, Architekturmuseum München, 2002
Intervention, *Die Kraft der Negation*/The Force of Negation, Theater der Welt, Cologne/Köln, Volksbühne Berlin, 2002
Frequencies-Hz, exhibition architecture/Ausstellungsarchitektur, Schirn Kunsthalle Frankfurt, 2001–2002
Videonale 9, temporary structure/Temporäre Struktur, Bonn, 2001
Synagogue Dresden/Synagoge Dresden, 1998–2001
Track 17/Gleis 17, Berlin-Grunewald train station/Bahnhof Berlin-Grunewald, 1996–1998

Börneplatz Memorial/Gedenkstätte Börneplatz,
Frankfurt am Main, 1994–96

TEACHING
University of Pennsylvania, Philadelphia, 2006
Institut für Theaterwissenschaften, Universität Gießen, 2003/2004
Hochschule für Gestaltung Karlsruhe, 2004
Architectural Association London, since 2000

RESEARCH PROJECTS / CURATING
Curating Architecture, Goldsmiths College, 2007
European Kunsthalle, Spaces of Production, 2005–2007
ErsatzStadt: Repräsentationen des Urbanen,
Volksbühne Berlin, 2005
Fluchtpunkt Kunst, Schauspiel Frankfurt, 2004–2005
The Truth About the Nearly Real (with/mit William Forsythe,
Markus Weisbeck), Mousonturm, Frankfurt am Main, 2002

LIST OF ILLUSTRATIONS / ABBILDUNGSVERZEICHNIS

BOCKENHEIMER DEPOT, PLAN VARIATIONS, 2003
Nikolaus Hirsch / Michel Müller
Page 29

RH IN THE MUSEUM, 2006
Nikolaus Hirsch
Page 32

EUROPEAN KUNSTHALLE AS EXQUISITE CORPSE, 2007
Nikolaus Hirsch, Philipp Misselwitz, Markus Miessen,
Matthias Görlich
Page 39

AUTOBAHN TOWER,
MUSEUM FÜR MODERNE KUNST FRANKFURT, 2006
Nikolaus Hirsch / Michel Müller mit Thomas Bayrle
Page 42

MAKING THINGS PUBLIC, PLAN, ZKM KARLSRUHE, 2005
Nikolaus Hirsch / Michel Müller
Page 48

UNITEDNATIONSPLAZA, AXONOMETRIC DRAWING, 2006
Nikolaus Hirsch / Michel Müller
Page 52

UNITEDNATIONSPLAZA, TYPOLOGIES, 2006
Nikolaus Hirsch / Michel Müller
Page 56

MOHALLA LAB, DELHI, 2007
Nikolaus Hirsch / Michel Müller
Page 59

HINZERT DOCUMENT CENTER, 2005
Nikolaus Hirsch, Wolfgang Lorch, Andrea Wandel
Page 77

TBILISI FAÇADE, 2006
Nikolaus Hirsch, Wolfgang Lorch, Andrea Wandel
Page 83

TRACK 17, BERLIN, 1998
Nikolaus Hirsch, Wolfgang Lorch, Andrea Wandel
Page 112

SCHLOSSPLATZ BERLIN, VISIBILITY STUDY, 2001
Nikolaus Hirsch with Nikolas Heep
Page 123

DRESDEN SYNAGOGUE, PERSPECTIVE DRAWING, 2001
Nikolaus Hirsch, Wolfgang Lorch, Andrea Wandel
Page 131

DRESDEN SYNAGOGUE, 2001
Architects: Nikolaus Hirsch, Wolfgang Lorch, Andrea Wandel,
Photo: Norbert Miguletz
Pages 137-141

HINZERT DOCUMENT CENTER, 2005
Architects: Nikolaus Hirsch, Wolfgang Lorch, Andrea Wandel,
Photo: Norbert Miguletz
Pages 142-147

FREQUENCIES-HZ, SCHIRN KUNSTHALLE, 2002
Nikolaus Hirsch / Michel Müller in collaboration
with Markus Weisbeck
Pages 148/149

VIDEONALE 9, BONN, 2002
Nikolaus Hirsch / Michel Müller
Pages 150/151

BÖRNEPLATZ MEMORIAL, FRANKFURT, 1996
Nikolaus Hirsch, Wolfgang Lorch, Andrea Wandel
Pages 152/153

TRACK 17, BERLIN, 1998
Architects: Nikolaus Hirsch, Wolfgang Lorch, Andrea Wandel,
Photo: Lukas Roth
Pages 154/155

MAKING THINGS PUBLIC, ZKM KARLSRUHE, 2005
Nikolaus Hirsch / Michel Müller
Pages 156/157

UNITEDNATIONSPLAZA, BERLIN, 2006
Nikolaus Hirsch / Michel Müller
Pages 158/159

BOCKENHEIMER DEPOT, PLAN, 2003
Nikolaus Hirsch / Michel Müller
Page 181

RH IN THE MUSEUM, 2006
Nikolaus Hirsch
Page 187

EUROPEAN KUNSTHALLE, MODELS FOR TOMORROW, 2007
Nikolaus Hirsch, Philipp Misselwitz, Markus Miessen,
Matthias Görlich
Page 192

FREQUENCIES-HZ, SCHIRN KUNSTHALLE, MEANDER, 2002
Nikolaus Hirsch / Michel Müller in collaboration with
Markus Weisbeck
Page 198

MAKING THINGS PUBLIC, PLAN, ZKM KARLSRUHE, 2005
Nikolaus Hirsch / Michel Müller
Page 203

UNITEDNATIONSPLAZA, SITE PLAN, 2006
Nikolaus Hirsch / Michel Müller
Page 210

UNITEDNATIONSPLAZA, CONFERENCE ROOM VARIATIONS, 2006
Nikolaus Hirsch / Michel Müller
Page 213

MOHALLA LAB, DELHI, 2007
Nikolaus Hirsch / Michel Müller
Page 214

BÖRNEPLATZ MEMORIAL, FRANKFURT, 1996
Nikolaus Hirsch, Wolfgang Lorch, Andrea Wandel
Page 228

HINZERT DOCUMENT CENTER, 2005
Nikolaus Hirsch, Wolfgang Lorch, Andrea Wandel
Page 232

TRACK 17, BERLIN, 1998
Nikolaus Hirsch, Wolfgang Lorch, Andrea Wandel
Page 267

DRESDEN SYNAGOGUE, DETAIL CORNER, 2001
Nikolaus Hirsch, Wolfgang Lorch, Andrea Wandel
Page 285